The Incidental Oriental Secretary
and Other Tales of Foreign Service

ADST-DACOR Diplomats and Diplomacy Series
Series Editor: Margery Thompson

Since 1776, extraordinary men and women have represented the United States abroad under widely varying circumstances. What they did and how and why they did it remain little known to their compatriots. In 1995, the Association for Diplomatic Studies and Training (ADST) and DACOR, an organization of foreign affairs professionals, created the Diplomats and Diplomacy book series to increase public knowledge and appreciation of the professionalism of American diplomats and their involvement in world history. Richard Jackson's delightful pastiche of Foreign Service vignettes and history is the 61st volume in the series.

RELATED TITLES IN ADST SERIES

Gordon S. Brown, *Toussaint's Clause: The Founding Fathers and the Haitian Revolution*

J. F. Brown, *Radio Free Europe: An Insider's View*

Herman J. Cohen, *The Mind of the African Strongman: Conversations with Dictators, Statesmen, and Father Figures*

Peter D. Eicher, ed., *"Emperor Dead" and Other Historic American Diplomatic Dispatches*

Donald P. Gregg, *Pot Shards: Fragments of a Life Lived in CIA, the White House, and the Two Koreas*

Brandon Grove, *Behind Embassy Walls: The Life and Times of an American Diplomat*

Cameron Hume, *Mission to Algiers: Diplomacy by Engagement*

Kempton Jenkins, *Cold War Saga*

Dennis C. Jett, *American Ambassadors: The Past, Present, and Future of America's Diplomats*

Charles Stuart Kennedy, *The American Consul: A History of the United States Consular Service 1776–1924*

Robert H. Miller, *Vietnam and Beyond: A Diplomat's Cold War Education*

David D. Newsom, *Witness to a Changing World*

Richard B. Parker, *Memoirs of a Foreign Service Arabist*

Raymond F. Smith, *The Craft of Political Analysis for Diplomats*

James W. Spain, *In Those Days: A Diplomat Remembers*

Jean Wilkowski, *Abroad for Her Country: Tales of a Pioneer Woman Ambassador in the U.S. Foreign Service*

For a complete list of series titles, visit adst.org/publications

The Incidental Oriental Secretary and Other Tales of Foreign Service

Richard L. Jackson

AN ADST-DACOR DIPLOMATS AND DIPLOMACY BOOK

Hamilton Books

An Imprint of
Rowman & Littlefield
Lanham • Boulder • New York • Toronto • Plymouth, UK

Copyright © 2016 by Hamilton Books
4501 Forbes Boulevard, Suite 200, Lanham, Maryland 20706
Hamilton Books Acquisitions Department (301) 459-3366

Unit A, Whitacre Mews, 26-34 Stannary Street,
London SE11 4AB, United Kingdom

Library of Congress Control Number: 2016938970
ISBN: 978-0-7618-6786-9 (pbk : alk. paper)—ISBN: 978-0-7618-6787-6 (electronic)

The views and opinions in this book are solely those of the author and do not necessarily reflect those of the Association for Diplomatic Studies and Training, DACOR, Inc., or the Government of the United States.

Praise for

The Incidental Oriental Secretary and Other Tales of Foreign Service

"A highly engrossing and insightful perspective of US diplomacy and Foreign Service life from the Horn of Africa to the Maghreb, from Greece to Washington and New York. Told in engaging vignettes of diplomatic adventures and misadventures by a practitioner of over three decades, with uncommon wit and humor."
—Hon. Timberlake Foster, US Ambassador to Mauritania, 1997–2000.

"Dick Jackson evokes the mystery, beauty and exoticism of Morocco that I myself experienced and was witness to four unforgettable years as US Ambassador from 1981–1985."
—Hon. Joseph Verner Reed, US Ambassador to Morocco, 1981–1985, and US Chief of Protocol, 1989–1991.

"Not since Gerald Durrell wrote *My Family and Other Animals* has the memoir, Foreign Service and Greece found such an erudite and humorous scribe."
—Dr. Karen Rhoads Van Dyck, Kimon Doukas Professor of Hellenic Studies, Columbia University.

"*The Incidental Oriental Secretary and Other Tales of Foreign Service* is a superbly written and fascinating look in the historical "rear view mirror" of Richard Jackson at our world since the 1960s; from the Horn of Africa and Libya in early post-colonial days to Greece and the Balkans during the Cold War, and Morocco in an era of development and the Gulf War. Mr. Jackson takes us back again for views of North Africa in the end of the 20th century and on to the recent economic collapse of Greece and his visits to modern-day Mongolia and the remote Western Sahara. Always behind the scenes are the U.S. and the State Department, other world powers, and the United Nations wavering between neglect and playing an often lethal game of global chess. Mr. Jackson shares his insights over five decades of many adventures and experiences, giving us countless observations, terrific analysis, lessons in history (the first time the Benghazi consulate was attacked in the '60s), and lots of his humor. He is Marco Polo for our times and he reminds us of a world gone not so long ago but one that clearly sowed the seeds of violence, chaos and disenfranchisement in our 'modern' world today. *The Incidental Oriental Secretary and Other Tales of Foreign Service* is as educational as it is thoroughly interesting"
—Hon. Michael Ussery, U.S. Ambassador to Morocco, 1988–1991.

"Dick Jackson came up with an incisive prologue, epilogue and annex for the second edition of my father's biography, *American Hero, the True Story of Tommy Hitchcock, Sports Hero, War Hero, and Champion of the War-Winning P-51 Mustang*, due out from Rowman & Littlefield in September 2016. He has now turned his hand to this subjective, revealing and dryly funny account of his own experiences in diplomacy and more."
—Louise Hitchcock Stephaich.

"It felt at times as if Dick Jackson was channeling Evelyn Waugh in his sketches of the characters he encountered."
—Hon. Marc Wall, U.S. Ambassador to Chad, 2004–2007.

For my Family

who have Laughed or Cried through these Often-told Tales,

Magnified Perhaps in Memory but Nonetheless Taken from Life

Contents

Foreword

I put down Dick Jackson's delightful *The Incidental Oriental Secretary and other Tales of Foreign Service* with more than a twinge of nostalgia. Much of the world he describes no longer exists. No American diplomat today drives through the interior of Somalia or negotiates with its tribal and community leaders. Long forgotten is the Kingdom of Libya and its aging somnolent monarch Dick Jackson knew in the 1960's.

If travel in these blood soaked lands is no longer possible, the quaint habits of diplomatic practice and State Department management which marked the earlier years of Dick Jackson's career have also disappeared. Unlike the young diplomats Dick describes, today's Foreign Service Officers on assignment in the Middle East and other war wracked areas work out of heavily fortified embassies and routinely face threats of terror and violence. Wherever they serve, America's diplomats live today in an age of information technology and sophisticated communications; they draw on multiple sources of intelligence and compete in multi-agency environments for the attention of Washington's policy makers. Today's diplomats are drawn from all strata of American society; they neither seek nor receive the privileges and respect of their forbears.

Dick Jackson's book chronicles the transformation of American diplomacy to its present realities. It is not a book of heavy lessons of foreign policy, statecraft, or bureaucratic and domestic politics. His "anti-memoire" is modest; it is a book of reminiscences of a career well spent, rich in detail, superbly written and often gloriously funny. Dick Jackson provides just enough historical context to let us understand where his anecdotes fit in America's modern experience with the world. To be sure, Dick does not spare the lash when it comes to the mistakes we Americans make abroad. He is outspoken in his call for "smart power," good analysis, deep experience, knowledge, and professionalism. He decries pretension.

Those of us who have devoted our lives to this nation's Foreign Service will find time and again in the pages of Dick Jackson's compendium, experiences and insights which match our own. Each of us answers questions from the public, friends and family about our careers. Invariably we speak of times in the public service when we faced challenges or dangers similarly to those Dick Jackson knew. All of us experienced the hard work of learning foreign languages and absorbing foreign cultures. But few of us are lucky enough to match Dick's power of storytelling. Few can elucidate as agreeably as he does the many truths about the way diplomats live, work, and the joys of the profession and the contributions they make to this nation's security and wellbeing.

—Hon. Frank G. Wisner, U.S. Ambassador to Zambia, 1979–1982, Egypt, 1986–1991, Philippines, 1991–1992, and India, 1994–1997.

Preface

When we recall our own memories, we are not extracting a perfect record of our experiences and playing it back verbatim. Most people believe that memory works this way, but it doesn't. Instead, we are effectively whispering a message from our past to our present, reconstructing it on the fly each time. We get a lot of details right, but when our memories change, we only 'hear' the most recent version of the message, and we may assume that what we believe now is what we always believed. Studies find that even our 'flashbulb memories' of emotionally charged events can be distorted and inaccurate, but we cling to them with the greatest of confidence.[1]

As a US diplomat for three decades and college president in Greece for a fourth, I've come to think of diplomatic memoirs among the least credible of literary genres. Unless you're Dean Acheson or Henry Kissinger, or perhaps particularly then, they are generally pompous, self-centered and transparent efforts to inflate one's own impact on passing events. Nor, in my own case, considering the downward spiral of countries where I have seemed to bring misfortune like Somalia, Libya and Greece, can my own role be considered anything but marginal, if not actually malevolent.

Memoirs also come freighted with dullness, self-absorption, and, worse, egotism in supposing that one's life story is for any reason more interesting, valuable or worth reading than the next guy's. Thus, I think of this account as an "anti-memoir," suppressing trivia of my own career and focusing instead on the breathtaking transformation of diplomacy, in just the short span of one career from the rollicking, mostly light-hearted endeavor on which I embarked into a kind of security-driven defensive crouch. When I revisit old haunts, like the American Embassy in Athens or the maximum security prison that is now our Consulate General in Istanbul where visitors are presumed guilty until probes and scans prove otherwise, I am drawn irresistibly back to days when diplomats used shoe leather to meet contacts over green tea in the medina or, yes, even on the golf course, rather than poring over other peoples' mail or email in soundproof, windowless spaces, known in the trade as "bubbles."[2]

Of course, the interaction of diplomats or, for that matter, anyone across cultures is by nature unpredictable, prone to misunderstanding and often hilariously funny. I've never forgotten, for example, crossing the broad Senegal River in a tippy pirogue with one of the first moonrocks in a strong box handcuffed to my wrist, a sure ticket to the bottom if we capsized, only to be jeered and laughed out of town by local Mauritanian dignitaries for whom it was just a rock like any other. Such bizarre occurrences came to seem normal over the years, and it is my hope that, in today's world of narrowed career options, something in these pages might still inspire adventurous souls into a career in public service. Certainly, reliving some of these experiences in the writing allowed me to revel in the joys of what it was like to be younger, in full harness and passionate about this or that position of the moment. Avoiding strict chronology, I've grouped together episodes from interminable stretches in Washington, as well as a surprising total of sixteen years in Greece which I trust the reader will not find chronologically discombobulating.

I've never forgotten how a balding Secretary of State Dean Rusk, harried and under pressure from Lyndon Johnson over Vietnam, told would-be new diplomats like me in his soft-spoken Georgia drawl that "the poetry of the Twentieth Century is the vision of the astronaut looking back at this emerald planet, lost and whirling away in the immensity of space." Like travelers in space, it is indeed a godlike privilege for diplomats to move from country to country interacting with street vendors and kings and arriving finally at a kind of planetary vision. Since the earliest diplomats and spies sallied forth from caves in paleolithic times, following protocols of the world's so-called second oldest profession, to confront trespassers, whether neanderthals or other primates, in their territory, perhaps marked doglike with urine, there has been a reassuring continuity in the practice of diplomacy. These early probes to distinguish friend from foe and to conduct primitive negotiations are not at heart so very different from dealing with Kim Jong Un and the Hermit Kingdom or confronting ISIS today.

As the world gets smaller, however, diplomacy has become an ever more serious, even grim, profession and, like most Foreign Service Officers over a full career, I have had friends and colleagues who lost their lives practicing it. While skirting here the weightier dimensions of diplomacy and global strategy, I do not want to validate the caricature of diplomats as "cookie-pushers in striped pants" by seeming to skate over their sacrifices or the woes that have befallen countries like Somalia where I first served. Nothing could be further from my intention.

NOTES

1. "Why our Memory Fails Us," Christopher Chabris and Daniel Simons, *New York Times*, December 2, 2014.

2. Nostalgia is, of course, often the bane of retirees, whatever the profession, and insidiously erodes memory, like Alzheimer's or any other disease. See F. Scott Fitzgerald, "So, we beat on, boats against the current, born back ceaselessly into the past," *The Great Gatsby*, Charles Scribner's Sons, 1925.

Acknowledgments

While the views expressed herein are purely my own and in no way reflect those of the Department of State, Anatolia College or wherever else I may have worked, here and there are passages that have been redacted by the State Department. As a former Foreign Service Officer, I was obligated to submit the manuscript for review prior to publication. The Department, in turn, shared it with two other agencies of government that I am not at liberty to name which probably insisted on the redactions. Far from opposing these relatively minor changes, I am most flattered that so many branches of government seemed to take my random and disconnected recollections more seriously than I do myself. It was thus a sort of validation for me that the events described herein did, in fact, occur and are not mere figments of my imagination. I, therefore, am thankful for the time spent on the manuscript by the State Department's Office of Information Programs and Services and hasten to formally state here for the record, as required, that "The opinions and characterizations in this book are those of the author, and do not necessarily represent official positions of the United States Government."

I would like also to acknowledge and highlight the contribution and outstanding role of the Association for Diplomatic Studies and

Training (ADST), particularly in the area of oral histories. The oral history concluded with me on August 17, 1998 by Charles Stuart Kennedy was a godsend in refreshing my cognitively challenged memory about episodes long past. The unexpurgated oral histories of some 2,000 retired American diplomats, housed in the Library of Congress, are a valuable, little known resource for scholars and anyone interested in US foreign relations. All are available on the ADST website at adst.org/oral-history/oral-history-interviews/. It is a source of great pride that ADST and its talented editor, Margery Thompson, decided to include this book in the ADST/DACOR series on Diplomats and Diplomacy. I must also not neglect to thank here my publisher and friend, Jed Lyons, at Rowman & Littlefield for his startling decision to publish this in the first place.

I would like here to particularly thank friends and colleagues who have taken the time to read and comment on this manuscript: Elias Kulukundis, Dr. William McGrew, Ambassador (ret.) Timberlake Foster, Brady Keisling, my stepdaughter Alexandra Ruso, and in the final stretch my son-in-law Spyros Petrounakos. Finally, I want to thank my talented daughter, Eliza, on whose drawings and sketches any claim to artistic merit rests.

—Richard Jackson, Wellington, Florida
May 13, 2016

I

Entry on Duty

When I went to Princeton more than half a century ago, there were still, among the Gothic spires and shaded walkways, echoes to be heard, even voices, of Scott Fitzgerald. His summary of the campus as "seven friends and the trees and buildings" perfectly described my own limited parameters.[1] I plunged into art, history, philosophy and literature in all forms. The world beyond the campus, much less beyond the United States, was *terra incognita*. UN Secretary General U Thant gave our commencement address, and only years later did I learn who he was and what he did, much less remember anything he said. Like many classmates of that time and place, I had an unshakeable faith that I would write the Great American Novel if only I could reach the Shetland Islands to do so.

I finally reached the Shetlands twenty years later, by then working on a more prosaic writing assignment described in these pages. In the meantime, influenced by my Princeton faculty adviser Carlos Baker, a biographer and slavish admirer of Ernest Hemingway, journalism seemed to beckon. Arthur Krock, the dean of Washington columnists then, was a family friend and advised me over lunch that only the Richmond News Leader could be the launch pad for someone with ambition and presumed talent. And so I dutifully headed south where I was received by Tennant Bryan, a silver-haired, patrician editor and publisher straight from central casting. He assured me in warm southern tones that "we here at the News Leader are just so honored to have a gentleman of your quality" and that there would be just a few formalities with the city editor. In a vast bullpen of clacking typewriters, the latter tossed me a few pages of jumbled facts and asked me to take three minutes to type them up in story form. A simple task, but I didn't type. When he kindly told me that I'd certainly picked the right lead sentence, my journalistic career was over.

And so, with a brother already serving in India, I decided Foreign Service it was to be. In those days the oral exam for entry on duty was legendary, a sort of free-form interrogation by a board of three, all presumably specialists in something or rather. Success for them was defined as toughness, and some boasted of admitting nobody or failing 50 candidates in a row. Each board developed its own techniques and questions, and some were said to hide ashtrays watching hawk-like to see whether candidates favored pockets, cuffs or the rug. In the absence of other career counseling, I consulted my father who had a jaundiced view of diplomats as cookie-pushers in striped pants. In his view, it would be the cut of my suit and the shine on my shoes that would count, not what I might know, and the Department would look for surface brilliance over substance. Worse, he insisted that nothing in my wardrobe would do and I must wear his London suit, old-fashioned detachable collar and specially made elevator shoes from Peale and Company, two sizes too small. He was short, while I am tall, strong-necked while I was scrawny, and I, no doubt, looked like a plucked chicken in such get-up, reddened like a lobster by an obligatory hour before-hand in the Turkish bath at his club.

Shakespeare writes, "Ye, who would judge a man, mark him by his first approach," and that is surely what the panel did. Tottering into the examination room, my borrowed elevator shoes caught the rug, pitching me forward onto the panel's table and springing loose the detachable collar. The surprised panel, their minds clearly made up, lost no time in building a negative case. I later learned serving on such a board myself that it is or was then standard practice with failures to document their unsuitability in excruciating detail in case the candidate was a complainer or there might be congressional interest. Clearly no Charvet tie or Peale shoes could save me as the Board noted the absence of economics on my college transcript and proposed to hone in on the dismal science for the remainder of the hour. Asked what ten steps I might take as finance minister to combat the then-hyperinflation in Brazil, I was quickly over my head and at a loss as they began to focus on whether my proposed interest rate changes would have this or that toxic side effects on the Brazilian economy.

Adding insult to injury, one of the panel members was the kind of Princeton graduate who harbors a lifelong animus about the University's system of selective eating clubs. If memory serves, our exchange went something like this:

Inquisitor: Did you belong to a club at Princeton?

Candidate: Yes, Sir, I did.

Inquisitor: Which one?

Candidate: The Ivy Club.

Inquisitor: Was it a good club?

Candidate: Yes, Sir, I think it was.

Inquisitor: What makes a good club?

Candidate: Sir, as the old song goes:

"Well, what are the good clubs?

They're the ones the good fellows join.

Well, who are the good fellows?

They're the ones who join the good clubs."

Clearly, my sophomoric attempt at humor had fallen very flat. He was not amused, and in fairness to him there were few options to the club system in his day (or in mine), and some who did not receive a hoped for invitation, or perhaps any, nursed their grievance for years. I had, in any case, not demonstrated the sensitivity expected in a would-be diplomat, and the rest of the hour was heavy going.

I did take the exam again after a year of economics and African Studies at the Fletcher School and somehow gained entry for persistence, although begrudgingly and without any particular "welcome aboard" that I can remember. Then, as now, new recruits received several months of orientation about which I recall little today beyond being frequently bused across the Potomac to the State Department by a feckless undersecretary for administration to pad out audiences for retirement and other forgettable ceremonies. The real suspense and intrigue surrounded the long-awaited list of open posts and fierce competition for perceived plums as bachelors bid for Stockholm, others sought London or Paris and the ambitious or patriotic headed for Vietnam. To the surprise of classmates, I happily bid for and received a first assignment to Mogadishu, Somalia. Never have I regretted exposure there to the whole picture, such as it was, compared to the worm's eye view I might of had in a visa mill like London or Frankfurt.

To fill the long months of medical and security clearances before I was called up for duty, I volunteered at the antiquated 1855 Saint Elizabeth's Mental Hospital in Southeast Washington where

Ezra Pound was famously impounded from 1946–58. My job was to draw on rudimentary French and Italian to visit with patients who did not speak English and sometimes to interpret for them with doctors and nurses. Several patients who had apparently not communicated with anyone in their own language for many years hardly seemed insane to my untrained eyes. One elderly lady, who had worked decades before in a match factory in Italy, still sang catchy tunes in Italian learned on the workshop floor. In fact, it was really a depressing and grim place, although I often joked in later years that it was ideal preparation for diplomacy.

In hindsight, entry on duty in those days was at best a random process with little counseling or analysis of options for what is one of life's most important decisions. In school, I had applied only to Princeton and afterwards unthinkingly did the same at Harvard Law. I visited Cambridge during final exams and observed a huge hall with hundreds of students clattering away at top speed on typewriters. Next door, a small group, clearly under pressure, were writing their exams in longhand. Further on still, a minority in the men's room were vomiting. These three circles of hell did not exactly draw me to a legal career, although it was a blow to pride not to be admitted. Today, I am a volunteer interviewer of undergraduate candidates for Princeton in the Florida county where I live and measure the passage of sixty years in the number of would-be students whose dream is to design the first quantum computer or to get their hot hands on a particle accelerator. It's, frankly, hard for me to hold my own in the conversation with them, let alone assess their potential or prospects at my alma mater.

NOTE

1. F. Scott Fitzgerald, *This Side of Paradise*, 1920.

II

Somalia

"If you stretch out your finger to a snake, he will jump up to
your wrist."
—Somali Proverb

In the Foreign Service of that time, the journey itself was still a
big part of the experience. Then, as now, Congress insisted that all
travel be on American flag lines, but American Export Lines not
only still existed, but operated twin luxurious liners, the Constitution and the Independence, which unlike today's get-there-yester-
day approach, American diplomats were actually encouraged to
take across the Atlantic in order to draw down a surplus of foreign
currency otherwise blocked abroad. So it was that my wife Stuart,
two-year old son Richard and I embarked for Naples on the Constitution. It was a time of vestigial formality when American Export
Lines would still offer a private table for American diplomats on
assignment abroad. We found ourselves at breakfast, lunch and
dinner in the congenial company of a young couple from my A-100
orientation class headed for Basra and an older, senior officer with
a new wife, Austrian I think, headed for Cairo where he would be

Administrative Counselor at one of our largest, most sprawling embassies. I'm sad to say that I believe he died there on the job.

Our younger friends, she a very talented artist later to do the sculptures on the National Cathedral in Washington and he a serious student of Arabic and Middle Eastern culture, brought great life to the table, as did my wife Stuart. At least four of us shared tremendous idealism, excitement and expectations, sailing for nine days in this languid luxury to first diplomatic assignments and as yet only imagined new lives. The third couple had been around the block and brought a certain decorum to the table, instructing us in the finer points of wine, protocol and other diplomatic niceties. Well intentioned and helpful as they were, there was thus a definite mentoring dimension to our three daily meals. We discussed, for example, the proper hierarchy and dress for separate courtesy calls by both officers and wives on arrival at our respective posts, as well as the contingency of how to handle the situation should those high on the pecking order not be available or willing to receive us in which case we were instructed to turn down the upper right hand corner of our calling cards as proof positive that we had actually made the effort and shown up, which as Woody Allen says is ninety percent of life. To this day, I still turn down the upper right corner if I find someone away, but doubt the signal is often registered and sometimes feel like a fossil.

Still, the journey was splendid and the mentoring and table banter jovial. I heard later about a classmate assigned to Milan whose unfortunate wife was admonished during her initial courtesy call on the Consul General's wife that "when we go abroad, we must put aside our high school ways." The mid-sixties were, in any case, a time of transition in the Foreign Service, accelerated certainly by Vietnam. Before the old guard shuffled off, I recall one crusty ambassador, in Brazil I think it was, famously complaining that "the people who were hired to press the pants are starting to wear them."

After the sea voyage, we flew from Rome to Moqadishu, from one world to another, with haunting stopovers in Khartoum and Aden. In the former, passengers disembarked into a small, crowded one room airport where vendors did a brisk business selling ivory hippopotami with their mouths open, and tall elegantly robed Sudanese drank pungent dark coffee at 3am. Inside and out it was 110 degrees Fahrenheit. Reaching Aden at about 6am, it was already light and passengers were herded into an outdoor holding pen encircled by barbed wire and nervous British troops with machine guns for a thorough examination of our documents. We had arrived during the Aden Emergency leading to independence in 1967 in the last days of the British Raj at this crossroads of Empire. There had been a series of bombings or assassinations and already polo ponies were being shipped home, so everybody was on alert. Later I had a good Somali friend and squash partner who was shot and killed at that same airport. We were glad to move on.

THE SETTING

"I once had a farm in Africa . . . ," Isak Dinessen plaintively begins her famous book, shrouded in memory and in an earlier life.[1] Arriving in Africa, as I did with my family, fifty years ago and fifty years after the Baroness carved out a coffee plantation in nearby Kenya, Somalia was an exotic land, now unrecognizable, of dazzling white Islamic-style houses etched against a shimmering Indian Ocean. Five years after the 1960 wave of African independence, including Somalia, there was boundless optimism about the future. Soapy Williams in Washington knew for sure that, with our resources and know-how, we could quickly pattern these new countries after ourselves in the democratic path.[2] The stages of economic growth, so well defined by Walt Rostow, were just benchmarks along the way, but, of course, wildly missed the mark on problems of underdevelopment and tribalism.[3]

Somalia, then considered one of the most hopeful cases, was still among the poorest countries on earth. Yet it was the only African state then seen as a true nation with one ethnic group, speaking one language, compared, for example, to the Congo with its 800 major tribes and distinct languages. Never mind that Somalis were also the vast majority in Djibouti, the Ogaden region of Ethiopia, and huge areas of Northern Kenya or that the five-pointed star on the Somali flag represented, and still does, its irredentist claims to these regions. These imposed straight-line borders, unrelated to age old migrations of pastoralists across them, were decided in Europe and have caused bloodshed and strife for more than a century.

American Embassies often tend to mimic their clients, and a generation of US ambassadors in Mogadishu and Addis Ababa fought tooth and nail in unequal bureaucratic combat, since American interests were anchored to the albatross of Kagnew Station, a large, regional eves dropping base in Ethiopia. Still, people tended to romanticize the Somalis, a handsome and articulate race sometimes called the Irish of Africa. The then-prime minister, Abdirazak Hagi Hussein, was young and charismatic and tended to flashy white linen suits. Until scandal tarnished him, Americans literally saw the man as a white knight in shining armor.

The American Embassy was a sleepy place in those days. Each year, following Italian tradition, the Somalis would open the prison gates, sparking a crime wave, but the excitement was short lived and the recidivism rate near total. In the rainy season, water poured from the roof down the stairwell onto the Embassy switchboard. It used to be an open secret that the operator was in local intelligence, assigned to monitor us, so these downpours always caused a certain merriment. The general tone was relaxed, and at the beginning of my tour many of the older officers still wore colonial whites, knee socks and all. My predecessor used to dress that way and, after lunch, he would stretch out right there on the office couch for a catnap.

Staff meetings were a highlight of the week and took most of the morning. Many of the stalwarts were cigar smokers and, in the end, everyone took it up, puffing up a storm just out of self-defense. By meeting's end, you could hardly see across the table. It was hot too, and in the interior at Lugh Ferrandi[4] they held the world record for the highest mean temperature of 114F, day in day out, over 15 years. Across the border in Djibouti's Dalool Depression it was said to have reached an absolute high of 165 F.

Another highlight of the week was closing the diplomatic pouch to Washington, and the Deputy Chief of Mission, accustomed to the amenities of Vienna and suffering from prickly heat rash, would meet with my boss, the Political Counselor, to fight over contents of the "Weeka," the regular classified airgram to the Department which apparently justified all of us being there in the first place. My office was in the adjacent corridor, and I could not help over-hearing their yelling and recriminations. When it was over, each, florid-faced, would retreat to their respective corners, and the Weeka would have to be hastily rewritten for a waiting diplomatic courier. Both the DCM and the Political Counselor were Europea-nists and, it seemed to me, fish out of water on the Horn of Africa. Once, navigating in the bush with my boss, he would stop whenev-er we encountered a nomad and ceremoniously present him with his calling card. Somali was not yet a written language, and the nomad had no clue what he had been given, but Bill insisted that his outreach might nevertheless still pay long term dividends for the Embassy.

Work outside the Embassy depended on random orders from on high, and one of my first assignments, originating in the Commerce Department, was a worldwide directive to go out and promote sales of that fine, old American product, Bourbon. I don't dispute the Embassy's executive management decision that it was more expe-dient to send the junior officer out on the street than try to remon-strate with Washington that Muslims, particularly in Somalia, don't openly consume alcohol, least of all Bourbon, and almost to a man could not afford it anyhow. In the event, I had much pleasure winding through the labyrinthine streets of old Mogadishu, talking with incredulous vendors, but no sales.

I had frequent occasion to work with both the Ambassador and his wife. The former was an affable and experienced diplomat who would lecture me often about the Russian soul. He had only one tic: on pain of banishment to the motor pool, nobody high or low could utter the name of Graham Greene. This was because, during a prior assignment, probably as Ambassador to Haiti, he had been caricatured as a bumbling diplomat by Greene, who missed few opportunities to stick it to Americans. It was little enough to ask, and he rewarded my silence on Greene with the job of Post Language Officer, responsible for organizing lessons for qualified personnel and, as a priority, finding him the best Italian teacher in town. No other criteria were specified, and I easily found her—well qualified as a native Italian speaker, beautiful, and married.

Everybody remarked that the Ambassador made amazing progress with his Italian, but after my own departure a huge scandal hastened his own. Corridor rumor in the Department had it that the aggrieved spouse appeared at the Embassy with a shotgun, and the Ambassador was hastily withdrawn. By chance, years later in Athens, I met the two of them, long since happily married and ashore from a cruise liner on which he held forth as an onboard lecturer on Mediterranean culture while his wife shaped up the passengers with aerobics and physical education.

The Ambassador's first wife during my time in Mogadishu had a simpler requirement: decent food prepared to her rather exacting standards. She had fired a succession of chefs deemed not up to the job. I was to find a replacement and, based on interrogatories laboriously written out by her, to weed out all but the finalists from an assemblage of mendicant would-be cooks. Mogadishu then, as now, was not a center for fine dining. There was a Chinese and an

Italian restaurant, both operated by enterprising but improvising Somalis, and two hotels with indifferent food. Most applicants were, therefore, military bush cooks, able to dish out a meal from Land Rovers, but short on the niceties. Some, depending on their region and the tides of war, could prepare a few British or Italian dishes, but there were few Djiboutians to be found with French culinary expertise. Following my script, I would dutifully ask each candidate, often through interpreters, which savourie he would propose at the conclusion of a formal dinner. The answer was never crisp, and the ambassadorial household continued to lack savouries throughout my time.

In our first weeks at our first post, my wife and I received a dinner invitation from the polished and very senior Somali Ambassador to the Court of St. James, a must-accept for a Third Secretary at the bottom of the totem pole and a supportive young wife at home in most any social setting. Only, we had ourselves invited a newspaper man, named Muusa, for dinner the same night. Guilelessly, I raised the conflict with the Ambassador, and he replied, "Gurigaa waa gurigaagi," my house is your house, bring him. On the appointed night, the Ambassador met us on his doorstep and told me in flawless British English, "you have introduced a snake into my house, take him out immediately before I kill him," gesturing to a dagger which all Somalis then carried tucked inside their socks. We dragged away poor Muusa, whose only fault was being from the wrong tribe, as fast as we could, in the process learning a troubling lesson that still resonates today.

IN HER MAJESTY'S SERVICE

"A Man who Praises Himself is like a Goat who Suckles Itself."
—Somali Proverb

In those days in Mogadishu on the East coast of Africa, we used to represent the interests of the United Kingdom. Britain had backed the wrong horse, from a Somali point of view, at Kenyan independence in 1963, leaving tens of thousands of Somali tribesmen stranded on the wrong side of the border in a desert region of northern Kenya marked by one of five points of the Somali star. And so, diplomatic relations were broken, Embassies closed and British diplomats sent packing on short notice as the United States, acting as next of kin so to speak, took up the varied burden of what they left behind as "protecting power." In the main, this consisted of a ramshackle collection of buildings, warehouses, war graves, and caretaker Somali personnel to be supervised, maintained and protected so far as possible against the inroads of Somalia's all-consuming climate.

As the lowest rung in the Embassy hierarchy, I was wondrously appointed Vice Consul in Charge of British Interests, and my modest office became officially the British Interests Section of the American Embassy. This is standard diplomatic practice, and the British would probably have done the same for us in similar circumstances, just as the Canadians once did in Iran and Switzerland, at least until recently, did in Cuba. Best of all for me, the job came with a long wheel-base British desert Land Rover equipped with an African roof, jerry cans front and back, and an hydraulic winch, in short everything I could possibly need. Mumin, my driver, with salary paid in full by Her Majesty's Service, was a splendid chap, always at my service. A devout Muslim and a huge man physically, he was kind and loyal to a fault, never trusting fellow Somalis he did not know. Most surprising, my windfall was in no way envied by my betters in the Chancery who cared little enough for British interests and left me to represent them as I saw fit.

Naturally, I made a point to celebrate the Queen's Birthday, at least in my own way, as the minimum I could do in view of my new stature. Local expatriate Brits for whom I was theoretically responsible were in short supply, although there was a sort of second class of British-protected persons, mostly Arab traders from the Trucial

States. Among the few real Brits, George Viveash, for example, had been Chief of Police in Aden during the troubles when the last British polo ponies were shipped out. Now, he labored to build up the Somali Police as a counterweight to the Russian-backed Army. Empty nesters, he and his wife Lennie coddled a full grown cheetah at home, which once in play good-naturedly blinded me for several days with its acid saliva, designed by nature to dissolve prey. Rudi and Erica Schumacher were planters, expelled at independence from Eden in Uganda, and so on.

Caring for far-flung properties of the British War Graves Commission was quite labor intensive and sensitive work, given the emotional investment the British make in the fallen of colonial wars. Remote graves and markers required upkeep in a manner of which Her Majesty might take pride. That is not to say that the odd British subject or, more likely, the bearer of a Commonwealth passport, showing citizenship in some outpost of former empire, might not occasionally show up and, as often as not, make impossible demands to be referred back to Washington for forwarding to Whitehall in London and back through an interminable round of bureaucracy. I came to feel empathy for our own early 19th Century consuls at Tangier on the Barbary Coast, waiting endless months for instructions delivered by slow ship. Arguably, however, these early diplomats had immensely greater power to take decisions and to improvise long before internet, secure phones, skype and congressional oversight committees.

There might be sunstroke cases, retired army officers who overdid it hunting in the bush, Pakistanis seeking repatriation or just any manner of complaints, petitioners for UK benefits or outright supplicants. My predecessor had to deal with a fellow who appeared at the Embassy dragging in the severed and still bloody head of a Cape buffalo, shot at Afmadu, for "official" measurement. The stain on the well-worn carpet to the left of the Vice Consul's desk was still there to prove it.

Apart from George and Rudi, whom I mentioned, most remaining British subjects clustered around Hargeisa in Somaliland, a former British colony and different from the Italianate south. And so, to show the flag, I often took the four-hour flight in an old DC-3 over nearly uninhabited plains, sometimes accompanied in the cabin by chickens and Berbera fat-tailed sheep. Hargeisa in those days had little to offer tourists, just a collection of houses along the wadi, or run as they would call it in Virginia. Activity centered around coffee houses where tribesmen chewed qat, a mild narcotic that gives you a buzz if you masticate for hours on end. Often there were tribal feuds in progress between the Rer Musa and Rer Ali. Causes were obscure, but camels were usually at the root of it, and many from each side died in ambushes and pitched battles over the years. Everything could be expressed in camels, and the vocabulary for them in Somali is among the world's richest. If you killed a man, you paid one hundred camels, castrated him one hundred camels, killed a woman fifty camels, and so on.

Besides being the only place in town to stay, the Hargeisa Club was a sort of refuge, almost a caricature of a British club eroding a few years after independence. It had its own tie with scrubby thorn bushes rampant on a blue field which bespoke worlds about the place. In rainy season, the dried out wadi flooded, cutting the Club off from town for weeks on end. And so the place was self-sufficient with two broken-down riding horses, a weed-filled tennis court, a dart board and a weekly movie. The single outdoor toilet was a massive "long drop," an open-air wooden throne built over an abandoned well which reverberated cavernously below with any movement. A crude sign pointed to the all too real danger of slipping through the throne. Beyond British members, a judge and a surgeon that I recall, independence had brought in the local police chief, a few generals and a major, but they came just for the Saturday movie and did not hang around. A Polish bush pilot fighting biblical locusts and a few prospectors rounded out the cast.

All took place at the same times and in the same order each day, drinks, darts, dinner, and variation was frowned on. I once overlapped there with a particularly boisterous Greek-American friend and fellow diplomat. Gregarious to a fault, he burst on the Club like a bomb, singing, playing the piano at odd hours, even founding a Sunday pancake eaters' society. Every evening the suggestion box next to the dart board was crammed full with member pleas, which were duly read aloud, that he be instructed to cease and desist from this or that. Apart from the joys of club living, the US Consulate was also pleasant enough, and Consuls with telescopes could learn much about the stars and sometimes turned to breeding camels. Transfers were not uncommon, however, and the Consulate is now sadly closed. I recall that once a new consul and his young family, fresh from a posting in Naples, experienced particular culture shock. His household effects, called HHE, were deposited in huge lift vans within his compound, and it took three days to unload them. Twice thieves broke in and, on the third night, guards speared one against a wall.

"Astride the long drop."

THE BRIGADIER

"A grave-digging hyena finds only rot."
—Somali Proverb

As I said, war graves were serious work, but I always felt that the Brigadier overdid it. It was, after all, his whole life. His command, if you call it that, ran from Zanzibar all the way to Hargeisa, covering most of the war cemeteries along the East African Coast and well into the interior. As for his men, they were loyal African troops, King's African Rifles and Somaliland Constabulary for the most part, with a sprinkling of actual British, casualties of the five great but unsuccessful campaigns against the "Mad Mullah," Sayyid Muhammed Abdille Hassan. The Brigadier never fully grasped, particularly after a drink or two, that these were not, however, living troops.

Under the rubric of Her Majesty's Service, the Brigadier became my nominal boss at least for the portion of my work involving graves. I use the word "nominal" advisedly because the US Congress under no circumstances would allow an American diplomat, even in remote Somalia, to take direct orders from a foreign power, no matter how special the relationship. Still, the Brigadier's seniority and sheer stubbornness put me in a difficult position. He would make an inspection visit every few months from the comfort of Nairobi, and along with Mumin we would tour the sites, commenting on the need for planting here or the state of a fence there. Once he caused us to bury a massive pre-World War I cannon rusting in the seaside humidity at the cemetery gate on grounds that it was not properly maintained and a disgrace to the Queen. I don't know what standard he expected, but the men worked for a week, and it is no simple thing to bury a field piece just like that under the equatorial sun.

It was the evenings that we dreaded most. We entertained him once a visit, inevitably a trial for my long-suffering wife, and it was always the same. First, he re-fought the Great War from the Marne to the Somme. Then, mellowing with drink, he turned to the present, by now well in command of his troops. It seems that he was coming under pressure on Zanzibar where a new radical government was making moves to expropriate the cemetery plot, by then valuable property within Zanzibar City. He would often alarm guests, pounding the table and fulminating about showing the Zanzibaris a thing or two and falling back to the mainland to re-group. Mornings after, indifferent to heat and obvious hangovers, he'd stalk out, moustache bristling, florid face covered in sweat, and nothing on earth would change his mind.

The trouble is that all this was not just idle talk and, at least once in my region, we did regroup. He had found three Englishmen resting incongruously in the Italian War Cemetery and was pre-pared to move heaven and earth to end their humiliation. Exhuma-tion was tricky business in that part of the Muslim world and against the local customs. Work was done by pariahs from a grave-digging riverain tribe under cover of night. Each man was moved separately by donkey cart to his old regiment. It cost a modest amount in Somali shillings or shillini, as they called them, for the lot.

Success seemed to fuel the Brigadier's ambition, and for a while he spoke of reuniting all the troops by regiment. This would have required an incredibly complex movement of men all along the coast, even some from the Ogadeni Haud where they too had fallen prey to the Mullah. In the end, he gave it up, but his fertile imagina-tion conceived a scheme equally costly and time-consuming. The man, it seemed, had an unerring eye for the logistically impossible, if not outright ghoulish.

What he instructed was simply this: That the plain and, to the rare visitor, dignified wooden crosses and stone markers at our main northern site be replaced with marble memorial panels, each inscribed with the deceased's name, if available, and an appropriate line from Rupert Brooke or Wilfred Owen. The work was exacting too, cataloging the men, getting the inscriptions right and placing orders from Italy. Once arrived, a jolting truck ride from the distant port of Berbera insured that many of the panels reached the cemetery site in smithereens. Among them, for example, was "Ali Raghe, died 1916, a child whom England bore, shaped, made divine" and "Hassan Farah Nur, died 1944, whose dying has made us more gifts than gold," all beyond repair. New orders were placed, but after my time the Suez Canal was closed during the Six Day War, and I never heard whether the work was completed.

Graves formed the bulk of my work with the Brigadier, but he was also obsessed with battle markers. Once, we received a sharp protest from London, transmitted with the usual delays through Washington, that a small stone marker, commemorating a battlefield during Britain's campaigns against the Mullah and located in a remote region along the contested Ethiopian border, had been defaced or disappeared. It was clearly not the famous site at Dul Madoba where the Mullah had decimated Richard Corfield and his entire regiment in 1913.[5] I was instructed to lose no time in making "discreet inquiries," and the region in question was a desolate moonscape five decades before the advent of drones or GPS and well before the Somali language was even in a written form. In other words, there was no way that British agents could have been positioned on this inhospitable ground or that illiterate passing nomads could have conveyed intelligence on the missing marker to MI-6 or Whitehall. I could only conclude that the Brigadier, with time on his hands in Nairobi, had planted a false report through Commission back channels to London, perhaps for no other reason than to jerk around a jejune American Vice Consul. It could only have been him.

In the event, Mumin and I crisscrossed the barren interior for nearly a week, frequently resorting to the Land Rover's winch and lower gear register for extreme conditions and hailing itinerant nomads, none of whom understood what we wanted or had news of the marker. We passed Bur Hacaba, a huge stone outcrop rising up sheer like Ayers Rock from the flat plain, and on our return to civilization I advised London through channels that discreet inquiries had been made and that the marker remained unaccounted for.

"Searching for the Missing Marker."

NUR ABBY

"Urine kills a man with bad kidneys."
—Somali Proverb

There were tumultuous changes starting in the sixties, and Nur Abby Hussein caught each one and rode it for all it was worth until his luck ran out. I did not know Nur in Somalia, but have pieced together the details of his early life. He was orphaned in tribal fighting in the North and at age 5 or 6 given over to distant tribal relations, nomadic pastoralists who, following the scarce rains,

moved camels and goats in an annual transhumance across northern
Somalia, into Ethiopia's vast Ogaden and back again. As the
youngest and without anyone acting in *loco parentis*, Nur lived on
sufferance, guarding goats and camels with his life against hyenas
and bandits, or shifta as they were called, as he wandered across a
parched landscape in one of the most inhospitable regions on earth.
Sometimes he saw no one for weeks on end, deprived of company,
education and language. Kidney failure is common in nomads without water from too young an age, and this too was to befall Nur.

His spartan existence, pushing the limits of endurance in a fragile balance with nature, lasted until Nur was about fourteen. Then,
in the port of Berbera where Somali herders brought their camels
for sale and export to Saudi Arabia, Nur was kidnapped and forced
to serve as galley boy on a derelict coastal vessel. As nearly as I can
tell, he stayed at sea for about five years, graduating to larger vessels and drifting about the world with goodness knows what forged
Somali papers or just stowing away onboard. I am unable to provide details of these years, nor did Nur speak of them later. I can,
however, vouchsafe that, without training in English, he acquired
an impressive seaman's vocabulary.

When I think of Nur in those years, I remember a young tribes-
man of striking appearance who once flagged us down in the middle of nowhere when I was driving with Mumin in the bush. It was
the custom for young men to buy extra hair from barbers, matting it
to their own with camel dung and rancid butter or ghee, signifying
readiness for marriage. This nomad had done just that, and his hair
formed a redolent arc of several feet of which he was justly proud.
Together with his spear in hand, aquiline features and lean frame,
covered only by a futa[6] at the waist, he stands out indelibly in
memory. Mumin was not pleased, but I gave the man a lift to
Mogadishu, a jolting four hours away. Asked on arrival where he
was going, he only said "Lido," a notorious dance hall on the outskirts of town. I happened to pass by that way the next day, and

there he was, standing on one leg in the same spot holding his spear, surrounded by city urchins. He seemed to nod but our worlds, never overlapping by much, were now far apart, and I knew that I, the instrument of his deliverance, had broken this man's fragile ties to earth. This too could have been Nur's story, but for the extraordinary events related below.

Midway through the decade, his tramp steamer set sail from the Port of Baltimore, stranding Nur ashore in an alien land. There were no Somalis in Baltimore then, unlike today when they dominate the taxi business. So, the perplexed police referred his case to the Department of State, and Nur's luck began to change. As it happened, John F. Kennedy had launched the Peace Corps in 1961, and Somalia was designated one of the initial pilot countries. As the program grew, there was insatiable demand for Somali language teachers to handle the growing number of volunteers in training. Despite his modest origins, Nur was pressed into service with expedited visas and work papers for the President's pet program. Since our family was in Washington by then and I had studied Somali *in situ*, Peace Corps friends put us in touch, and Nur lived in our modest basement for many months. His wild nomadic looks, charisma and way with women upset suburban neighbors, but made him a magnet for PCVs. Soon he moved to his own place, grander than ours, although we stayed in touch. With just a few months of seniority himself, he supervised more recently arrived fellow countrymen, lording it over them.

Meanwhile, back in Somalia, General Siad Barre, whom I had known as Defense Minister, pulled off a military coup on October 21, 1969, just a day after the assassination of President Ali Shermarke. It was no surprise that the Peace Corps were the first to be expelled by the suspicious and pro-Soviet general, shutting down the Somali program, including language training and putting Nur back on the street. Here the story takes an unimagined turn, however. Black and African studies were becoming trendy in US higher ed. and were dominated by Nigerians, Ghanaians and other West Africans. No Somalis were yet in the field, and fewer still were already managers, and "academics" like Nur were in sudden demand. He received credit for lifetime experience and a full scholarship from a California university in return for a pledge to serve as an on-campus student resource and eventually an instructor.

Here I must digress briefly from the story of Nur. One of my schoolmates at a small, all-male boarding school in New England was a real sportsman who, incredible to the rest of us, used to sneak out nights for illegal cockfights over in Marlborough where he did very well, serving as his own handler and fighting his own game chickens against all local comers. His birds were the real deal, said to be descended from the legendary Bone Crusher, a streaky-breasted red dunn, and from a black-breasted red champion who had famously killed three in two minutes. Marlborough was not then or ever a center of world cockfighting, and when I say he did very well, he cleaned up. Boys at school used to make bets with him and, while I did not personally ever observe it, apparently paid off during the mandatory high Episcopalian daily vesper services in the school's Norman chapel. His expulsion was, of course, spectacular, and my friend was sent down for remediation at the Johnny Hun School in Princeton.

There, he repeated a year and, against all odds, Johnny Hun worked its magic and he was admitted to Princeton, bringing along his Saudi roommate from Hun and joining my gaggle of sophomore roommates. I understood that Saudis were different when, finding that the best rooms were already spoken for, Saud proposed to purchase the entire dormitory, Princeton's venerable Brown Hall. Nor was he just any Saudi, but a genuine HRH from the House of Saud, Prince Saud bin Faisal bin Abdulaziz al Saud, who became the world's longest-serving Foreign Minister from 1975 until King Salman replaced him on April 29, 2015. He died just two month later on July 9. I once chatted with Saud about horses and cockfighting on the General Assembly floor before he excused himself to make a rousing and now legendary speech about jihad. I saw him again only once at the Royal Dar es-Salaam Golf Club in Rabat in the time of King Hassan II.

In any case, I know that, after Saud's time at Princeton and Columbia, his many younger brothers and cousins abandoned the East Coast and went west for education to the California universities. There, they encountered and sponsored a well-networked young Muslim instructor of African studies from a friendly, neighboring country. California had clearly agreed with Nur, and he was in even more demand on the West Coast than he had been in Washington. On the negative side, however, Nur was completely unreconstructed in matters of gender and had blundered in marrying the head of the Militant Black Nurses of Northern California. Together, I'm told that they came close to killing each other on several occasions. Accusations of spousal abuse may also have harmed Nur's academic prospects, and he was open to change.

So Nur went willingly when the Saudis took him home to Jubail, the largest industrial city of the Middle East, the biggest civil engineering project of modern times, and the region's largest and world's fourth largest petrochemical complex. Bechtel, the project manager, was eager to please the princes, and Nur found his niche, recruiting thousands of unskilled laborers from his tribe in Somaliland. There, he was treated like a godfather, and there was even talk of politics, although General Siad Barre still ruled with an iron hand. Nur travelled widely for his work and delighted in taking my wife and me to a swanky Washington restaurant, grinning as he showed off a huge wad of hundred dollar bills. He still carried a dagger in his sock, even or particularly in our nation's capital.

In the end, renal failure, which I've already mentioned and to which nomads are prone, struck Nur. He flew in a brother, whose new house in Hargeisa he had bankrolled, for a deluxe US tour capped by a kidney donation. The brother enjoyed the trip hugely but proclaimed on the last day that he'd come for the experience only and had no intention of parting with a kidney. I don't know how long Nur lived on, but wish he were here to fill in the many gaps in this sketchy account.

SHIPWRECKS I HAVE KNOWN

"A Drowning Man Shouldn't Grab for Crests of the Wave."
—Somali Proverb

An unexpected aspect of my work for Her Majesty was the care and feeding of frequent shipwreck victims of the treacherous winds and barrier reefs along Somalia's unprotected coast which, transposed onto a US map, stretches from Maine to Florida. These almost invariably involved Commonwealth Protected Persons, a second class passport category accorded to former British colonial subjects during the transition from empire. After my time, there were a few instances of real British yachtsmen foundering on the coral reefs and even seized by pirates for ransom, but I never had such a case. Nevertheless, the British Interests Section of the American Embassy, meaning Mumin, me and an Adeni clerk named Ahmed, had to be in constant readiness, sometimes difficult to maintain when the Brigadier was in town. Two shipwrecks particularly stand out in memory.

In the first instance, I remember being at work in the office on Social Security benefits for an ancient Somali-American who had returned to Mogadishu to marry a nubile teenager, when Omar, the captain of an ill-fated Omani dhow, first strode in. He must have been well over six feet, muscled up and sun-burnt, the way sailors from Muscat and Oman usually are. In his disheveled white robe and turban, dagger at his waist, he was clearly a match for whatever might come his way. Probing dark eyes and a beard completed the picture and, while he did not actually beat his chest, this was the impression that he conveyed. Peering from behind was his son, Ismael, a boy of about four.

Omar launched into a tale of woe in guttural Omani Arabic, haltingly interpreted by Ahmed. The owner and captain of his own dhow, a rough wooden sailing vessel common on that coast, Omar had sailed from Lamu, Kenya's easternmost port, counting on the south winds which blow steadily for six months of the year to bear him safely to the Persian Gulf. The dhow, an open-decked veteran of many such crossings, carried the usual cargo of goats, lumber and some forty passengers. The voyage had gone smoothly until somewhere off Warsheikh, a few hours northeast by Land Rover from the capital, an unexpected storm forced the primitive craft onto the reef. Omar played down the loss of crew and passengers, but it is clear that most had little chance with the offshore reef, waves and shark-infested waters, particularly a party of black veiled Hadhrami women travelling on deck, whose custom and religion forbade swimming.

Omar himself cleared the reef with his wife, infant daughter and son, striking out for the distant shore. Soon, he surrendered his wife to her fate, struggling on with daughter and son. Abandoning the former, he reached land after a grueling swim pulling his son behind. After wandering along a desolate coast, famed for the most aggressive hyenas in all Somalia, they were rescued by nomads and reached Mogadishu after a week's march by camel caravan. I could detect no remorse in Omar's account, but rather acceptance that the wreck was the will of Allah and immutable fate. For him the priorities of survival were clear, and he and Ismael had responded to the challenge as men. And who is to say that we, westerners, would not have floundered and perished together, by wave or shark, with none like Ismael escaping to tell the tale? We found them lodging and, through channels and in the proper time, passage back to Oman where Omar doubtless resumed his trade.

Calamities have a way of coming all at once, and it seemed like only days, weeks at most, before another befell us. On that coast, there are no real seasons, only unbroken days of sun, heat and sand. It all runs together in your mind without the usual guideposts of season, and memory fails you there year by year. Last month's gala dinner becomes last night's and the Saudi Ambassador who seemed to leave last week really left a year ago, and so on. Life becomes a jumble of days without the kind of seasonal memory-aids we normally rely on. The donkey's bay at dawn, the smell of sweat in the streets, the haggling of vendors, all are seamless parts of life, the way it expends itself effortlessly there on the Equator.

Still, I can recall just when the second calamity occurred. I was at my post in the Embassy interviewing candidate cooks for our first lady when into a packed waiting room of mendicant bush cooks burst a strange assemblage of castaways. At length, a leader distinguished himself and pronounced words I was to hear daily for two months, a litany of swear words learned as a sailor, and the sum of his English. After these greeting pleasantries, we began the task of piecing together their sad history with help from a local Indian gentleman whom providence had placed in their path. His grasp of their particular tongue or theirs of his was far from complete, however, and many details of their ordeal are missing.

We learned, however, that their craft, a motor-less coastal sailor, had set out from Male in the Maldive Islands 1337 miles west of India, laden with produce and passengers bound for a neighboring island some thirty miles distant. A violent tropical storm struck en route, blowing the vessel seaward into the Indian Ocean. There, caught in the prevailing winds and without hope of return, it traversed the entire Ocean, running before the wind in good weather for most of the way. After nearly 2,000 miles and, by their estimate, forty-one days at sea, the craft foundered on the Somali reef somewhere off the remote Mijertiin, south of Ras Hafun, but closer to shore than the site of Omar's wreck. Several passengers died during the crossing of exposure, thirst or illness. An old man and a child perished reaching land. The others, some eighty marooned Maldivians, were found by nomads along the arid coast and were eventually moved by trade trucks to Galkayu. From there, they were transferred by the Somali Red Crescent to the capital and, finally, the Embassy.

While the Maldives were by then independent and soon to become another UN mini-state, Whitehall for reasons of its own still considered Maldivians protected persons, in other words the Embassy's responsibility as long as we represented the UK. So it was that requests for guidance and assistance moved with the diplomatic bag from Mogadishu to Washington, on to London and in this case finally to Male in the Maldives and back the same way before decisions could be taken, probably one of the longest chains of command in diplomatic or consular history. Such bureaucracy was incomprehensible to the Maldivian victims, many debilitated and afflicted with sores. Each day, they came in as a group, exhausted their limited English vocabulary and probed through the flustered interpreter for news.

Mogadishu mobilized to help, as only a small place can. The Interior Ministry donated lodgings, medicine and surplus food, rare in that impoverished land. The Red Crescent gave clothing and blankets, the Hadhrami Benevolent Society raised cash, the American Embassy ladies baked pies and cakes, and many others helped as well. And then we waited and waited for a bureaucratic response through channels. Finally it came, approval for their return by the cheapest possible transport to Male. Better than their original crossing, but not by much, this meant a bone-crushing eleven-day truck ride in muddy season to Berbera, uncertain passage from there by dhow to Aden, and steerage home on any available bottom. The Maldivians left us after nearly three months in Mogadishu, with all the usual swear words, followed this time by embraces.

THE IMPORTANCE OF LANGUAGE

"If you cut off an ear, the hole remains."
—Somali Proverb

Somali is an intense, guttural language, and I was proud to be the first American, at least in the State Department, to speak it. I studied under the legendary Muusa Haji Ishmail Galaal, collector of these and other Somali proverbs, not only because I thought that I might win friends and influence people but also, more self-interested, because the Department offered a huge salary increase to officers officially tested at a fluency level in this obscure language. At the time, Somali was still without a written form, and the country was divided among three competing orthographies: modernists favored the Latin alphabet and access to western knowledge, Islamists as they were then called without today's connotations, on the other hand, considered Arabic to be the language of God and insisted on its script, and, finally, nationalists believed that, as a new and independent nation, Somalia was entitled to its own unique form of writing and devised the distinctive Osmanya script for this purpose. Blood was sometimes shed over this conundrum and, for my part, I was left to record the barks and glottal stops of my daily lessons in whatever hieroglyphics or shorthand I chose. It was a fascinating window into the culture with regular grammar, a rich vocabulary for camels and livestock and a total absence of niceties like "please" and "thank you," reflecting the directness of the people.

Things progressed and, as I developed a rudimentary grasp of Somali, I soon found myself assigned on July 4 and at other gatherings to make idle chitchat with Gen. Mohammed Siad Barre, then Defense Minister and later the longtime President and strongman, a taciturn individual who paid scant attention to my memorized proverbs. On the Washington front, the more I insisted, the more bureaucratic resistance developed to actually testing me. The organizational chart at the Foreign Service Institute (FSI), then as now, consisted of a body of "scientific linguists" responsible for overseeing clusters or families of related languages with native speakers to do the actual teaching. Somali fell completely outside this structure with no scientific linguists, no native speakers and no test materials. Furthermore, lack of an agreed written form eliminated any check on one's depth of knowledge, making the test result dependant on the spoken module alone.

Finally, a linguist with deep knowledge of the Shona languages of Southern Africa agreed to come to Nairobi as part of a regional inspection tour of Embassy language programs, but under no circumstances to visit Mogadishu. Somalis, it should be noted in advance, are believed to have had their earliest origins in the Arabian Peninsula, and their language belongs to the small Cushitic linguistic family along with Galla in Ethiopia and Afar around Djibouti, closer to Semitic languages like Hebrew and Arabic than to those of Africa and completely alien to the Shona family in which my interlocutor was versed. In any case, when the appointed time came, I went happily to Nairobi and, unlike entrance exams for the Foreign Service, soon found myself completely in the driver's seat.

The scientific linguist had retained two native Somali speakers from the expatriate population in Kenya to administer the test, but failed to distinguish that one came from the far north and one from the far south of Somalia and that they spoke totally different dialects. Much worse and unbeknownst to the struggling linguist, they came from opposing tribal clans and, I could see immediately, held each other in the greatest contempt. Unwilling and perhaps even unable to communicate between themselves, they argued incessantly, and the linguist quickly lost any semblance of control. Having studied in the capital city close to the center of the country, I was invariably and embarrassingly given maximum benefit of the doubt by these two first-time examiners and mortal enemies.

Frustrated, the linguist finally took me aside to say that I was at a higher level of proficiency than he had anticipated and that the litmus test of fluency in a language is the ability to convey humor. He proceeded to lay out a particularly inane American baseball joke which I was to convey to the two Somalis. I could not remotely have done so and, even if I could, you must understand that baseball is not played in Somalia and the joke would have fallen on deaf ears. So, I spoke to them of the beauty of women's gums, by which Somalis set great store, they laughed uproariously, and I received an unconscionably high, near-fluency rating and returned to Mogadishu with a huge pay increase.

I don't for a minute regret taking advantage of this bizarre situation and think of it as the only time over three decades of service that I was able to successfully "game the system." Still, the wages of sin can take unexpected forms. Shortly thereafter, I was reassigned to Tripoli, Libya where I made desultory efforts to study Arabic, loosening my already tenuous grip on Somali, but nevertheless continuing to enjoy the higher salary. More than a year later, I received an urgent telegram, known then as a "rocket," to report back to Mogadishu for duty within forty-eight hours. In a pre-computer age, Department files had identified me as the only Somali language resource, and I was to stand by to interpret during the January 1968 Somali visit by Vice President Hubert Humphrey. The Vice President, whom as it turned out I never laid eyes on, was a rapid and voluble speaker whom, behind his back, some called "motor mouth." The sheer fantasy of interpreting for him in that language was frankly terrifying, but, having pushed for the test and received the pay increase, I could not refuse the Department's order and was soon airborne.

Once again in Mogadishu, I realized that this was no ordinary visit. Somalia and Ethiopia were in a virtual state of war along the border, inflamed by the recent announcement of yet another American tank sale to Ethiopia, and Humphrey's long-scheduled visit had been cancelled because of threats to the Vice President and only reluctantly rescheduled at the last minute by the Secret Service. Tension was high within the Veep's security entourage, and happily for me a Somali was soon found to interpret for him, while I was locked in a small, windowless room to monitor threats to the Vice President on the Somali police radio, particularly incidents along his motorcade routes.

There came a time that Humphrey was enroute to the Somali President's residence at Afgoi, which means cleft or harelip in Somali, some distance from the capital. Actually, the place is quite well known for stunka fighting each year when two riverain tribes come together to beat each other with sticks, a holdover from earlier times when the victors carried off wives of the vanquished as booty. Even in my time, they would sometimes insert razors into the sticks, and the local diplomatic corps used to troop out each year for the spectacle. I had some familiarity with the road to Afgoi, usually choked with donkey carts, camels and livestock and was not surprised when the radio exploded with angry yelling and shouts. It was impossible to decipher the pandemonium, and security officers crowded around eager to turn back the Vice President's motorcade. I thought I heard the word for donkey and made an educated guess that an advance patrol was clearing the road of livestock, and allowed the motorcade to proceed. It was, nevertheless, a very uncomfortable moment, and the scientific linguist had clearly done me no favor.

IN THE REARVIEW MIRROR

The first real job probably burns brightest in memory for everyone, whatever the profession. Not that it's necessarily all downhill from there. Still, newly married, newly employed, newly a father and in an unimaginable, exotic place like Somalia then, the unfamiliar sights, sounds and smells still stand out in sharp relief. After being overeducated for fifteen years, maintained on an allowance from my father, he of the Peale shoes and bespoke shirts, and generally dependent on others, the freedom of being on one's own in such a faraway place was exhilarating. Nor did diplomatic protocols, strictures and niceties inhibit joy of life at the edges of the known world. You could snorkel on a reef at lunchtime or in the cool of evening play tennis late into the night, lounging around a clay pizza oven afterwards. A lamp strategically held over tidal pools on the reef would unfailingly attract enough lobsters to feed a picnic.

Camping too was an experience and, encircling the campfire, you could see the yellow eyes of hyenas, kept safely at bay by the fire and our fearless dog Booboo. It was, in short, a time of innocence, and as the youngest couple there my wife and I were spoiled as sort of Embassy pets with many willing mentors at a close-knit, small post in a challenging and isolated place. And if it seemed claustrophobic, there was always Mt. Kilimanjaro next door to climb. Coming from sea level, the latter was a challenge, however, and I keeled over at 17,000 feet and had to be escorted down gasping while my wife continued on and summited or at least close to it. Never mind that, taking off for Kenya, we had blithely and irresponsibly left our two year old son Richard with good friends in Moqadishu where in our absence he came down with break-bone fever, but thankfully was well cared for and soon recovered.

Somalia, flush with independence and full of hope, was a paradise in those years, and watching its long downward spiral has been painful for anyone who was there, let alone for the Somalis themselves who continue to live through it. Both pain and guilt too, since most of us moved on to other countries and languages, and few returned to help in Somalia's protracted hour of need. There is surely plenty of blame to go around. Extractive Italian colonialism distorted the time-honored tribal balance by reinforcing clans in the capital region at the expense of the periphery. The Organization of African Unity (OAU) made Somalia a pariah state by refusing to rectify colonial borders despite majority Somali populations outside its frontiers.

The Cold War was the final straw. The Soviet Union, with a major naval base at Berbera, poured in armaments, and then, with the overthrow of Emperor Haile Selassie in Ethiopia, the superpowers switched client states and it was the US turn to do so. The result was a failed state: a cataclysm of famine, warlords, Islamists, pirates and periodic US-sponsored invasions from Ethiopia. In 2011 alone, 260,000 Somalis starved to death, half of them under age six. The Dadaab refugee camp across the border in Kenya, threatened with closure following the September 2013 Westgate Mall attack in Nairobi and again in May 2016, became the largest refugee center in the world where half a million mostly Somali refugees lived in appalling conditions. Cry the beloved country.[7]

NOTES

1. Isak Dinessen, *Out of Africa*, 1937.

2. G. Mennen Williams, former Governor of Michigan and Assistant Secretary of African Affairs 1961–1966.

3. Walter Rostow, Chairman of State Department Policy Planning Council, 1961–66, and National Security Advisor under President Johnson, 1966–69.

4. Today known as just Luuq.

5. Richard Corfield (1882–1913) was a British Colonial Police officer stationed in South Africa, Nigeria and Somalia. He was killed on August 9, 1913, at the Battle of Dul Madoba by Sayyid Muhammad Abdille Hassan, who subsequently wrote "The Death of Richard Corfield," an epic poem on Corfield's final hours, memorized by generations of Somalis.

6. A traditional Somali garment similar to the Indian longi.

7. The title of Alan Paton's classic novel of South Africa, *Cry the Beloved Country*, 1948.

III

From Kingdom to Jamahiriya

THE SETTING

State Department Personnel had obviously branded me as viable for the former Italian colonies only and not to be trusted in Rome, *bon pour l'Orient* as the French say. After Mogadishu, we were reassigned to Asmara in Eritrea, also once an Italian colony but at that time part of Ethiopia and eventually independent, although the assignment was changed to Libya where Italian occupation had been of the scorched earth kind, particularly in Cyrenaica. In fact, the Italians from 1912 to 1943 were only the most recent, but unquestionably the most brutal, in a long line of occupiers from Phoenicians to Greeks, Romans and Ottoman Turks. Tobruk and other major tank battles of World War II were fought there as well, and deep in the desert, perfectly preserved in the arid climate, was the "Lady be Good," an American B-24 Liberator bomber which inexplicably crashed there on April 4, 1943 after a bombing raid on Naples.

After the War, the UN Trusteeship Council wrestled with the fate of Libya, which could not just be handed back to the Italians. Amid general misgivings, it was cut loose as an independent state in 1951, among the poorest in the world with annual per capita income of only $48.[1] Its major export was esparto grass, an additive in making fine textured paper. This was only slightly supplemented by scrap metal sales after the War. The great surge of oil discovery from 1960–62 attracted almost every major oil company including the famed Seven Sisters, and by our arrival in 1966 Libya had skyrocketed to a booming daily production of three million barrels of light sweet crude, the most prized petroleum requiring only minimum refining. This was staggering wealth for an Alaska-sized country with only 1.4 million inhabitants, many of them nomadic herders.

The King, while benign and from a religious dynasty with Algerian roots, was elderly and ascetic, basically living as a recluse in palaces at Tripoli, Benghazi, Baida and Tobruk.[2] In his absence, corruption flourished and a suddenly-rich minority lived in a style even Hollywood or Miami might envy. As for the man in the street, I never met anyone who considered themselves Libyan, but instead all were first and foremost Tripolitanian, Fezzani or Cyrenaican, incompatible regions with divergent histories, thrown together randomly by the UN at independence. Each appeared contemptuous of the others with eastern tribes, then as now, scorning the Turkified and effete manners of Tripoli and both discriminating against the black African population of the Fezzan.

Apart from oil, the only other game in town was Wheelus Air Base, a sprawling US Air Force installation highly visible just a few miles outside Tripoli on the main coastal road. It was, in effect, a medium-sized American town with schools, churches, hospitals, bowling alleys, theaters and supermarkets, simply parachuted into Libya and walled off against intruders. This was the height of the Cold War and Wheelus, which came with huge areas of empty desert for live bombing and target practice, was considered vital to NATO readiness. Pilots stationed in congested Europe, where they could not bomb or strafe at will, had to complete an ambitious quota of bombing and gunnery practice at Wheelus each month or lose their combat-ready certification and take a pay cut.

Thus, there was a daily rotation of F-4s, F-5s and other aircraft in and out. Sometimes, nomads would unwittingly intrude into the range areas resulting in fatal accidents, which required intricate diplomacy and compensation handled through a special political-military office. More mundanely, the latter was also busy deciding which privileged Libyans would gain access to the sought-after Wheelus medical and dental facilities or to the almost inexhaustible stores of liquor, cigarettes and other tax free offerings at obscenely low prices in the Base Commissary.

We had, in short, rocketed through time and space from an impoverished but proud tribal society to a place of intrigue and subterfuge where the greed and corruption of today's world were on full display. Oil magnates jostled with generals for access, and we were no longer the youngest couple and pets of a close knit Embassy community. Instead, USG agencies fought tooth and nail for turf, and careerists elbowed their way ahead. Beyond the Embassy gates, the late Bunker Hunt was not so quietly reaping a cool $5 billion from the Libyans in just those years before Qadhafi nationalized oil. It dawned on me belatedly that, for all the talk of service and hardship, ambassadors in their flag-flying limos had only limited clout when it came to the petrodollar crowd, most of whom had direct lines into Congress and the White House.

WITHIN A PROPER EMBASSY

Gone certainly were the free-wheeling days of representing Her Majesty and foraging in the bush with Mumin. The Tripoli Embassy was an unprepossessing, even shabby structure, not far from the King's Palace in the garden district of Tripoli. While it seemed grand to me at the time and I recall being summoned to the front office of the Ambassador and DCM with no little shock and awe, I revisited the place years later and was struck by how memory magnifies and gives benefit of the doubt. In fact, on a second look, even the Ambassador's once magnificent suite now appeared cramped and unworthy of a superpower. The Ambassador, David Newsom, was by then Undersecretary of State for Political Affairs, the Department's top career post at State, and I was travelling with him but kept my thoughts private about the seedy venue of his former glory.

Work too was more specialized than I was used to and, still the low man on the Embassy totem pole, I was assigned to biographic reporting. In those days, with Libya awash in oil money and rampant corruption, this was like picking low-hanging fruit from the bough. It involved developing extensive profiles on Libyan cabinet members and leaders, many of them reprobates known for sexual and financial peccadillos and all manner of venality. My salacious reports were apparently well received in Washington and fueled a growing cottage industry devoted to psychological profiles of foreign leaders and employing a staff of resident shrinks without access to actual patients or the proverbial psychiatrist's couch. My reports served as grist for their evaluations, although I had taken only a single psychology course to fulfill a college science requirement, doing my meager research at Princeton on superstition in the pigeon. Years after my time in Libya, the new industry reached its zenith under President Ronald Reagan, who preferred films to dry written reports and regularly screened Hollywood-quality psychiatric profiles on Muammar Qadhafi and Kim Il Sung, as well as less reprehensible foreign leaders with whom he met.

The biographic portfolio also recalled my stunted career in journalism and was a fine vantage point to observe the comings and goings of a larger embassy, including the military brass from Wheelus, SHAPE and NATO and executives from an alphabet soup of oil companies who constituted the bread and butter of the mission. Weekly country team meetings, far removed from the cigar-filled back room atmosphere of Mogadishu, were august events for senior officers only and snippets of their deliberations filtered down imperfectly by word of mouth. My boss, Holsey G. Handyside, like Outerbridge Horsey, had a Foreign Service name for the ages, as well as boundless energy and, although a short man, used to take the flight of stairs up to our offices in a single stride.

Libya at that time had as many as four capitals. Tripoli, where we lived, was the largest and most cosmopolitan with vestiges everywhere of Italian occupation and centuries of rule by Ottoman Turks. Benghazi, so much in the news today, was the eastern port and power center of Cyrenaican tribes. Baida, in the Jebel Akhdar or Green Mountains, was an artificial capital designated by the King and the improbable location of the Ministry of Foreign Affairs. Finally, Tobruk, near the Egyptian border, was where the King spent much of his time in solitude and was thus a kind of *de facto* capital as well.

The sheer distances required the Ambassador to have an aircraft, and an aging 6–8 passenger, twin engine Beechcraft aircraft stood at his beck and call at Wheelus. A ministry of foreign affairs with its permanent undersecretary, director for the Americas, protocol chief and other key officials is basically the main access point or one-stop shopping center for diplomats. So, to have it 500 miles away as the crow flies in a remote mountain town was a huge anomaly, let alone a logistic nightmare for embassies without their own planes. Of course, we had a one-officer post in Baida whose incumbent was kept busy importuning his Ministry homologues on how we hoped Libya would vote at the UN on, for example, independence of Puerto Rico, Security Council candidates or UN reform.

These demarches were all well and good, but no substitute for face-to-face contacts. So it was that every month or six weeks we would make the three and a half hour flight to Baida, taking off at dawn and often returning after dark. There was a healthy competition among the political, economic, consular and administrative officers to prove who could schedule the most calls while in Baida. Each had burning issues of one kind or another to discuss, whether access to American prisoners in Libyan jails or diplomatic licenses and parking privileges. I believe the record was eight Ministry calls in a single day's trip.

Libyan protocol was unbending in its insistence that three glasses of bilious, bitter Libyan green tea were *de rigueur* during each call. To consume less was to give serious affront to the host, so these calls, inconsequential as they may have been in the larger scheme of things, nevertheless involved considerable hardship and discomfort if not outright sacrifice for one's country. Assuming that you carried out an ambitious six calls, no mean feat because the Libyans did not necessarily want to see us in the first place, that would total 18 glasses of tea. Whatever the amount, the turbulent return flight bumping back over the Jebel Akhdar Mountains was invariably torturous and even the stalwarts barfed uncontrollably into USAF-provided air sickness bags.

Nor was all the work as routine as I have described. For example, I came to know the expatriate head of a local air conditioning company who confided in me his success in winning a contract to air condition the fortress-like Soviet Embassy. My modest role was only to turn him over to a specialist in the field, but it is a satisfaction to know that in those Cold War years the Soviet Embassy became a prolific source on what transpired within its honeycombed walls. The diplomatic corps was, of course, larger than in Somalia and generally bored, eager to play tennis, golf at Wheelus if invited, or to picnic in the vast Roman cities of Leptis Magna and Sabratha.

Deep in the desert, there were even markers and monuments of Roman design but with Berber carvings of lions and elephants which, until recent millennia, had inhabited what was once the breadbasket of the Roman Empire. Without the Brigadier on my back, I was now free to appreciate these exquisite markers and monuments. Once on a camping trip with friends from another agency of government we were guided by a bedouin deep into the

Libyan desert through an impenetrable sandstorm or "ghibli" to an obscure archaeological site fusing Roman and Berber designs.

The British Embassy, in contrast to the humble Interests Section in Somalia of just Ahmed, Mumin and me, was quite grand and stands out in memory. While the Ambassador received his knighthood for persuading the Libyans that they really needed the British Bloodhound Air Defense Missile System, his top lieutenants were pungently named Smellie, Swett and Pugh. No matter that a year later Col. Qadhafi personally ripped up the Bloodhound contract, the Ambassador's knighthood was for life. On the other hand, Smellie, who was later himself deservedly also knighted, went on to head MI-6 in troubled Northern Ireland where for several years he never slept twice in the same bed.

Libya was clearly in an unimaginable transition, and the two major events of my time were the June 1967 Six Day War and the 1969 Qadhafi coup, although I was working on Libya in Washington when the latter transpired. The sheer rate of change, vast oil money and disparity of wealth and life styles seemed to bewilder and disorient many Libyans, creating a kind of Wild West, boom town atmosphere. Women were mostly left behind, and it was not unusual to see cars with interior locks removed so that women could be left securely inside while men folk shopped. I also once observed a female guest secrete what looked like a whole leg of lamb from the Ambassador's buffet beneath her flowing robes. A ruder shock, at least for the thief involved, occurred when the small Peace Corps program, where my wife Stuart worked as assistant to the Director, summoned volunteers to deliver stool samples to Tripoli for analysis. On the bus from Gharian, a mountainous area still inhabited by troglodytes, a thief grabbed a surprised volunteer's paper bag and sample and jumped off at the next stop to inspect his prize. Peace Corps disappeared soon afterwards with the Qadhafi revolution and in hindsight may have been an oxymoron to begin with in an unpopulated desert country with 3 million barrels of oil per day.

THE KING AND I[3]

The Vietnam War, far from the preoccupations of King Idris and his inward-looking subjects, was continuing to escalate under Lyndon Johnson throughout the sixties. Twenty million gallons of Agent Orange were being used to destroy 25 million acres in Vietnam, both to eliminate jungle cover for the Viet Minh and to deprive the countryside of food, thus tripling the population in US-held cities. American embassies around the world were under pressure to put the best face possible on these abominable tactics and to counteract accusations from the Non-Aligned Movement and others. Thus one day bells went off in the Embassy communications center signifying arrival of a high precedence telegram, either Niact Immediate or Flash. In fact, it was a stern instruction from the beleaguered Johnson Administration for every American ambassador wherever the US had an embassy to lose no time in delivering a detailed five-page demarche on defoliation in Vietnam to the head of state, in this case the aging King Idris.

And so it was that the Ambassador was obliged to fly the 1,262 mile round trip to Tobruk to carry out these instructions from on high. The King seemed truly ancient and looked and moved more like a shrouded sage from classical Greece than a desert warrior. He died in 1983 in Cairo at age 94, so was probably 78 at the time. The Ambassador, always a straight shooter, informed the King of the subject and importance of his mission, and the wily Monarch, probably fearing the worst, proposed lunch first. It included a capitaine, flown in from Paris but probably fished first from Lake Chad, lamb, pilaf, cakes, dates and fruit.

"The Demarche."

Ensconced after lunch in a kind of private solarium, the King reclined on a couch and finally assented to the Ambassador's presentation. After the midday meal, with the heat of early afternoon and the droning of bees from a nearby apiary, the King was soon asleep. The Ambassador, seated by his side, launched into the demarche, faithful to his instructions. Paragraph by paragraph, he read from the extensive text as an interpreter rendered it into classical Arabic. Words like strategic hamlet, rural pacification and defoliation evidently had no Arabic counterparts and echoed strangely in that vaulted chamber. In the room, all else was still save the droning of bees and the Monarch's rhythmic breathing. Outside, the sun sparkled on the Mediterranean and, to the South, sands stretched away endlessly to the Great Rebiana and Calancio Sand Seas, reinforcing the impression that Vietnam was indeed a world away.

In about an hour, the Ambassador completed his task and, before long, the King awoke refreshed and proposed tea, thanking the

Ambassador warmly for his presentation. Tea arrived with multi-flavored honey to sample. In fact, honey and beekeeping were dear to Idris' heart, and the royal staff included a head beekeeper from Dundee and an under-keeper from somewhere in the Highlands. Both were fixtures of the household and labored to produce fine Scottish honey there amid Saharan sands. I'm told they were dour individuals, whether from regular stingings or the hive-destroying Ghibli winds. On his return to Tripoli, the Ambassador cabled the Department laconically, "Carried out subject demarche. King seemed quite responsive to some points," although because of its classification I was not privy to the actual message and did not have an "obvious need to know."[4]

It may be that the King's fondness for honey was related to his dental problems, as he was certainly the most prominent and, I believe, one of the most frequent clients of the Air Force dental clinic at Wheelus. As I understood it, the King had consulted an Italian dentist during World War II and the terrified man had let slip an electric drill, stitching up and down the Royal tongue. As a consequence of this shoddy treatment by the Italians, the King was pleased to accept proffered dental assistance from Wheelus but only on condition that no electric drills were allowed in his mouth.

Thus it was that for many years, until just before he was overthrown and all dental assistance terminated, work on the Royal mouth was carried out with old-fashioned wooden mallets, chisels and other period pieces. Such a return to Nineteenth Century practice was particularly galling to younger dental school graduates doing their military service at the well-equipped Wheelus clinic, but they nevertheless rendered the old man *pro bono* service each month in the national interest. With the passage of time and confidence-building measures by the dentists, his fears gradually subsided, however, and towards the end of his reign, he authorized use of the latest high speed water drill and was well pleased with the results. Such are often the unsung diplomatic victories, out of sight and unknown to the public.

THE SIX-DAY WAR

One of the great pleasures of assignment abroad is to explore the wider region, and my wife and I made a poorly timed trip to Hurgada on the then-unspoiled Red Sea coast of Egypt just days before the Six Day War erupted on June 5, 1967.[5] Flying south from Cairo, we were the only foreigners on the plane, and the friendly Egyptian pilot invited us to enjoy the sweeping view with him from the cockpit for the entire flight. We had a close look at what was considered a very strategic area including military bases, proof if any be needed that the Egyptians were really clueless about the impending Israeli attack. We arrived back in Tripoli just before the outbreak of war after a week snorkeling on crystaline Red Sea reefs.

As first reports came in of Israeli destruction of aircraft and airfields across Egypt, the Libyan authorities advised the Embassy that security of American aircraft at Wheelus Field could no longer be guaranteed, and two squadrons of fighters down from Europe for gunnery practice took off in combat formation, two at a time, as well as other aircraft on the base.[6] This mass exodus of nearly 200 aircraft and sheer volume of sound was seen and heard throughout Tripoli just as reports began coming in of planes bombing the airport and other sites in Cairo with pinpoint accuracy. The inescapable conclusion, soon accepted as absolute fact by all Libyans, was that the attack had been launched directly from Wheelus and carried out by Americans. The coincidence was simply too great for Libyans to entertain any other explanation, as was the psychological jump for them to acknowledge that a small state like Israel could so easily defeat the largest and most powerful country of the Arab world.

Chaos soon erupted in the streets and particularly along the coastal highway leading to Wheelus. In the short term, there was a period of rioting and looting during which the American Consulate General in Benghazi was besieged and burned by an hysterical mob, forcing its ten employees to take shelter in a solid steel vault, left over from the building's days as a bank. There, they survived, despite intense heat, smoke and tear gas, for nearly ten hours until rescued by tanks and armored cars from a nearby British base.[7] Many Libyans were injured forcing themselves through the jagged gates and window bars that protected the building. Then, as now, Benghazi and its surrounding region of Cyrenaica were a hotbed of tribal enmities and hatreds.

In this atmosphere of violence and uncertainty, all Americans except "essential" Embassy staff were evacuated for several months to the US or, like my wife and young son, to a holding pattern in Italy until conditions were deemed safe for their return. One day, before a ceasefire was declared on June 11, I recall being asked to accompany the Embassy Budget and Fiscal Officer on a truck from the Embassy to Wheelus, conveying classified papers, currency and items of particular value for safe keeping on the Base. I understood that one strong box contained gold bullion belonging to another agency of government but was not able to verify this or to ever understand why any Embassy section would be holding gold bars. We left at 4 am along the coastal highway to minimize risk of encountering looters or roving bands. Along the way, cars and several giant trucks were still burning from the previous day, but the road was empty except for roadblocks with young and jittery Libyan soldiers fresh from the countryside fingering assault weapons.

Gradually, with a ceasefire in place, order was restored and life began to return to normal, although the humiliation of such a total Arab defeat resonated with the Libyans and colored their approach to most things. Ambassador David Newsom, one of the most respected American diplomats of his era, anticipated the enormous pressures on the King and Libyan leaders to close Wheelus Base and, despite opposition from the Pentagon, took the initiative to start negotiations on its future. A practiced listener, he drew out the negotiations endlessly until gradually tensions cooled and finally the talks collapsed altogether.

It was a diplomatic *tour de force* which allowed Wheelus to slowly return to full operations and me, as note taker, to observe a master craftsman at work. Money was, of course, involved and the US paid the Libyans a tidy rental for the facilities, but ultimately it was about pride and being taken seriously as equal partners. With their burgeoning oil revenues and minuscule population, the Libyans had no need of additional money and did know what to do with it. As it was, King Idris was putting money from oil into unwanted investments like the vast Idris public housing project with giant apartment buildings that stood empty for decades when nomadic tribesmen preferred their bedouin tents and rejected outright the concept of permanent housing.

Although Wheelus Base had been temporarily saved and normalcy restored, the reverberations of the 1967 War destabilized the already fragile Libyan state, ushering in an uneasy period of transition and leading ultimately to the 1969 coup and four decades of repression under Qadhafi.

LABOR DAY 1969

As the negotiations wound down, American families returned, schools reopened and the Air Base resumed operations. The King appointed a young technocrat, Abdel Hamid Bakkush, as Prime Minister, in place of the usual tribal Shaikhs. Bakkush struggled to win over Libya's restive youth who gravitated instead to Col. Nasser next door in Egypt. Soon, tribal elements fulminated to restore the old order, and Idris abruptly dismissed Bakkush and his government. For many, including Lt. Qadhafi, an obscure lieutenant in the signals corps, the writing was on the wall that meaningful reform would only come through confrontation.

My boss, Holsey G. Handyside, predicted military intervention in a lengthy report one year before the coup.[8] He lacked specifics or a timeframe, however, and his report was filed away long before the coup actually occurred. As I later learned in Washington, the rival intelligence briefing books which were then prepared each day for the President by the State Department, the CIA and the Defense Intelligence Agency (DIA) frequently contained dire warnings of multiple coups around the world. These were quickly forgotten if nothing happened, but readily cited if any proved accurate. Conversely, a coup or invasion without warning invariably led to a clamor, to ferret out and blame whoever "lost" country x, y or z. Such intelligence warnings were rarely actionable, however, yet this regular over reporting still persists today. President George W. Bush, for example, famously received one such warning in his daily CIA book just a month before 9/11.

I was reassigned, in any case, well before the Qadhafi coup to the Bureau of Intelligence and Research in Washington, working there on Libya and other countries of North Africa. I can vividly recall that, as a recent returnee from Tripoli, I was called in for a briefing by the new Ambassador-Designate to Libya, Joseph Palmer. He was one of the most senior career ambassadors and totally drained by three years' service as Assistant Secretary for Africa during the Biafran Civil War. The latter was the first exposure of Americans to the full horrors of war close-up every day on TV, and public pressure on Palmer for America to intervene on behalf of starving Biafran children was intense. He was clearly looking forward to a quiet last ambassadorship, and Libya with major American interests including oil and Wheelus, as well as reasonable amenities, was to be his reward.

Palmer asked me very directly whether there was the slightest possibility of an irregular change of government in Libya, and I hastened to disabuse him of such an outlandish idea, reassuring him that the Libyan Armed Forces were extremely limited and not possibly capable of the complex logistics required to simultaneously secure its capital cities separated by such vast expanses of desert. So much for conventional wisdom in the Foreign Service and my own perspicacity.[9] What I told him, however, was widely believed at that time, and it was by no means just me that was clueless. Palmer appeared well pleased with his briefing, but arrived in Libya shortly after the military coup, had a miserable time there and retired early from the Foreign Service in 1971.

I can remember the coup well because it fell on Labor Day, September 1, 1969, and the Department was empty, its long corridors echoing with the footsteps and hushed voices of the few Libyan hands trying to piece together fragmentary reports of what was going on. Only days and weeks later did the identity of Col. Qadhafi and his Revolutionary Command Council emerge and, even then, they were unknown names. King Idris, who was often out of Libya, had been in Turkey for some time for medical treatment. Instead of returning to Libya to suppress the upstart lieutenants, he proceeded to the famous Greek spa at Kamena Vourla to take the medicinal waters, well known since Roman times. From there, he made his leisurely way to Cairo where he lived in relative obscurity in a palace provided by Col. Nasser until his death at age 94 in 1983.

The King was beyond reach of the Libyan People's Court which sentenced him in absentia to death in 1971. It is a paradox, however, that, while Qadhafi saw Nasser as an inspiration and father figure, the latter gave asylum to Idris and refused to share planning for the 1973 attack on Israel with the Libyan leader. There is even reason to believe that Nasser may have been involved in planning for a separate colonels' coup in Libya and, like everybody else, had been surprised and preempted by Qadhafi.

Certainly, there was much finger-pointing about an intelligence failure following the coup, and some brazenly claimed to have known the plotters and to have predicted the outcome, but there is little evidence of this. While 4–5 US military communications officers were training the Libyan Signal Corps in Benghazi from which Qadhafi and many of his inner circle came, the Embassy was denied access to these personnel prior to the coup and they themselves had little understanding of political events. Two RCC members had been trained at Fort Belvoir near Washington and may even have initiated coup planning while there, but otherwise appear to have made little impression. [10]

On the ground in Libya, staff was literally living in the Embassy for months on end and there were still hopes that some sort of new relationship could be established. The new Ambassador and his deputy were traditional, old school diplomats more than twice the age of Qadhafi and his circle, so that outreach across generations must have been a challenge. A downward spiral began when the Libyans became aware of Wheelus personnel involved in smuggling out a Jewish businessman and, separately, two Libyans closely associated with the old regime.

Inevitably, the Peace Corps was soon expelled, Wheelus was shut down and negotiations began in earnest over oil royalties with American and other companies whose expertise the Libyans still required. Following an impasse, the venue moved to Tehran and OPEC, resulting in an historic increase in world petroleum prices. In the process, US companies in Libya were either nationalized or closed down. The Soviets soon replaced the US and Britain as Libya's chief military supplier, and Libya began to forge a global network of terrorist links stretching from Latin America to the Philippines. More importantly, Libya was isolated and frozen in time under Qadhafi, emerging into a vastly different world only in 2011.

FAST FORWARD

Astute readers may have noticed that, recalling time and events in Libya, I have relied less on personal experience and focused instead on the bigger picture, since I was but a small frog in a much larger pond and these events have had lasting consequences for the United States and the region. By contrast, my biographic reporting portfolio, while extensive regarding the sheer venality of individual Libyans, was at best a worm's eye view. I would be the first to admit that rummaging through files of sexual abuse, financial peculation and even murder by senior Libyan officials probably may well have biased me against them.

It is certainly true that, as victims of successive occupations and tribal divisions, the Libyans were more withdrawn and opaque than nationals of other countries where I have lived. It is, in fact, a common refrain in oral histories from colleagues in Libya that there was only limited opportunity for interaction, let alone real friendship with Libyans, or for the kind of diplomatic dinners and receptions with local officials that is standard fare in most places. One senior Embassy officer, stationed in Tripoli during the years just after the Qadhafi coup, describes Libya as "the most xenophobic country I've ever been in."[11] An exception to the general standoffishness were young Libyan businessmen, particularly graduates of universities abroad, with keen interest in free liquor and opportunities to meet Western women.

In my own case, I cannot recall, during three years in Libya making more than two Libyan friends. One, a taciturn pipe-smoking judge, seemed to enjoy philosophical discussions, but gave little away during his abstract musings. The other, a former actor and psychic from the Fezzan, was at ease with westerners. He once invited me to serve as an honorary judge for a Libyan beauty pageant, an oddity in that country, which I accepted while no fan of such contests. The contestants were all modestly attired, and I'm sure that the competition was completely rigged. Beauty is, of course in the eye of the beholder, but by my lights the only radiant beauty placed last, winning an undesirable one-way ticket to Homs. Two by far lesser beauties, at least in my view, received round trips to Rome. Improbably, after my time in Libya, I heard that my host went on to become a senior official under Qadhafi.

Watching 2012–15 Congressional hearings on Benghazi, the Libya we inhabited nearly fifty years ago seems like a different planet. And yet, the differences may not be so very great. Libya was and remains a place adrift with conflicting visions of itself. The backdrop of desert, endless beaches, mountains and incomparable Greek and Roman ruins, of course, remains the same. So, too, does distrust of the foreigner and the history of attacks against American and other diplomatic and consular facilities. I mentioned earlier the 1967 attack on the US Consulate in Benghazi during which the American staff of ten was finally able to escape with their lives, but many in the invading Libyan mob were killed or injured. The American Embassy in Tripoli was also burned to the ground in 1979 by a mob encouraged by Qadhafi, and the remaining staff were barely able to get out through a secret passageway to an adjacent building.

Libya is, in other words, a stark reminder of the contradiction between effective diplomacy and the hostile environment faced by many of America's 294 posts around the world, described in architectural terms in Jane Loeffler's excellent book.[12] On the one hand, diplomacy and dialogue are not possible from the confines of a maximum security prison, while on the other Foreign Service personnel cannot be put at unacceptable risk. The case of Ambassador Chris Stevens and his three colleagues who perished in Benghazi in 2012 is a turning point likely to shape the conduct of American diplomacy for years to come. I knew Chris as a young Peace Corps Volunteer in Morocco and worked with him in the Department's Near Eastern Bureau. Self-deprecating and conscientious to a fault, he was fluent in Arabic and committed to service in North Africa. The Benghazi tragedy and the subsequent killings bring the total of

Foreign Service personnel killed or lost in the line of duty and listed on the State Department's memorial plaque to 248 as of May 16, 2016.

Libya, with its uncertain future and security vacuum in major cities, will be a proving ground in the war against Islamist terror and the hemorrhaging of refugees and migrants. It is already unrecognizable to people like me from an earlier epoch, and the episodes recounted here simply could not have occurred in today's environment. Striking a balance between carrying out the nation's business abroad and protecting the staff who do it will require a bipartisanship so far lacking in our dysfunctional Congress where rancor and partisanship cloud sound judgment and scholarship when it comes to foreign affairs. That is to say that readers of E.E. Evans-Pritchard's classic *The Sanusi of Cyrenaica* (Oxford University Press, 1949) and analysts of Britain's devastating 1920 defeat at the Battle of Kut were probably less likely than most to be surprised by the downward spiral today in either Libya or Iraq.

For me personally, Libya was by no means a bad second post, in which you can begin to feel confidant and self-reliant in a career, really independent for the first time in life. It was a long way from cemetery work and chasing markers in the desert, more mainstream with exposure to issues that the US still faces today, as well as to the bureaucracy of a larger embassy, military commands and a massive oil sector. Life as a smaller frog in the pond was, in short, not bad with much to learn and lifelong friends to make.

NOTES

1. Mason Sears, *Years of High Purpose, From Trusteeship to Nationhood*, University Press of America, Inc, Washington, DC, 1980.

2. Amb. David Newsom recounts that, having been born in Algeria, the King, in his view, never really felt comfortable in Libya. David D. Newsom, Oral History, Association for Diplomatic Studies and Training (ADST), June 17, 1998.

3. The chapter title is purely whimsical since I only once met the King. I did, however, have a classmate in elementary school and later again as a class and club mate in college who was one of the children in the original 1951 Broadway production of *The King and I* with Gertrude Lawrence and Yul Brynner.

4. Amb. Hume Horan recounts a similar instance which occurred during an audience with King Idris several years earlier under a previous ambassador, who recited a long laundry list of issues, obviously drawn up in Washington, while the King slept soundly following an ample lunch. That ambassador subsequently advised Washington that "the King had taken due note of the Ambassador's points but had not chosen to commit himself to an immediate response." Hume Horan, Oral History, Association for Diplomatic Studies and Training, November 3, 2000.

5. Also known as el Gardaqa.

6. Holsey G. Handyside, Oral History, Association for Diplomatic Studies and Training, April 19, 1993.

7. John Kormann, Oral History, Association for Diplomatic Studies and Training, February 7, 1996.

8. Holsey G. Handyside, Op.Cit.

9. Richard Jackson, Oral History, Association for Diplomatic Studies and Training, August 17, 1998.

10. Holsey G. Handyside, ibid.

11. Harold Josif, Oral History, Association for Diplomatic Studies and Training, October 4, 1999.

12. Jane Loffler, *The Architecture of Diplomacy*, Princeton Architectural Press, 2011.

IV

Foggy Bottom*

HARDSHIP DUTY

People often talk of culture shock in terms of exposure to exotic places and languages, but in my experience the greatest shock is almost always coming home. Gone are the garden villas, the armored cars, the drivers and household staff, the cost of living allowances, danger pay and hardship pay for deprivation of bowling alleys, pizza parlors and other essentials of American life. In their place are the daily, gridlocked commute or succession of bus rides from the suburbs, the high cost of living and, for most diplomats of whatever nationality posted at headquarters, debt.

Technology and popular culture also have a disconcerting way of leapfrogging ahead of you while you're chasing markers in the Horn of Africa or considering VIP dental admissions to the Wheelus clinic. So it is that, hip as you may be, there are cultural reference points—books, music, movies—that simply never reached you in Kazakhstan, Angola or even Greece. Speaking of technology, when I first returned from Libya, I happened to visit the Operations Center, the central nervous system of the Department where the emergency phone calls and cables signaling crises around the world first land. An acquaintance, just back from Vietnam I think he said, was on duty and like me trying to master the new technology. In his job, you can't not be prepared, and when the flash cable arrives at 3am reporting the latest *coup d'etat* there comes the momentous decision whether to wake the Secretary or his or her top people. Although there is probably little they can do about it in the wee hours, at a certain level of gravity they have a need to know, although I never saw criteria for wake-up calls spelled out.

On this occasion, in 1968, a prototype Long Distance Xerox (LDX), a complicated machine with unfamiliar bells and whistles, had just been installed. It was late afternoon, and a flash message from Paris with draft instructions for the Vietnam peace talks had to be LDX'd to the White House for President Johnson's urgent review. Johnson had an evening engagement, and frantic calls came every few minutes from the NSC staff protesting the delay as flustered diplomats pressed button after button with no result. Finally, an irate Lyndon Johnson came on the speaker phone, hopping mad, with an unbelievable string of Texan epithets and invective directed at the State Department and anyone within hearing range. I had no business as a bystander to this meltdown and withdrew, but assume that, by LDX or old fashioned courier, the instructions were eventually conveyed, although peace was not to come in Johnson's time.

The Department of State itself, like most corporate headquarters, is a sprawling, anonymous place taking up an entire city block. Its endless hospital-like, antiseptic corridors, usually devoid of traffic, with desk officers where they should be at their desks behind closed doors, conjuring up surgeries in progress, with transplant or appendectomy patients anesthetized on desks. Certainly the enormity of the place is in jarring contrast to the human scale of small or medium-sized embassies abroad. Visually, it is also, in its banality, a somewhat disappointing nerve center for the one remaining superpower.

To heighten the sense of anonymity, I was cursed with a Foreign Service namesake, middle initial and all, which led to no end of bureaucratic confusion. If memory serves, his career path was Santiago, Juarez, Singapore, Fukuoka and university training on early computers at MIT. At any rate, we used to receive Christmas cards, sometimes years late, bearing these postmarks before they got on the correct trail. Far more alarming and possibly handicapping in a career sense was the frequent commingling of personnel files. This was not discovered for many years, after which I was obliged to periodically review my entire performance file in order to cull out my namesake's material. In the meantime, I had received totally undeserved letters of commendation for my supposed cooperation with the Bureau of Narcotics and Dangerous Drugs, membership in the ten-gallon-a-year blood donor club, and a citation for the keynote speech at a conference on Atlantic codfish held in Reykjavik. I can only suppose that my double must have stumbled on equally bizarre and out of character performance reports for my work with war graves in Somalia or biographic profiles of reprobates in Libya. More annoying, for years we received midnight harassment calls from a collection agency in St. Louis about a washing machine the man apparently purchased at Sears Roebuck. Nor did I ever meet him to settle the score.

The Department was a great leveler and equal opportunity employer. Overseas, American embassies and ambassadors generally command a certain standing, if not necessarily outright affection, representing as they do the last remaining superpower. Ambassadors or consuls general of just a week ago are, however, just like anyone else in the vast State Department cafeteria, searching the crowd for familiar faces and at a loss without their staff. Many too are like lost souls stalking the corridors in hopes, without seeming contrived, of encountering old Matt or Ralph, colleagues from a previous post, who might be in a position to put in a good word for their onward assignment. A whole separate contingent of these hall walkers lurk outside the medical division seeking doctors' clearances, magic slips that they are certified for duty abroad after bouts with rare tropical dysenteries, worm infestations or other parasitic infections.

Some even claimed during the sixties that, like Grand Central Station in New York, there was a small and surreptitious homeless population within the building that had somehow infiltrated through the employment office and merged with diplomats and staff, feeding at odd hours in the cafeteria and sleeping wherever couches were unlocked. I always found this improbable, but it was hard to explain debris and other traces of freeloaders making use of the facilities. They had vanished, however, by the time that highly classified laptop computers began to disappear and building security was increased to the point where even retired diplomats like me no longer have routine access.

Eavesdropping in the cafeteria line was always instructive, and you could hear snatches of random disoriented conversation like:

"Tom, do you remember me? I was admin. officer in Rangoon."

"Sure, Joe, where are you now?"

"I do bananas in the Division of Tropical Fruit."

or worse:

"John, what are you doing here? I thought you were in Addis."

"You may not have heard, but Margie left me for an Ethiopian, and I'm getting out."

or still worse:

"You don't remember me, do you Al? Lang Henderson."

"Lang, is that really you?"

"Yes, I picked up this disease in Niger. You know it bleaches out the hair and skin."

THE VIEW FROM A DESK

To occupy a desk, meaning to be the operations officer or first point of contact for a single country or, if the countries were insignificant, for a cluster of countries, was thought, at least in my time, to be the launch pad for a diplomatic career. And so it was that I soon found myself in charge of Sudan, Mauritania and Western (formerly Spanish) Sahara, huge desert areas, but by no means high on the list of US priorities. The position involved reading daily reports from the field, backstopping US embassies or ambassadors home on consultation and responding to the rare public inquiries or would-be American travelers to those out-of-the-way regions.[1] I should clarify that Western Sahara was not an actual country but rather a trackless desert region, claimed by both Morocco and an Algeria-based guerrilla group, and subject to occasional border skirmishes and UN peace keeping efforts.[2] Thus, there was no embassy to backstop and potential prospectors for oil or surfers chasing the perfect wave were told in no uncertain terms to stay out of the line of fire and that the US Government would not be responsible for whatever misfortunes might befall them.

As in any bureaucracy, however, work flows into a vacuum, and I believe that the Sudanese and Mauritanian Charges d'Affaires appreciated my modest efforts to help them navigate official Washington. Both were virtually one-person operations in the process of establishing embassies, let alone reaching out to and cultivating congressional staff. More than once, Foreign Ministries in Khartoum or Nouakchott fell behind in paying salaries and rent, and it fell to me to plead with irate Washington landlords for patience, although strictly speaking this is a function of Protocol.

In the case of Mauritania, the only event then drawing the slightest worldwide attention was a rare solar eclipse in 1973 for which an outcropping in one of the remotest regions would offer the best worldwide vantage point for astronomers.[3] Ambitious to make myself known in the bureaucracy, I prepared a series of Eclipse Planning Papers (EPPs) in the years leading up to the event, receiving kudos for my initiative from the Bureau. In the event, long after I had left the desk, several hundred astronomers did set up telescopes somewhere in the Mauritanian desert and were hospitably received in tents by the Mauritanian Government. The phenomenon otherwise passed unnoticed except within the tightly knit solar eclipse community and was soon forgotten, although somewhere deep in the archives of the State Department, perhaps in the moldering archival annex at Suitland, Maryland, there must still be a bulging folder of EPPs.

If you had not been stationed in your areas of responsibility, which I had not, you could hardly be credible as the Department's resident expert, so one of the great perquisites of being a desk officer, at least prior to the era of budget cuts, sequestration and layoffs, was an orientation trip to the actual countries. Of course Western Sahara was off limits, but with Mauritania and Sudan at westernmost and easternmost points of the Continent and flight patterns then vertical through Europe rather than horizontal across Africa, my orientation was quite extensive.

Sudan, my first destination, remains shrouded for me in disappointment and sadness. Disappointment because, as Africa's largest country with nearly a million square miles, oil, untapped minerals in the Red Sea and agricultural potential to be a breadbasket for the entire Continent, it has squandered these bright prospects through mismanagement, oppression and bloodshed. Sadness because the next year my friend and host in Khartoum, Curt Moore, along with the newly arrived Ambassador, Cleo Noel, were assassinated, together with the Belgian Chargé d' Affaires Guy Eid, when Black September, a Palestinian terrorist group, stormed the Saudi Embassy on March 1, 1973. In the heat and dust of Khartoum, a diplomatic reception hosted by the Ambassador of Saudi Arabia was underway to honor Curt Moore, the longtime Chargé d' Affaires who was completing his tour, relinquishing the Embassy to the newly arrived US Ambassador. They never had a chance.

All in all, Khartoum and its sister city across the Nile, Omdurman, were exotic but deeply disorienting, sweltering along the Nile, fusing past and present with echoes still of Kitchener and "Chinese" Gordon. The patriarch of the large Greek community, now long since fled from Sudan, had died while I was there, and the only coffin certified for international travel was in the US Embassy, designated in the Foreign Affairs Manual (FAM) only for emergency evacuation of American citizen (AMCIT) remains. The heat quickly made the case a diplomatic cause celebre, but Curt Moore stood his ground, impervious to piteous entreaties and wailing from grief stricken Greeks. Had he not, an American might have died the next week and there would have been hell to pay. In any case, the FAM was implemented, and I assume the patriarch was buried locally.

"Orientation," in State Department parlance, means getting out of the capital to see the "real" country and its people. I suppose in France that might mean the Loire Valley and its chateaux, but that opportunity never came my way. I was packed off instead to Port Sudan, a long flight traversing many of Sudan's million square miles. There I was taken in hand by the US Consular Agent, a Greek named Andreas, who operated a kind of Hellenic convenience store and did customs clearances and other odd chores for the faraway Embassy. In his carelessly open safe I glimpsed for only the second time in my life carefully stacked bars of gold, the provenance and purpose of which I could only surmise.[4]

Despite my remonstrances that orientation was serious business, Andreas had stocked a small fishing boat with beer, and we spent the remainder of orientation diving in the pristine, but shark-ridden waters of the Red Sea. Departing, I visited the eerie, abandoned city of Suakin, a UNESCO world site, on the coastal plain north of which the barren Red Sea Hills rise up to forbidding peaks. There, at a remote army camp, Sadiq al-Mahdi, Imam of the sufi Ansar sect and twice Prime Minister of Sudan, had been incarcerated since the 1969 military coup by Col. Jaafar al-Nimeri. A graduate of Oxford, Sadiq smuggled out an erudite reading list and somehow embassies in Khartoum responded surreptitiously with Marcel Proust's *Remembrance of Things Past* and other eclectic reading matter. Until his release, Sadiq became a kind of latter day Ezra Pound at St. Elizabeth's Hospital, and a small diplomatic cult following developed around nurturing his prodigious intellect.

Sudan was, in short, an exotic place of intrigue. To see the world's largest variety of migratory birds over the Nile at dawn or explore the British-built Gezira Scheme, the world's largest irrigation system producing cotton and groundnuts, was to glimpse the world as it might be, the complexity of human ambition and the obstacles to both. Visiting a remote desert industry producing molasses and, improbably for Muslim Sudan, its byproduct rum, I had the feeling of stumbling into a re-enactment of Dante's *Inferno*. Inside the cavernous space, the floors, walls and ceiling oozed molasses, the temperature registered 120 F, and the fumes were overpowering. Workers were dazed and nearly indistinguishable in the gloom, with eyes yellowed by malaria. Until then a sound sleeper, I departed Sudan with bouts of insomnia recurring from time to time right up to the present.

"Crossing the Senegal River with Moonrock."

Mauritania could not have been more different. This was 1970, and the previous year the US had put a man on the moon, returning to earth with a few moonrocks as the ultimate proof of American technology and prowess. The State Department was given a small quota for display to selected foreign heads of state and top officials. Senegal, which I had to transit to reach Mauritania, had received one such rock via special courier in order to impress the legendary Leopold Sedar Senghor, the dean of African fathers of their nation, and also to reach a younger generation of Senegalese leaders. Since the moonrock was already in Dakar and had been exhibited there to a blue ribbon but highly skeptical audience, I was asked to escort it to Nouakchott so that Mauritanians too could marvel at our achievements.

The rock, while small and unprepossessing, was encased in a strongbox which local security insisted be attached by handcuffs to me at all times as if someone might attempt to steal it. Travel consisted of a long jeep ride past the picturesque fishing town of Port Louis and on to the broad Senegal River. From there, two Senegalese boatmen paddled me across to Rosso in a pirogue or primitive dugout canoe. The thought did not escape me that, in the event of a crocodile attack or simple capsizing, it would have been a spectacular addition to the State Department's memorial plaque of diplomats lost in the line of duty to have drowned in the Senegal River, dragged to the bottom by a moonrock.

Thus, it was a relief to reach Rosso, an important regional center in southern Mauritania, inhabited by a population of largely Senegalese tribal origin and quite distinct from Moors in the rest of the country. As it happened, the Governor of Rosso was hosting an outdoor lunch for local notables to which I was somehow invited. It consisted of a huge platter heaped with rice and goat which some thirty all-male guests shared using only their right hands to eat in the Muslim fashion. Common courtesy obliged me to shift the handcuffed moonrock in its strong box from my right wrist over to the left in order to eat in the prescribed manner.

President Nasser of Egypt had died in the days before, and conversation focused interminably on controversial variations in the Islamic funeral liturgy with which many traditionalists seemed to take sharp exception. After the repast, it was my turn to show the Governor and his guests the moonrock, but I was met with uproarious guffaws and derision. There was no way that anyone from the Governor on down was prepared to believe that man had walked on the moon, much less brought back a piece of it. I didn't even remove the precious rock from its strong box, since to the untrained eye it looked just like any other rock strewn across Mauritania's endless desert and would have made an even bigger fool of me in their eyes. Afterwards in the heat of the afternoon, guests slept where they were on the ground around the now empty platter before tea was served.

Nouakchott, which I later visited several times, is a surprising capital. Seen from the air, it was little more than a core of stone buildings surrounded by clusters of nomad tents, and the only patches of green in the scorched landscape were the Spanish and US Embassy lawns. Since then, however, drought and desertification have tripled or quadrupled the population. The country was a graveyard for aid schemes, and you could see skeletal pumps, tractors and entire slaughterhouses, all bleaching in the sun. Optimism about seeding the rare rain clouds that scudded across the desert before precipitating over the Atlantic had long since evaporated, and even the Peace Corps was down to a single chicken sexer at the time of my visit. So it was that, after a few days of obligatory consultations with Embassy staff, local officials and friendly embassies, I was dispatched inland to discover the real Mauritania, surrendering the moonrock to Embassy Nouakchott. Hopefully, the ambassador there would have better success than me convincing Africans of our technological prowess on the basis of a paltry rock, a challenge verging on hubris. I imagined him saying to the conservative President Moktar Ould Daddah, "Psst, let me show you my rock" and wished him all success.

We passed Akjoujt with its massive copper refinery, now defunct, and overnighted in Atar, the ancient capital, where I distinctly recall a six-inch scorpion, tail-up and ready to strike, on the shower floor of my fifth floor hotel room. The real Mauritania of our destination turned out to be Chinguetti, an ancient oasis with a broken down Foreign Legion fort. There life seemed to unfold as it had since date palms first grew and camels came to water, some of it handwritten on ancient gazelle skin and preserved for centuries if not millennia in a one-room museum. Sounds of laughter in dark passageways and of people and animals preparing for the night could be heard under a canopy of dazzling stars. In daylight too, the place had a certain purity, shimmering like broken glass in the sun. At noon, time lost all meaning, minutes fusing into hours, suspended in stillness and heat. You wondered how you got there, why, and whether you would leave. Perhaps that is what locals meant when they kept telling me "see Chinguetti and die." The night time sky made me feel close to Antoine de Saint-Exupery whose pioneering postal flights between Toulouse and Dakar passed between these very same stars and deserts that he loved and wrote so movingly about.

Little Yahya, "he who will never die" he proudly told us, took our party in hand pointing out the local mosques and other sights. He indicated a woman drawing water from a well who, he matter-of-factly told me, was a slave. In fact, widespread slavery has existed in Mauritania for centuries, and was only abolished in 1981 and not criminalized until 2007. To date there has been only one prosecution and many former slaves or haratine, without other means of livelihood, remained with former owners in exchange for room and board.

Yahya steered us inexorably to a network of underground caverns formed by ancient rivers. The Chinese, he said, had dared to descend into them and surely we Americans would too. I had already noticed that Chinese were ubiquitous in Nouakchott and could be heard across town at their morning tai chi, although no fraternization was then allowed. Reluctantly, I accepted Yahya's challenge to avoid loss of face and descended by rope to the bottom of a long-abandoned well. There, he led me through a giant watercourse of sand with cathedral-like chambers and narrow passages resulting from sand slides. Eventually our single flashlight gave out and Yahya, doubtful of rescue, was convinced that his final entombment was at hand. I had confidence, however, in my Embassy friend and escort, DCM Steve Buck, who wisely remained above ground, and after a few hours imagining unseen adders and scorpions and for a fee, a man appeared with a miner's lamp.

Orientation was the highlight and reward of duty on a desk, although I can also vividly recall a bizarre White House reception. The diminutive Lion of Judah, Emperor Haile Selassie, King of Kings, was paying a state visit to Washington and, on short notice, President Nixon had announced a press conference and reception. To fill out the audience, government workers involved with the region were summoned at the last possible moment to attend. Gilding the lily, someone at the White House had even thought to invite the Miss World contestants who were then touring in Washington, and the room was soon packed. Both the Emperor and Nixon were diminutive, and the audience was pressed together, like a New York subway, craning their necks to see the heads of state. I remember simultaneous and intimate contact with a statuesque Miss Ivory Coast and a petite Miss France who faced backwards to observe the proceedings through a mirror held over my head.

Such events did not occur every day, however, and, finding underemployment more stressful than an overload, I curtailed my time on the desk, before both the great eclipse and the tragic assassination of our top diplomats in Khartoum. By sad coincidence, my wife and I had hosted a dinner to honor Ambassador Cleo Noel not long before his departure for Khartoum which Daniel Arap Moi, then Vice President and later the longtime President of Kenya, attended, more congenial than his austere image.

A SPY AMONG US

I left the Desk early for ten months of intensive Greek language training at the Foreign Service Institute (FSI) which I have known over the years, both as a student and later as a dean and faculty member. It was housed for many decades in a high-rise building, never designed as a schoolhouse, in Roslyn, Virginia, but eventually moved to the sprawling campus of Arlington Hall, once a girls' school where the Japanese codes were broken during World War II. The move was negotiated by Secretary of State George Shultz, without whose steadfast support it would not have occurred. Today, it is grandly named the George P. Shultz National Foreign Affairs Training Center (NFATC), sometimes irreverently referred to as Fat City.

Geographic separation protects trainees from the reach of a desk, but there is also an out-of-sight-out-of-mind phenomenon whereby two year's absence to learn Chinese or Arabic, for example, does not necessarily translate into promotion. All in all, the military does considerably better than State at linking professional training to promotion and assignments. The splendid new NFATC campus could have been an opportunity to encourage research and intellectual debate like the National Defense University, or even the service academies, but in recent years there has been a trend toward vocational training as well as suspicion of whatever might be considered intellectual, academic or elitist. Shultz was clearly a visionary, but bureaucrats who came after were not and rejected ideas to fold in the Historian's Office and External Research, potentially making NFATC a center for ideas and creative ferment.

Ten months of Greek training, eight hours a day, week after week, was at once tedious and deeply rewarding. While it is artificial to learn a foreign language in an English-speaking environment like Arlington, Virginia rather than by immersion in a country where it is actually spoken, the FSI method does work for the 70 odd languages taught there and has been copied by most private language schools. Ten months spent together in small, claustrophobic classrooms not surprisingly nurtures close friendships as well as the opposite among both students and teachers. Tensions too are predictable between slow and fast language learners with teachers usually favoring the latter.

The same faculty also of necessity serve as examiners, usually favoring their students over walk-ins who learned Greek elsewhere or were of Hellenic origin. I certainly benefitted from this, receiving a 4+/4+ with 5/5 marking native fluency. As in the earlier case of Somali, this too came back to haunt me in later years, as I will soon recount, when I again was over my head in this bottomless language.

Still, after all these years, I can remember the tongue-twisting sentences that we were obliged to memorize in week one of training. Greek comes in many gradations, not all mutually intelligible, for example classical, church, highbrow (*katharevousa*), middle brow (*kathemiloumeni*) and popular (demotic). It was in *kathemiloumeni*, favored by the colonels who had then seized power, that I learned to say: "Please, Madame, can you tell me where I may hide my parachute." (A phrase that I never had occasion to use which might still cause panic in more remote villages.) Or even more farfetched: "I'm sorry to tell you that all of the seats in the first class section of the train are taken." (Giving the false impression that the class was preparing for assignment, not as diplomats, but as railroad conductors.)

The persistence of these phrases, funnier sounding in Greek than English, forty-five years later is proof, if any be needed, that memory invariably dredges up the truly useless rather than goodness knows what on which our lives might actually depend. It also shows that FSI language teaching started modestly from WW II military manuals, as well as providing a clue to my own age.

While it may be an old-fashioned point of view, I have always believed that language and area expertise are the core skills that distinguish Foreign Service Officers from colleagues in the innumerable other government agencies elbowing for space at the table. Thus, I was quite content later to return to FSI as Dean of the School of Area Studies, now abolished for budgetary reasons and, even then, suspect for its intellectual pretensions. Dare I say, amidst current talk about dumbing down American education and culture, that our nation's diplomats are clearly not themselves exempt? At the time, the School of Area Studies each year served some 2,000 students from State and forty-seven other federal agencies preparing for assignments abroad. Instruction was provided on individual countries and regions through two-week intensive modules and weekly half-day classes for language students.

The staff was an eclectic but congenial mixture of certified academics and diplomats with recent exposure in countries about which they taught. Sometimes, senior ambassadors would have a political falling out with whatever administration was in power and were viewed as pariahs by Personnel, so I was able to snag several who proved to be inspired teachers and were grateful for a place to wait out a change of administrations. One, whom we made interim Chair for Africa, had been Ambassador to Nigeria and brought in the 1986 Nobel Laureate for Literature, Wole Soyinka, as a lecturer. Staff meetings with long winded academics and senior ambassadors were a far cry from the usual stilted, show-and-tell sessions across the Potomac at State. Debate was generally animated and, as often as not, beyond my ability to control or rein in.

Department Chairs for Asia, Africa, the Middle East, Latin America and Europe were all respected academic authorities and frequent speakers at universities and think tanks around Washington and beyond. Organizationally, I had an unusual relationship with the Chair for Middle Eastern Studies, Dr. Peter Bechtold, for whom I worked as Coordinator for all courses on North Africa, but also supervised as Dean. In addition to his deep knowledge of the Middle East, Peter was a recognized expert on the culture and societal implications of soccer and was in huge demand as a commentator, night and day, every four years when the World Cup was held.

The Chair for European Affairs in many ways stood out among the faculty, whether for dry humor, tantrums or overweening academic hubris. Of Scottish descent, he was also by far the tallest at six feet, six inches and drew further attention to himself with tweedy academic dress, spectacles and a droopy moustache. Invariably, he received the highest student ratings but was hopelessly disorganized and almost always late, whether for classes and staff meetings or in submitting schedules and course prospectuses. He probably spread himself too thin as a senior faculty member of long standing at the Johns Hopkins School of Advanced International Studies (SAIS) and a respected analyst on Vatican and UK affairs in the State Department's Bureau of Intelligence and Research (INR).

Such unevenness packaged in an overbearing personality was a continuing management issue, since Dr. Kendall Myers was at once hugely popular and an obvious adornment to our permanent faculty, while at the same time either absent or a handful to control during meetings and never ready with training reports by the time students departed for posts abroad. His forgetfulness about deadlines, appointments or borrowed books was legendary. Nor, pulling himself up to his full height, would he let us easily forget that his great grandfather, Alexander Graham Bell, had invented the telephone. He was always receiving invitations from US ambassadors and embassies abroad for speaking engagements and lecture tours which usually conflicted with scheduled courses at the Institute.

We often conducted specially tailored mini-courses on their countries of assignment for Ambassadors-Designate with Prof. Myers presiding over those dealing with Europe, most of whom were political appointees and often *prima donnas*. He took care to stay in close touch with these ambassadors once they reached their posts, sending them little notes with clippings and articles of interest, so it was only natural that they in turn would request his presence for further in-country training. In any case, at the School of Area Studies (SAS), we took things day by day, the stellar along with the downright infuriating.

To put things in perspective, however, the Institute and SAS within it was a relatively stress-free, relaxed environment in which Dr. Myers' general good cheer and humor outweighed his forgetfulness and eccentricity. Some even disparaged the School's admixture of academics and diplomats as a "white wine and brie crowd," and in fact we did sometimes round out the academic week with an occasional thank-God-it's-Friday party (TGIF). On one occasion, as a pricey office joke, they served Kendall-Jackson Grand Reserve Chardonnay, fusing together his first and my last names.

Once a year, SAS would also organize a family picnic, and one such excursion was to the Eastern Shore where a highlight was to board Prof. Myers' handsome sloop, again for white wine and brie if memory serves me.

You will understand, therefore, my absolute astonishment, several years later while serving in Thessaloniki, Greece, to read in bold letters in the international press of Kendall Myers and his wife Gwen's arrest on June 4, 2009, not just for espionage but in the service of Cuba's Fidel Castro for nearly three decades. As a diplomat, I met many spies of various nationalities, but Prof. Myers was by far the least probable. His colleagues and even closest friends, if he really had any, are surely still groping for answers.

How could this woolly-headed idealist, who received only medals, never money, from Castro have been so taken in? How could his legendary absentmindedness have concealed the tradecraft of a spy for three decades? How could a brilliant intellect and respected analytic mind have seen Cuba's socialist workers' paradise through such rose-colored glasses? And most of all, how could an American with such distinguished ancestors as Alexander Graham Bell have betrayed his own country?

Toby Harnden, a British journalist and occasional contact of Myers, has since uncovered some disturbing inconsistencies.[5] In 1975, under the influence of alcohol and without apparent remorse, Myers ran over and killed a teenage girl in Washington, severely injuring her two companions. Later, he was arrested for growing marijuana. Myers also enjoyed an expansive lifestyle, for example selling his mother's apartment for $3.2 million and paying $350,000 for a specially-designed, Swedish thirty-seven foot sloop intended to sail the couple into an imagined retirement in Havana.[6]

He also fought tooth and nail with his first wife to avoid sharing university tuition costs for his only daughter. He further caused a diplomatic furor with protests from Whitehall in 2006 when he denounced the special relationship with Britain during a public lecture at Johns Hopkins. Erratic behavior, conviction in 1977 for negligent homicide, and a drug history are a toxic brew, raising questions about security procedures and how Myers was allowed virtual carte blanche to the nation's secrets.

The School of Area Studies happily was a completely sanitized environment with zero classified documents and no secrets at all, so it was not as if Myers was stealing from right under my nose as Dean between 1991 and 1995. In hindsight, one might have flagged his eccentricities and mood swings for greater attention, although they were perfectly obvious for all the world to see. There was also and probably still is a tendency to cut eminent academic chairs a bit of slack for such traits, rather like the academic quarter or half-hour when it comes to punctuality. Harnden reports that Myers was under orders from Havana never to talk about Cuba,[7] and I never heard him mention the island or express the slightest interest in the region, even when his colleague for Latin America would offer provocative analyses at faculty meetings. Damage assessment is a different matter, however, and, as Harnden also points out, Myers held a top secret security clearance from the Bureau of Intelligence and Research (INR) beginning in 1985 and an even more restrictive Sensitive Compartmented Intelligence (SCI) clearance since 1999, as well as having exposure to State and Agency trainees bound for Europe.[8]

The general consensus is that the range of secret intelligence that he provided to Castro, whom he met personally for four hours in 1995, far exceeded the parochial needs of that small island and would have been used by the Cubans to curry favor with Russia, perhaps insuring for themselves a continued supply of free petroleum.

Kendall Myers was of Scottish descent and, like Sir Craig Smellie, also stood a full six feet, six inches and was a spy. Yet he could not conceivably have had the backbone, like Sir Craig, a master spy's spy, to have shifted houses night after night during the Troubles in Northern Ireland. Nor would Sir Craig, even believing deep down as he did in eventual independence of Scotland, ever, ever have betrayed the British Crown. Myers had a set speech, self-promotional in the extreme, which he would trot out on every possible occasion, that he was some kind of unique "amphibian," by which he meant that, with equal ease, he swam in the seas of academia and walked on the terra firma of foreign policy. I thought it was just empty verbiage, but have to acknowledge that he did seem to navigate diverse worlds of academia, government and social Washington and possessed an immense rolodex of contacts. His fall from grace was, therefore, precipitous, bringing to mind John Milton's:

> Him the Almighty Power
> Hurled headlong flaming from the ethereal sky
> With hideous ruin and combustion, down
> To bottomless perdition, there to dwell
> In adamantine chains and penal fire . . .[9]

Kendall Myers was sentenced on July 16, 2010 to life imprisonment without possibility of parole and his wife Gwen, in a plea bargain, to between six and seven-and-a-half years. Myers is serving his sentence at the ADX Florence SuperMax facility in Fremont County, Colorado, sometimes known as "Alcatraz of the Rockies." It is the highest security facility in the United States and perhaps the world, serving a small population of the most dangerous and hardened criminals. Together with Myers at the SuperMax are, for example, Larry Hoover of the Gangster Disciples, Barry Mills of the Aryan Brotherhood, Zacarias Moussaoui from 9/11, Faisal Shahzad of the 2010 Times Square car bombing, Richard Reid the "shoe bomber," Umar Abdulmutallab the "underwear bomber," Ramzi Yousef of the 1993 World Trade Center bombing, the Unabomber Ted Kaczynski, Terry Nichols of Oklahoma City, and Robert Hanssen of the FBI. Past notables have included "Sammy the Bull" Gravano and a host of Al-Qaeda operatives.

Unspeakable as his crime was, it is hard to imagine the jovial, man-about-town Kendall Myers dealing with the Islamist rage of Moussaoui or the paranoid delusions of Kaczynski. On the other hand, Myers studied at Brown University and received his doctorate from Johns Hopkins, while Kaczynski graduated from Harvard and went on for his Ph.D. at the University of Michigan, all good schools. While opportunities for learned discourse are probably minimal and under total hi-tech surveillance, it is intriguing to imagine furtive dialogues between the two in the sunken concrete exercise pit at SuperMax. And yet the behavior of both was so appalling and their elite educations so totally useless that they might just as well decide to ask for tuition refunds from their respective *alma maters*.

THE VIEW FROM ON HIGH

Most assignments in the Foreign Service, even for ambassadors, are for three years unless you happen to have unusual influence, what the Greeks call "mesa" and the Chinese "guanxi," or vital expertise and can prolong time in a plum job. On the other hand, if the post is particularly dangerous or insalubrious, shorter postings are often the rule. I believe, for example, that the Antarctic observer mission in McMurdo Sound is still only one year. Critics, however, sometimes maintain that the return on investment (ROI) for taxpayers can be negative if the first eighteen months are spent learning the country and people of assignment and the remainder on securing a follow-up job through an intricate, formal bidding process and outright corridor lobbying. I once neglected these rituals at my own peril and landed in a series of random, short-term or bridging jobs.

The first of these, improbably given my background, parachuted me into the arcane Office of Soviet Affairs, then still in the grip of the Cold War. Rigid travel restrictions, exactly matching those on Americans in Moscow and Leningrad, were imposed on Soviet officials in Washington and New York, many of whom were under-cover KGB and GRU agents. My worm's eye job was to review all requests for travel by Soviets beyond a radius of twenty-five miles from the center of either city. Whether to visit the Russian Ambassador's country residence in Glen Cove, Long Island or to speak at a university, all requests had to be examined for destination and length of stay to insure that they in no way exceeded excursions authorized for our people in the Soviet Union. To keep track of all of this, I maintained a huge map of the United States with red pins representing individual Soviet officials in authorized travel status outside Washington or New York. [10]

Deviations in either the exact itinerary proposed or length of stay were, of course, matters for the FBI, and there were also large no-go areas of the country for which requests would not be entertained on security grounds. Requests were most frequent and most frequently refused for travel to commercial and trade events by personnel from the huge Soviet state trading company, AMTORG, itself a major platform for espionage. The single accomplishment I can recall from this four or five month interregnum was a ground-breaking agreement for one Russian fisheries expert to visit a fish plant in Bellingham, Washington while one of our fish guys travelled simultaneously to Vladivostok. Both were virgin territory for exchanges but the travel distance was at least as close as we could get within the continental US.

My next interim assignment, after plotting itineraries for Soviet diplomats and spies, was immersion in six months of intensive economics training. As often happens when the Congress tries to make things better, in this case to ensure the quality of government training programs, they achieved the exact opposite by insisting that the six month training fully replicate four years of university study. Thus, a full semester course was squeezed into each week with two-hour exams every Friday, whether in econometrics, integral calculus or money and banking. There was little time to digest the mass of material, and now literally all I can remember is the impecunious money and banking professor who sought in vain throughout all Washington to find a masseur willing to trade a massage for a lecture on money and banking, illustrating, of course, the folly of barter systems.

When the honchos in Personnel began to speak to me about applying my presumed new skills in the Division of Tropical Fruit, I outwitted them by joining the staff of the Undersecretary for Political Affairs, the highest career official in the Department of State, who just happened to be my former Ambassador in Libya. Sadly, I never had recourse to my newly acquired skill set and taxpayers had zero return on their investment in me.

While the State Department's Eighth Floor has elegant reception, ceremonial and dining rooms with museum-quality antique furniture, the Secretary and Undersecretaries inhabit the Seventh Floor, the real center of power. From there, one has an Olympian view of what occurs on the floors below and how the building meshes into the vast machinery of US government. It is a perspective that ambitious Foreign Service Officers are encouraged to seek out in order to lubricate their further rise through the ranks. Be that as it may, it was also an ideal spot for people watching. I listed above some of the luminaries doing time at the Colorado Super-Max, but on any given day a diverse and in some ways more intimidating cast of characters would surge, albeit with escorts, through corridors of the Seventh Floor. One might, for example, share the elevator with the Dalai Lama, who always made a point to greet fellow riders during our ascent together, or attend a meeting with Bishop Desmond Tutu or Chief Buthelezi about implementation of the Sullivan code of ethics for American companies in apartheid South Africa. It was a privilege to be present for historic discussions, chaired by the Undersecretary, with personages such as Joshua Nkomo, Robert Mugabe and once even Ian Smith leading up to the Lancaster House Conference in London and eventual, troubled independence of Zimbabwe in 1980.

While my specific responsibilities were for Africa and international organizations, including the UN, the staff all pitched in during crisis situations and no one could be oblivious to tumultuous global developments, as well as acute rivalries swirling within the administration. There were obviously real differences of philosophy and personality between Secretary Cyrus Vance and the more hard-line National Security Advisor Zbigniew Brzezinski. Their frequent lapses in communication pushed critical issues down to the next level for resolution, and Ambassador Newsom managed the Iran hostage crisis, day in, day out, during the time I was there, meeting often with the hostage families and unlikely figures like Ross Perot of E Systems who was behind various hostage rescue schemes. Once, the Shah of Iran, Reza Pahlevi, was admitted to the New York Hospital for emergency medical treatment and, to preserve anonymity, incongruously registered himself under the name of David D. Newsom, unbeknownst to the Under Secretary.

Mr. Vance's lawyerly work habits were legendary, and he would begin his day at 7am with a briefing from the Under Secretary on overnight developments, meaning that special assistants had to come into the silent building at ungodly hours of the morning to sort through several cubic feet of overnight cables, press and intelligence reports to get Amb. Newsom up to speed before his meeting with the Secretary. Having watched the man carefully plan and prioritize as head of his own embassy in North Africa, it was a revelation for me to realize the difference between the field and headquarters and how the higher one rises in the hierarchy, the less one controls even one's own daily schedule and agenda. He was, in any case, often sent to cover critical meetings in Washington or New York without sufficient time to prepare, if not dispatched on short notice abroad. Washington is famously paralyzed by snow, and I can recall picking him up by Land Rover when necessary,

including Sundays, to deal with the hostage crisis or events following the assassination of US Chargé Spike Dubs in Afghanistan.
Much of this was captured by Robert Shaplen, a senior reporter
from The New Yorker magazine, in a three-part profile, derived
from full access over several months to meetings and documents. [11]

At that time, many of the geographic bureaus for each region of
the world as well as the functional bureaus like political-military,
international organizations or human rights, all based on the floor
below, were headed by political appointees, with strong and conflicting points of view. These inevitably rose to the Under Secretary's office for resolution of time-consuming but childish turf
wars. Representing the Under Secretary, special assistants attended
weekly bureau staff meetings where we were regarded as spies and
quislings, making ourselves even more unpopular by returning me-
mos and cables to be rewritten.

Yet the work was not always petty and confrontational. There
was then, and I'm sure still is, a closely guarded daily book, prepared at the end of every day to alert the President to urgent situations around the world. Input was almost always sent up from the
geographic bureaus by close of business and carefully scrubbed by
the Executive Secretariat. One day about 7pm, I received a frantic
call from the Secretary's office; it was a slow day, no items had
been submitted and lights were already out in the bureaus. It was
unthinkable to tell the detail-oriented President Carter that in all the
world nothing had occurred to merit his attention, and I was given
twenty minutes to come up with an item. All I happened to know at
that moment, in sufficient detail to write for the President, was the
deteriorating situation among refugees from tribal fighting in Somaliland and distribution of powdered milk in makeshift camps
around Hargeisa. President Carter was nothing if not methodical in
his work habits, and used to pore over his daily book on arrival in
the Oval Office at first light. As the only item in that day's book,
the refugee camps thus received his full attention, and I was

astounded on my own arrival at work to find a long handwritten fax from him requesting information on specific quantities and sources of milk and other supplies being distributed. The President's deep curiosity was inspiring, but one felt guilty taking up his time with just a placeholder item. Nor could I imagine a similar exchange with, for example, President Reagan.

A quick trip with the Undersecretary back to Libya was relief from the perfervid atmosphere of Washington for us both. Before the Qadhafi coup, the Libyans had commissioned and paid for a fleet of Lockheed C-130 Hercules aircraft. Because the planes had dual civilian and military uses, they had been embargoed at the plant in Marietta, Georgia when the "Brother Leader" seized power in 1969. The issue had been a sore point with the Libyans ever since and now, ten years after the coup, this was the first, and for many years to come the last, authorized trip to that country by a senior US official. We were scheduled to meet directly with Qadhafi on the matter, but were informed at the last minute after landing in Tripoli that his mother had died, a regular diplomatic excuse he is known to have used on several occasions. It would have been intriguing to observe this bizarre personage up close, and I later learned from a former Greek Ambassador to Libya that, during a visit to Qadhafi's bedouin tent, the Libyan leader had so much admired the Ambassador's shirt that he was forced to take it off and return shirtless to his Embassy. We, however, met only with his deputy and by then rival, Col. Abdulssalam Jalloud, a slick operator who offered nothing of substance; and so the last probe of Libyan intentions failed not long before relations were broken after the bombing of Pan Am 103 and the total destruction on Qadhafi's orders of the American Embassy in Tripoli.

In many respects, the Olympian view from the Department's upper reaches, was disquieting. Particularly in crisis situations, decisions and policy outcomes seemed to me often chaotic and random, depending on individual personalities and shifting coalitions within the Government. Concepts of permanent, immutable US interests that structure relationships with individual countries, politics stopping at the water's edge, or the Holy Grail of a coherent overall foreign policy often turned out to be little more than reassuring bromides favored by Washington think tanks, but more often observed in the breach than in practice.

Later, I was to view the same issues from the different perspective of Director for Egypt and North Africa, proving the adage that what you see depends mostly on where you sit. For example, complex US issues and interests with individual countries often became hostage to vagaries of the Middle East peace process which dominated Washington's attention. While effective negotiation required absolute secrecy and the element of surprise, it was hard to be seen as a serious interlocutor, for example by the Egyptian Ambassador, if you were out of the loop on peace negotiations. Countries on the periphery, like Morocco or Tunisia with centuries old relations with the US, also complained of being valued in American eyes only through the prism of their relations with Israel rather than in their own right. I remember, for example, often chiding these countries about not fully staffing interest sections in Israel which we had inveigled them into establishing.

Policy considerations aside, never in my wildest dreams could I have imagined escorting the Pharaoh by helicopter from Andrews Field to the White House Lawn. At the time, Hosni Mubarak seemed to me a down-to-earth army officer who enjoyed telling out of date American jokes, probably showing off his knowledge of English and our culture. Like Haile Selassie in Ethiopia, however, and many leaders before him, Mubarak had brought unmistakable change and stability to his country, but in the end became out of touch and a prisoner of his own absolute power. This was on display in the pomp and circumstance of the Gore-Mubarak Partnership which required meetings with a huge entourage in Cairo or Washington every six months. The goal was to leverage our $2.1

billion in annual assistance to Egypt to bolster economic efficiency
in a daunting race against Egypt's rampant population growth. The
latter is readily apparent when you overfly the Nile Delta where
isolated farming villages in some of the richest soil on earth now
fuse together into a nearly seamless urban sprawl.

The State Department tends to have a stronger work ethic than
many sister agencies in the federal government, which became obvious during my last trip to Cairo. The established routine was for a
staff entourage to fly out the night before the Vice President's
arrival, set up a beachhead and meet a remarkably fresh Al Gore,
ready for work, on his arrival at 6am the next day. I had, as usual,
put in a day's work at State in a presentable suit and gone directly
to the airport. My colleagues from Commerce, Treasury and the
FBI, on the other hand, had taken the day off to prepare and
boarded the plane comfortably attired in flashy leisure suits and
running shoes. Not surprisingly, all checked bags were lost in transit, and arriving at our hotel late at night my colleagues were
obliged to haggle with a bespoke tailor who demanded $1,100 from
each for overnight service. As the Vice President descended the
ramp next day, they looked like three stooges in ill-fitting, double-
breasted Egyptian silk suits of purplish and greenish hues. My own
bags caught up with me two weeks later in Morocco, just missing
stops in Algiers and Tunis, and I never heard what happened to
theirs.

A contentious issue which sometimes arose at the Cairo meetings and also occupied me in Washington was construction of the
new ring road or beltway around Cairo, badly needed to relieve one
of the world's most congested cities. The problem, evoking memories of my work with war graves in Somalia, was that the roadway
unavoidably had to pass through an ancient Jewish cemetery on the
outskirts of Cairo which involved relocation of certain graves and
was of the utmost concern to the ultra-Orthodox community in
Israel, as well as to the public at large since disturbing the dead is

anathema in the Jewish faith. The United States became deeply involved in these delicate arrangements including daily travel by Orthodox Rabbis from Jerusalem to supervise work around the graves and return by nightfall to Israel, bringing with them kosher food and drink for each day. Neither the Rabbis nor the Egyptian construction workers spoke each other's language, and misunderstandings were frequent.

My small role was to travel to New York to regularly brief a council of senior Orthodox Rabbis on the status of the work. The contrast with the State Department's antiseptic corridors and offices was total. I would proceed to a building in the garment district on New York's West Side, taking a freight elevator to an upper floor and emerging into a vast women's clothing factory with hundreds of seamstresses and models in various stages of undress. I would then be escorted through the chaos to a closed conference room where about a dozen solemn Rabbis awaited me around a table. After a briefing on the work, conducted over fruit juice and actual fruit, I would return the way I had come, but have never forgotten the surreal contrast between the factory floor and our solemn deliberations behind closed doors concerning ancient Jewish bones in Egypt.

LOOKING BACK

For most diplomats, of almost any country, a posting to their capital city is usually a kind of purgatory. The immediacy, sense of purpose and status, not to mention insulation from plumbers, expedited vehicle registration and many of the simplified details of daily life at an embassy yield to the myriad demands of an anonymous commuter life. Washington is, of course, home base for several postings in the course of a normal career, but by no means necessarily home. The very concept of home, that mythical place of childhood memories and old friends poised to welcome the wanderer back, recedes with successive postings abroad until the standard query, "where is home," has no true answer and causes confusion.

With its museums, wide spaces and gardens, Washington is a tranquil and secure place to raise children, but at the same time a transient and one-company town. Status, for the most part, lies in one's government job title or membership in this or that inner circle, and for transients and outsiders it can be a soulless, unforgiving place. Many diplomats, and not just Americans, do nevertheless retire there when the time comes; padding out the audience at think tanks and accepting such invitations as still come their way.

A Washington posting also has an aspect of keeping up with the Joneses. Classmates and old friends who have stayed in place deepening their roots and networks and moving forward as bankers, lawyers or other professionals tend with time to inhabit a different space. Many will have done well financially compared to those in civil or foreign service, and just reciprocating hospitality can be a challenge. Then too, over the years, the old school friend, while still professing interest, tends to be less and less interested in tribal structures of Mauritania or the latest cataclysm in Sudan.

There is also the issue of work-life balance, so much in vogue today. The myth is that, after an unending whirl of diplomatic receptions and protocol abroad, Washington is a welcome haven for exhausted families to recover and re-knit. The truth, I think, is the exact opposite. Families are generally on their own and stranded in remote suburbs while the FSO may have 2-hour commutes, 12-hour work days, Saturday in the office, and Sunday for lawn mowing, mulching and tree work. By contrast, the joys of couples sharing diplomacy abroad stand out, while the divorce rate in the Foreign Service, higher than the general average, usually surges in Washington. Most colleagues, myself included, were thus eager to get back abroad to resume what we thought we had signed up for, as well as to pay down debt accumulated at home.

NOTES

*Washington is unavoidably home base for the Department of State and, in the course of a full career, one can expect to have several tours of duty there; in my own case three. For simplicity sake, I have compressed highlights and low points from these into this single chapter. The name Foggy Bottom by which the State Department and its surrounding region is colloquially known probably dates to an earlier more pestilential era when our nation's capital was little more than a swamp and foreign diplomats assigned there received handsome hardship pay for their service.

1. See John Hopkins, *White Nile Diaries*, I.B. Tauris, London, 2014 for a description of what travelers in these remote lands may sometimes encounter.

2. The Popular Front for the Liberation of Saguia al-Hamra and Rio del Oro (POLISARIO) based in the area of Tindouf in southwestern Algeria.

3. This was decades before the Hubble and Kepler telescopes and vast earth-bound observatories when all observations had to be conducted *in situ*.

4. Later research convinced me that Andreas had other clients as well and that the gold was part of emergency preparations for evacuation of the large Greek community which came all too soon as the situation unraveled in Sudan.

5. Toby Harnden, "Spying for Fidel," *Washingtonian*, October 2009.

6. Ibid.

7. Ibid.

8. Ibid.

9. John Milton, *Paradise Lost*, 1667

10. While tedious in the extreme, my work in Soviet Affairs was also something of a family tradition in that my father, William H. Jackson, was assigned to the US Navy Coastal Command in New York City from 1941–42 where, using a ladder, he marked on a wall-size US map all German U-Boat sightings along the Eastern Seaboard. Like me, he found the work boring, but went on to write a critical intelligence brief recommending that anti-submarine warfare be transferred to the British in order to destroy U-Boats coming out of submarine pens in the Bay of Biscay.

11. Robert Shaplen, Three Part Profile on Under Secretary David D. Newsom, *New Yorker* magazine, 1980.

V

Multilateral Diplomacy

TURTLE BAY

The United Nations is indeed a perplexing place; yet, when the Under Secretary recommended me to the US Ambassador there, without second thought I happily returned to New York where I was born and lived as a child. Compared to Washington, with its monuments and stately avenues, the sense of possibility, of being able to do anything at any hour of the day or night in New York, is incredibly energizing. Ambassador Don McHenry, an understated professional and team-player, was in the process of restoring order after his more flamboyant predecessor Andrew Young had flamed out over unauthorized contacts with the PLO. Going from bilateral diplomacy, where you have a single set of counterparts and diplomatic colleagues, to the United Nations with some 180 permanent missions (193 today) and a huge multinational UN bureaucracy was at first exhilarating but, over time, frustrating as UN committees considered nearly identical agendas year after year with few changes in annual resolutions and little if any real world impact.

My brief as a political advisor covered the General Assembly's Fourth or Decolonization Committee, a Security Council sub-committee for sanctions against apartheid South Africa, as well as the Non-Aligned Movement (NAM) consisting of 101 countries. The latter leveraged its influence over the General Assembly through bloc voting on an agenda predetermined outside the UN. This was a smart strategy for small states, many with populations under 100,000, to maximize their power, but in other respects defied logic. The Decolonization Committee, for example, would annually review progress toward independence of seventeen territories still under colonial administration. The smallest of these, like Pitcairn Island with 60 inhabitants or the Cocos (Keeling) Islands with 435, were vastly outnumbered by the bureaucracy of UN delegations, interpreters and staff engaged in monitoring their progress.

Similarly, the independentista parties of Puerto Rico, while then supported by only 6 percent of the Island's people, were always invited to testify before the Committee and to attend NAM meetings, where they were lauded as freedom fighters. In other words, while the "right to self-determination," enshrined in General Assembly and NAM doctrine, implies free choice, in practice the only allowable outcome was independence and the process thus devolved into a weapon to bludgeon former colonial states still administering vestiges of empire too small for statehood. Nor was there particular concern with self-determination by the local population when the Non-Aligned bloc rushed to support Argentina, a NAM member since 1973, in its war over the Falkland (Malvinas) Islands.

Despite a stale and repetitive agenda, the United Nations was still a place of pageantry, intrigue and, on rare occasions like the Cuban missile crisis, a safety valve for the world. Statesmen would congregate in New York each year for set speeches at the opening of the General Assembly and every possible permutation of bilateral meetings among themselves. While they did not endear themselves to New Yorkers, bringing the city's already clogged cross town traffic to a standstill, it was a chance for small states lacking worldwide embassies to make themselves better known and for great powers to exchange views in a neutral venue. The US Mission was strengthened during the General Assembly by "public members" appointed in Washington like Congressman and later presidential candidate Paul Tsongas who had been a Peace Corps volunteer in Ethiopia and cared deeply about the Horn of Africa. We talked sometimes late into the night about differing Ethiopian and Somali perspectives on the Horn.

Another such appointee, to whom I was assigned as "control officer," although he was virtually uncontrollable, was former Ambassador to Spain and Connecticut Governor John Lodge. Lodge was a rock-ribbed conservative, and one day I was sitting behind him in the General Assembly when the Polish delegate launched into a diatribe against the United States. His outrageous remarks called out for rebuttal, and I rushed back to USUN to write one and clear it with the new Ambassador, Jeane Kirkpatrick, who doubled my text with additional arguments. I got back to Lodge two minutes before his time to speak and he instructed me to cut the text in half so that he would not be gaveled down and humiliated for exceeding his allotted time. While I was frantically deleting Ambassador Kirkpatrick's additions, he added what he called a final "peroration" at the conclusion, over which I had absolutely no control. When he reached that point in his speech, Lodge declaimed in a stentorian voice, "We Americans will not truckle to the godless yoke of red communist atheism. We will not stoop in the hellholes of totalitarian fascism," leaving the General Assembly in stunned silence and outdoing even the most ideological hardliners of the Reagan Administration.

The late Mayor Koch, never one to shrink from controversy, would sometimes also use the United Nations as a foil for the city's politics. I had once escorted him, as a visiting New York Congressman, around Northern Greece by Land Rover and, as a joke, told him that I had brought it to New York because of the potholes. His Honor, generally someone of great humor, seemed to have lost it in New York and was definitely not amused. Soon afterwards, he caused a firestorm by proposing tongue-in-cheek to inscribe on a wall owned by the City near UN headquarters, "Let the great nations and the mighty of the earth bow down and magnify the glory that is Israel." It was good politics in New York, but poorly received in the UN Delegates' Lounge, an inner sanctum resembling the lounge from "Star Wars" where one had to be ever cautious not to fall into conversation with PLO, Cuban, KGB, Sahraoui Democratic Arab Republic (SDAR), North Korean or other odd types whom American diplomats were instructed to eschew in those years.

As note taker, I occasionally accompanied the Ambassador to the Thirty-Eighth Floor offices of Secretary General Kurt Waldheim. While the Ambassador always had a laundry list of important issues to raise, Waldheim was inevitably more interested in gossip about what people were saying about him on the lower thirty-seven floors of his own building. Flash forward, in a later life, which I will come to, I was president of a college in Thessaloniki, Greece which had been seized as the regional Nazi headquarters during the war from which Waldheim is believed by some to have played a role in the deportation of Greek Jews to Auschwitz.

The annual fall General Assembly was always a tumultuous time of crossed signals, massive traffic jams and heightened security. The Secretary of State would usually take up residence in New York for a week, meeting and entertaining visiting heads of state and dignitaries. I remember one particularly prickly Pakistani diplomat, Agha Shahi, who went on to be twice Minister of Foreign Affairs. Relations with Pakistan were in a downturn and Shahi was to meet with Haig after the Secretary's speech to the UNGA. I was to be the escort and note taker. I made small talk outside the Secretary's closed door for nearly an hour with an increasingly impatient and rank-conscious Shahi.

Haig had already received criticism for his speech and when we were shown in Shahi said ingratiatingly that it was quite a speech. Taking the innocent pleasantry for sarcasm, Haig exploded, "you sure know how to hit a man when he's down." There followed a jumbled conversation on possible Sikorsky helicopters for Pakistan from United Technologies, where Haig had previously been President and CEO. When it was over, I began to receive frantic calls from Washington to provide a verbatim transcript ASAP. When I did so, I received even more frantic calls to immediately destroy every copy of the report. The Secretary had apparently misspoken himself. In the evening, Haig was to host an annual reception for VIPs and UN diplomats on the top floor of the US Mission. It was poorly attended, and he cut short and returned to Washington early. After all guests had left and Mission staff were taking their time to close down the bar, who should arrive to show there were no hard feelings, but Agha Shahi. Again, I made excruciating chitchat with the self-important and fuming diplomat as I escorted him out. As Milton writes, "They also serve who only stand and wait."

Opinions of the United Nations, usually expressed with fervor and emotion, run the gamut from last hope for world peace to unwieldy failed bureaucracy to invasive world government backed by black helicopters. The reality is more nuanced, and the organization that emerged from the ashes of war at San Francisco in 1945 clearly raised unrealistic expectations. In the early years, the Soviet Union out-vetoed the United States three to one in the Security Council, blocking progress on most issues. In the mid-seventies that ratio was reversed as the Soviets courted the Non-Aligned bloc and the US was often isolated, particularly on issues of the Middle East. Further, the Soviet Union had client states like Vietnam, Laos, Afghanistan, Cuba or Nicaragua who could be counted on to vote with it well over ninety percent of the time, while by contrast NAM counties friendly toward the United States like St. Lucia,

Morocco, Lebanon, Singapore, Ivory Coast or Liberia would only rarely vote with us more than thirty percent of the time.

This conundrum has led to radical shifts in US policy toward the UN under different administrations and ambassadors like Vernon Walters, who saw it as a valuable sounding board and vehicle for outreach and intelligence, or others like Patrick Moynihan and Jeane Kirkpatrick, who attempted to hold individual countries to strict account for statements at the UN or NAM. Their attempt to directly link voting records at the UN to levels of American assistance in each country was particularly popular in Congress, already suspicious of the United Nations and eager to slash budgets.

On the other hand, assistance to some countries was a negotiated trade-off for military bases, overflight rights or other privileges and making UN voting the litmus test for our assistance often risked tipping a fragile balance. This, in turn, created regular disputes with the Department of State, although most UN ambassadors were full members of the cabinet and thus able to hold their own and, on occasion, to transform the UN Mission into a nexus for foreign and domestic policy. George H. W. Bush notably used it as a springboard to the Presidency, while Cabot Lodge had also made an unsuccessful run for Vice President, and Patrick Moynihan was elected from there to the Senate. Edward Stettinius and Madelaine Albright actually went directly on to become Secretaries of State.

A CASE OF MISCAPITALIZATION

The transition from the Carter to Reagan administrations and from Don McHenry to Jeane Kirkpatrick in New York was particularly tumultuous, and I had a ringside seat for it. The outgoing team had worked to build bridges with the developing world, generally disregarding rhetorical excesses in the UN and NAM, whereas the newcomers were all about cost cutting and strict accountability for declarations in any public forum. Jeane Kirkpatrick herself had come to the new President's attention through her famous or infamous article, "Dictatorships and Double Standards" in *Commentary* Magazine, and was propelled into office by unstinting support from neoconservative intellectuals sometimes called the *Commentary Crowd* and centered around its editor, Norman Podhoretz, and others like Irving Kristol. One by one, political appointees of a liberal stripe, some even holdovers from the era of Andrew Young, began to disappear and offices went temporarily dark. Seeing colleagues with whom one had worked on UN committees depart in such haste, there was an atmosphere of hostile takeover, and even mid-level and non-political career officers, like me, were none too sure what the future held.

Ambassador McHenry was given short notice to vacate the ambassadorial residence in the Waldorf Astoria Hotel, and I recall a frenzied lunch there for his remaining skeletal staff during which he was literally taking down personal items from the walls and packing his bags. Ambassador Kirkpatrick arrived in a matter of days, suspicious of holdovers and unsure of what she would find, which ushered in an uncomfortable period of mutual sizing up. She was an extremely quick learner, but came to the job new to multilateral diplomacy, or any diplomacy for that matter, as well as to managing a complex mission. I recall accompanying her as note taker for a meeting with the visiting Foreign Minister of Ivory Coast. He began the conversation by saying, "what I am going to tell you is very sensitive and for your ears only" which, of course, in diplomatic-speak means "please convey this message to the Secretary of State and, if possible, the President." He was absolutely crestfallen when the Ambassador instructed me in no uncertain terms, "I want no record of this conversation. Put away your pen." His message, the less-than-earth-shaking contents of which I've long forgotten, was never to reach Washington, defeating one of the poor man's main goals in traveling from Africa to the General Assembly.

As time went by, less and less work flowed to my office, and it was clear that the new Ambassador relied primarily on a small coterie of non-career advisors whom she had handpicked to come with her to New York. This left more than enough time to peruse the dozens of nondescript cables and administrative notices that fill a bureaucrat's daily inbox and are usually discarded unread. In fact, the inbox exercise is a staple of the Foreign Service entrance exam during which candidates are given fifteen minutes to deal with a bulging inbox, testing their ability to separate wheat from chaff. So it was that I happened to focus on a circular notice from the State Department announcing something called the UNA Chapman Cox Sabbatical Program, which offered a year on full salary plus generous expenses for a worthwhile and creative project. Looking out my office window at the United Nations building across UN Plaza, I could see delegates coming and going, security checks in progress and the flags of member states flapping in the breeze. How providential, I thought, that such an opportunity bearing on the UN, in whose affairs, particularly relating to the NAM, I was then immersed, should come to me at just that moment from the United Nations Association.

I had not personally had occasion to work with UNA, which functions as an extended network and support group for promotion of the original San Francisco ideals and greater public awareness of the United Nations and its specialized agencies. I knew people close to it, however, and was optimistic that, if I could just develop a proposal of direct interest to the UN, I might well be competitive.

As we have seen, the Qadhafi coup had already started the meteoric rise of oil prices, and, since the 1973 Non-Aligned Summit in Algiers, the NAM and its related economic grouping, the G-77, had used the oil weapon to bludgeon the West. The 1979 NAM Summit in Havana and three year chairmanship of Fidel Castro further radicalized the movement and injected it big time into the Cold War, with Moscow claiming the non-aligned states as "natural allies" of the Soviet Union. By the time I arrived on the scene, the NAM had clearly put the US and West on the defensive by tabling hundreds of resolutions each year which the non-aligned majority had agreed on at meetings from which the US, which pays by far the largest share of the UN budget, was excluded. Jeane Kirkpatrick was about to bring this contradiction into sharp relief with her threats to cut off American aid to states voting against the US or even to block payment of US assessments on which the UN budget depended. There was also the specter then of eight NAM states dominating the Security Council or, more remotely, achieving an absolute majority of nine.

With a book proposal along these lines in hand, originally titled "An Aligned View of the Non-Aligned," I launched my application, also instigating letters and calls to recommend me to the UNA main office, not far from the US Mission building in New York. They, in turn, said that they would be pleased to send along endorsements to the UNA offices in Washington, which were undoubtedly the point of contact on the matter. Having done what I could, I returned to my inbox and, as time passed, began to forget the UNA and my quixotic application in the usual humdrum of committee meetings and briefing the new staff in the Ambassador's office, many of whom were also political appointees, new to government and the UN.

My surprise was thus total when I received a call from Washington informing me that not only had I been selected to receive a prestigious sabbatical, but my presence was mandatory at a luncheon the following day in one of the State Department's private Eighth Floor dining rooms to be hosted by the Under Secretary for Management. No further details were vouchsafed to me, and I hastened to thank the kind folks at UNA, who congratulated me warmly and said that they were delighted to have helped. Arriving at the appointed time and place, I was completely blindsided to be introduced to my benefactress, Mrs. Una Chapman Cox. The circular notice had been a simple case of miscapitalization, a mere typo-graphical error by a printing crew in the bowels of the State Depart-ment. There was absolutely no connection to the United Nations, much less to the UNA with which Mrs. Cox appeared to be com-pletely unfamiliar.

Mrs. Cox, it turned out, was a delightful, diminutive rancher from Texas whose property outside Corpus Christi, only slightly smaller than the King Ranch, was well endowed with cattle, gas and oil. She was the only lady I ever met with a personal zip code. As she explained to us, she had travelled to India just after the War to bag a tiger and, putting ashore in Bombay in the confused last days of the British raj without proper documentation for her guns, she was promptly incarcerated in the local jail. In her distress, the American Consul there came to her rescue, keeping her company and providing food and wine before eventually securing her release and reunion with her cruise ship several stops ahead. Reflecting on this episode later in life, Una had decided to show her gratitude for the astute Consul's intervention by making a sizable grant from her own private foundation to the State Department for public benefit projects that would advance its work and image.

It was the prospect of funding for her program on a permanent basis that explained the elaborate luncheon, general commotion and even TV cameras in the claustrophobic private dining room. There were two other sabbatical winners, with projects to travel and lecture across the country to make the State Department and its consular services better known to American audiences. Mrs. Cox announced at the outset that her decision on permanent funding to the tune of five million dollars, a huge sum at that time, would depend on whether she liked our first three projects and their overall quality. We were each asked to summarize them for her, and my turn came last after my two colleagues had described a variety of speaking engagements and travel about the United States to make Americans more aware of the State Department and its consular services to citizens like her abroad, all of which appeared to meet with her approval. By contrast, our exchange went something like this:

Una Chapman Cox: "Now, son, what's your project?"

Me: "Mrs. Cox, It will be a book analyzing the growth of the Non-Aligned Movement and the impact that it has on the operation of the United Nations, in particular the Security Council and the General Assembly, in the context of US-Soviet competition at the UN and Moscow's campaign to promote the Non-Aligned Nations as the "natural ally of the Soviet Union.""

Una: "Pshaw, that's one book I'm never going to read!"

Una (finished with me and happily turning her attention to the flustered Under Secretary): "Mr. Secretary, them Mexicans are taking all of our good Texas turkeys and what are you folks going to do about it?"

Under Secretary: "I beg your pardon?"

Una: "I said the Mexicans are poaching our Texas turkeys and I'd like to know what the State Department is going to do to get them back."

Under Secretary: "Well, I'll certainly look into it for you, Madame."

The Under Secretary, eager to get his hot hands on Una's $5 million, had obviously received the customary staff memo with carefully scripted talking points that are standard for Seventh Floor "principals." That is, "Mrs. Cox may say . . . and you may wish to respond . . . etc." Except Mrs. Cox was one of a kind, an irreverent free spirit who kept departing from the stilted script. Apparently more a bureaucrat than a hunter, the poor Under Secretary was clearly out of his element and flummoxed. Between our two lack-luster performances, I was frankly amazed that, when the lunch ended, the Department emerged with grant funding in perpetuity, and I came away committed to write an arcane book on a topic that, in my wildest dreams, I would never have undertaken but for a single three-letter miscapitalization.

Returning to New York, I was initially euphoric about the prospect of remaining in the city for an unstructured year of reading, writing and travelling whenever I needed for research. I had a splendid apartment in Chelsea, long before it was discovered by galleries and boutiques, with parking for the Landrover just in front. Soon, it dawned on me, however, that to properly research and write a meaningful book on the obscure interactions of the NAM and UN, as well as statistical analysis of voting patterns, would be real work compared with shuffling paper from an inbox to the outbox or waste basket. Happily, however, diplomats from well-disposed NAM countries welcomed interest, even American, in their much maligned movement and were surprisingly helpful. The resources of the UN Library were also available to me, although their colossal documentation caused me to question what I had gotten myself into.

As I went from a suspect legacy of the outgoing Democratic administration to an independent researcher working on the UN and NAM, Jeane Kirkpatrick, herself a Georgetown University professor and certified academic, began to take an interest in the project, sharing her time and background materials, as well as, when the time came, a generous jacket blurb. Another luminous intellect who helped unstintingly was George Kennan, who had been in Yugoslavia as US Ambassador during the 1961 founding conference of the Non-Aligned Movement, along with Tito, Nehru, Nasser, Nkrumah, Sukarno, Archbishop Makarios et al. His historical perspective and critique of the manuscript were invaluable. Una Cox, having agreed to sponsor our grants, also became a friend and supporter. She insisted that the three grantees visit Trinity College in San Antonio, an institution which she had funded and which had one of the highest per student endowments in the country. Sadly, Mrs. Cox passed away during my sabbatical, but called whenever in New York to offer encouragement.

My mentor on non-aligned affairs was Bob Shaplen, the *New Yorker Magazine* writer with whom I had worked on his long profile of Under Secretary Newsom. Bob was an old Asia hand, deeply versed in India and Indonesia, and a close friend of Soedjatmoko, Rector of the UN University in Tokyo. As a reporter on assignment, he would guide me through the intricacies of the 1983 NAM Summit in New Delhi. In the meantime, he invited me for lunch at New York's Harvard Club midway through the project. It is a huge baronial hall decorated with African big game heads, probably donated by Harvard grads whose tastes and apartments could no longer accommodate family trophies. Or one could speculate that Theodore Roosevelt, Harvard Class of 1880, shot the entire lot.

In any case, after a couple martinis, as was his wont, Bob asked to see the manuscript such as it then was. I reluctantly handed it over, and we were immediately admonished by the waiter that Harvard Club policy precluded display of commercial papers in the public rooms. Shaplen maintained in an outraged tone that it was a literary work and not commercial paper and insisted on seeing the Maitre D'. By the time I could wrestle back the manuscript, which I should never have brought, the scene had become the center of attention for several hundred lawyerly-looking and bemused Harvard grads. As we left, Bob introduced me to a regular table for *New Yorker* staff, inquiring if they had witnessed our "humiliation." The legendary editor, William Shawn, quipped with typical *New Yorker* humor, "Well, Bob, at least you were not showing cloth samples."

A crucial piece of the book would be coverage of the next NAM summit, following Cuba's three-year chairmanship, for clues whether these 101 countries would moderate their behavior after a high water mark of radicalism under Fidel Castro. Saddam Hussein had secured the meeting, scheduled for 1982, in a bid to break out of Iraq's international isolation and was doling out $1 billion each year as a sweetener for member states. He miscalculated, however, by invading Iran in September 1980 in a war that was to cost a half million lives. As fighting escalated and spread into Iraq, Saddam continued to insist on holding the conference as a diversion for his war-weary population. Only at the last moment was it re-scheduled for New Delhi in March 1983, when Iran threatened to strike Baghdad during the conference and the spectacle of two member states locked in mortal combat seemed to the more moderate members to undermine the Movement's commitment to peace. On July 21, an Iranian F-4 fighter carried out a suicide attack destroying the Al-Rashid Hotel, where the Summit was to have been held from September 6-8, 1982. The matter was thus sealed, and Fidel Castro made the final announcement cancelling the Summit on August 3. It caught me midway in consultations about the NAM in Europe en route to Baghdad.

So it was that, with time on my hands, I did finally reach the Shetland Islands with diminished ambitions to ponder on the Isles of North Uist, Lewis, Harris and Berneray, ironically not the great American novel I had once dreamed of writing, but instead the inner workings of the NAM bureaucracy. The subject matter was incongruous on the windswept isles, so far from the arenas of New York, Baghdad and New Delhi. Still, I could understand why it is that Prince Charles, seeking refuge from the architectural and environmental wars, finds solace in the silence of Berneray. And what traveler to Harris has not acquired tweed there at the source? Mine, handwoven in the Outer Hebrides from Scottish Grown Wool according to the label, I took with me to New Delhi where a tailor endorsed by the local Washington Post man made a jacket for less than the cost of the cloth. Last year, returning to Florida at summer's end, my closet was a major oil slick where sheep fat impregnated into the fabric for wear in the Outer Hebrides had liquefied in the sub-tropics. Globalization has its pros and cons.

In any case, the delayed summit resulted in my return to Ambassador Kirkpatrick's staff for six months to fill the gap and complete the book. There I found relations with the NAM in an uproar since her infamous letter of October 6, 1981 reading the riot act to Permanent Representatives of 64 relatively moderate NAM states for signing a declaration which criticized the US by name nine times and dozens of times by implication. The extra time, however, made possible several brainstorming sessions at the Council on Foreign Relations which adopted the final product as a Council of Foreign Relations Book. [1]

I had already covered the 1981 NAM Foreign Ministers' meeting in New Delhi and knew well the challenges for an American, even an independent writer, to access the proceedings. While the non-aligned have a category of Permanent Observers and Official Guests including countries like Mexico, Austria, Finland, Sweden, Switzerland and even Spain, the United States is definitely not among them. By its charter the NAM was defined in contrast to the United States and the Soviet Union, so neither country could officially be present, although Moscow had reliable proxies within. Thus, delegates from even friendly countries like Singapore or Morocco could not afford to be seen in too deep conversation with an American, and gathering information was a discreet process of casual or impromptu meetings. This was not in the realm of cloak and dagger, but still one had to be patient and keep a low profile to fill the pages of a book. Security and protocol were breached at least once, however, during the Foreign Ministers' meeting when, in the early hours, smoke filled New Delhi's plush Oberoi Hotel and I was evacuated along with Foreign Ministers and Ambassadors Extraordinary and Plenipotentiary into the Indian night clad in every conceivable form of sleepwear.

The Delhi Summit turned out to be the largest and most elaborate in NAM history, well worth the wait. While the days of NAM dominance were already numbered by the impending collapse of the Berlin Wall and Soviet Empire, the Summit did succeed in curbing some of the excesses of the Castro years. I was able to take copious notes hanging around the periphery of the Conference and talking with Indian academics and experts including one of the grand old men of non-alignment, former Prime Minister Morarji Desai.[2] I rewarded myself with an idyllic month in Goa poring over my scribbled notes and completing the final chapters. Calangute Beach where I settled, like Nepal or Matala in Crete, had been besieged for over a decade by hippies but was now blissfully empty. Nearby, one could venerate, or at least contemplate, the Holy Relics of Saint Francis Xavier at the Basilica of Bom Jesus where his silver casket was on permanent display and his bejeweled bones were brought out once every decade to mark his death in 1552. Indeed, I relished the sheer incongruity of pondering the UN and NAM voting patterns in that setting, alone on one of the world's great beaches. The only client in sight, I was set upon from time to time by a half dozen professional ear cleaners with their rusty instruments. Unwilling to risk a punctured ear drum in faraway Calangute, I resisted their entreaties and returned to New York in time to meet my publisher's deadline and prepare for onward assignment to Morocco.

As Foreign Affairs Quarterly noted in a fulsome jacket blurb, it was "ironic that the Non-Aligned Movement should receive its clearest and most comprehensive treatment from an American author." This is surely because the movement was so divided into rival factions that analysis by anyone from a member state would have been discounted. For me it was doubly ironic in view of the misunderstanding that had locked me into the topic in the first place. In any case, publication attracted attention on the non-aligned circuit and led to a number of unlikely speaking invitations around the world. I first presented the book, now blandly re-titled "The Non-Aligned, the United Nations and the Superpowers" at the insistence of a conflict-adverse under secretary and a publisher hoping that the word "superpowers" might sell books, to an august gathering at the Council on Foreign Relations. There I was humbled when an Indian student of non-alignment told me that he had fasted for a week in order to heighten his sensitivities to what I was about to say.

Newly posted to Rabat, Morocco, I was soon seconded as a speaker at an academic conference on non-alignment at Novi Sad in Yugoslavia. There, as elsewhere, I was an object of curiosity as an American, and therefore by definition "aligned," writing about non-alignment or, worse, posing as some sort of "expert" or even spy on the Movement. Years later, when the book was dated and its contents far from my mind, I was sent to lecture the diplomatic corps of newly-independent Bosnia on the NAM. The Foreign Service Institute improbably trained Bosnia's fledgling diplomats at Oberammergau, and there I held forth on a movement by then in steep decline and unlikely to loom large in their future.

IN RETROSPECT

Beyond the clamor of the Security Council, the chaos of the General Assembly and the unabashed Cold War rhetoric of that time, the main attraction of a UN assignment was, of course, New York itself. Often these postings go begging because of the high cost of living and exorbitant or dubious schooling for children. Endless and often pointless night time meetings of the Security Council are also a deterrent for some. Born and raised in New York, however, I was happy to disprove the aphorism that "you can't go home again." Whether or not one actually takes advantage of the city's boundless possibilities, their very existence was exhilarating for at least this middle aged returnee from Moqadishu, Tripoli and Washington.

The sheer vitality of the city comes from millions of New Yorkers hurtling about below ground, thronging the streets, and racing to and fro by car, plane, boat and helicopter. The scale and triumph of order over bewildering complexity inspires optimism and hope undiminished by 9/11. Still, the World Trade Towers that I used to circle most mornings training for the New York Marathon will always be a painful memory. Their beauty and the play of light on their angles in the early morning sun made them wondrous symbols of what man can accomplish and also destroy. The latter and the loss of 2606 lives, originating in the Middle East where I had lived and worked, was unspeakable.

The Marathon, which I ran in 1982, was an indelible experience, crossing, as it did, a swaying Verrazano Bridge with a mere 16,000 fellow runners that year, passing through Hassidic Brooklyn and approaching Central Park through Harlem where, with the field spread out and with no other runners in sight, the friendly cheers of encouragement could only be for you.

Overall, a year out of the system, regardless of how I happened to stumble into it, provided the intellectual capital to survive another couple decades in government service. While a diplomat's life and perspective on other countries and cultures is immensely privileged, it is also often frenzied and lacking time to read and reflect. Investment in a year out, such as Una Chapman Cox generously made possible, paid lifelong dividends, expanding horizons and outlook.

The book project turned out to occupy most of three years that I was assigned to the US Mission to the UN, with one full year working from a loft in Chelsea. In practical terms, authorship of a book is not necessarily esteemed in Foggy Bottom where I've always felt that a strong anti-intellectual undercurrent prevails. I have to admit, however, that I too have sometimes viewed PhDs assigned to my office as mildly handicapped and in need of remediation to adapt to the pace and terse prose of embassy reporting. Still, a published book does provide an extra half inch to stand on in certain circumstances and to plump out an argument. This is less true, of course, as interest in the book has waned along with fortunes of the NAM. While the latter continues reflexively to meet every four years, the rationale for a neutral alternative between superpowers has long ceased to exist. Sadly, the same can perhaps be said of the UN as well, where the tendency today is in most cases to bypass Turtle Bay.

NOTES

1. Richard L Jackson, *The Non-Aligned, the UN and the Superpowers*, Praeger Publishers, 1983.
2. Morarji Desai (1896-1995), an Indian independence activist and later Prime Minister, was the grand old man of Indian non-alignment.

VI

The Fabled Kingdom

THE ORIENTAL SECRETARY

One of the vestigial privileges of a diplomat is to pick up a vehicle for export directly from the factory, avoiding taxes and receiving a hefty diplomatic discount. So, I approached Morocco circuitously, driving south from Paris with my son and daughter in a new Peugeot 404. Passing Tours, where Charles Martel turned back the northernmost Moorish invasion in 732 AD, and moving from the lush green countryside of the Loire Valley into the increasingly arid South of Spain with outcroppings of Moorish influence well beyond just Granada and the Alhambra all along our route, we traversed fault lines of a tumultuous history. Arriving for the first time, and in a shiny new car, in seedy and somewhat sinister Tangier also underscored the transition, as did a nighttime drive over deserted roads to Rabat. There, city lights were ablaze with tens of thousands of Moroccans parading in the streets after breaking the Ramadan fast. We had arrived in a different and exotic place.

Morocco is one of the most beautiful countries on earth, with its rich traditions and history against a backdrop of expansive seashore, high Atlas and Rif Mountains and trackless Saharan wastes. So seductive, in fact, was Morocco that I remained there an unprecedented, and probably not career-enhancing, eight years for three consecutive postings. Nearby Tunisia was the Land of Lotus Eaters in Homer's *Odyssey*, but it could just as well have been Morocco. My successive assignments in the same country violated conventional wisdom that the ambitious path for a diplomat is the short tour, preferably in hardship and/ or dangerous posts, with broad exposure to potential mentors and senior officials. Had I known that eight years in Morocco lay ahead, I would certainly also have plunged deeper into Arabic, although French was usually a viable, but less endearing, alternative.

In fact, while skipping about the world every few years from place to place may satisfy personal ambitions and glorified tourism, I've always felt that it was at the expense of the taxpayer and the quality of American intelligence about any given country. Costs of moving entire households over and over, retraining, and all the allowances involved are enormous. Equally, a two-year tour with the second year devoted to competing for a next assignment prevents in depth knowledge of a foreign country.

Take Morocco, for example. Casablanca, the largest city, has gone from 250,000 inhabitants after World War II to as many as five million today, and while I was there Morocco's population balance tilted for the first time to an urban majority. Yet, the country's outlook and rhythms remain rooted in agriculture and, during cyclical droughts every six or seven years, there is a welling up of malaise and complaint. A newly arrived political officer picks up these signs of dissent and, confident that his or her diplomatic skill and charm have elicited an intelligence breakthrough, hastens to advise Washington that the sky is falling. There, transient desk officers initiate a review of whither Morocco. John Waterbury, a scholar of the region, wisely wrote in 1970 that Morocco remains a "country waiting for an explosion that never comes."[1]

As a corrective, the British until recently had "oriental secretaries" in exotic or obscure posts who would be in place for 8–10 years at a time and return often over a career, picking up nuances that transients miss. The US Congress, of course, would never permit this with its fear of American diplomats "going native" and succumbing to dread diseases like localitis or clientitis, further proof, if any be needed, of a basic lack of trust in the nation's diplomats. They have no such scruples, however, in assigning servicemen and women to repeated tours in a war zone.

So it was that by chance, lacking any special preparation or knowledge of either Arabic or Berber, that I became a sort of inadvertent Oriental Secretary simply by virtue of staying on and on for so many years. Moroccans are immensely hospitable, but typically formal and not the first to offer a newcomer friendship or trust. Rabat, the capital city, teems with diplomats, and Moroccans who have in the past invested in such friendships tend to pull back when new friends disappear every two or three years. They value above all continuity and usually turn first to the person they have known longest and learned to trust, regardless of rank. It also helped that, in my case, the first of four ambassadors with whom I worked was unusually gregarious and focused on the widest possible outreach to Moroccans, often taking me along as a resource person, note taker or translator in French. With his departure, many such senior contacts looked to me in my own right. Within the Embassy too, waves of subsequent arrivals gave benefit of the doubt to "old Moroccan hands," attributing to me a dubious country expertise.

The Morocco around me was an absolute monarchy. King Hassan, of Sherifian descent from the Prophet Mohammed, occupied the four-centuries-old Alaouite throne and was informed about and controlled the minutest details within his Kingdom. Critics found his iron-fisted rule repressive and authoritarian, although there was also good reason for it. In July 1971 and again in August 1972 he was very nearly killed in two attempted coups d'etat. The first episode was a full-scale ground assault on the Skhirat seaside palace where a reception marking the King's forty-second birthday was in full swing and one hundred were killed and two hundred wounded, including guests and diplomats, while the King hid in a secret closet. In the second instance, his plane was badly strafed by Moroccan F-5 Air Force jets and only when Hassan coolly ordered his pilot to radio that the Sovereign had been killed and beg to spare the crew, did he escape.[2] The King was ruthless in reprisal, eliminating the perpetrators and brutally punishing their families and anyone even remotely connected. Ahmed Touil, for example, a low-level air force fuel depot attendant who unknowingly fueled the attacking fighters barely survived 15 years at the Tazmamart death camp despite vigorous efforts by the Embassy and constant pressure on Congress from Touil's Iowa-based American wife, Nancy.

These violent escapes, as well as the subsequent deaths of his closest confidants, his brother Abdallah and Uncle Moulay Hafid, appeared to turn Hassan inward, limiting his former accessibility. He, nevertheless, continued, as has his son King Mohammed VI, an annual pilgrimage or Harka throughout the realm to royal palaces in each imperial city, typically winter in Marrakesh, spring in Fez, summer at Skhirat and fall in Rabat with shorter stays elsewhere in the Kingdom. For centuries, Moroccan history has been a constant struggle for control between the central power or Makhzen in the imperial cities and the warlike outlying tribes in the countryside or Bled as-Siba.[3]

More recently, support for the monarchy has been strongest in the traditional countryside with a massive rural to urban exodus and latent Islamism eroding consensus in the cities. For both, however, the Harka remains the time-honored way for the Sovereign to show himself to his subjects, and power continues to reside wherever the

King happens to be in the course of his annual pilgrimage. Bureaucrats in the ministries of the capital thus may well not be informed of his thinking on any given subject and must walk a tightrope with foreign diplomats between not seeming uninformed on the one hand or offering misinformation on the other.

King Hassan II was at once a world class strategist and an avid golfer, not necessarily an oxymoron. His addiction to golf led to a proliferation of first rate, but underused courses throughout the Kingdom. With a huge entourage, he would swoop into the Royal Golf of Dar es-Salaam outside Rabat and whatever nine of its forty-five holes he fancied to play would be closed to members and the public. Short of a major international golf pro or golfing heads of state, he would usually play alone and rarely had to putt out. He was followed at a respectful distance of maybe twenty yards by a clump of ministers and royal counselors, anyone of whom he might beckon in an instant to come forward to discuss matters of state. The contrast of the King in his latest golf attire and the cabinet and bureaucrats following behind, despite the heat, in full business suits bespoke absolute power. The King was usually attired by the Italian couturier, Francesco Smalto, although it was later revealed that Smalto procured more than just clothing in both Morocco and Gabon.

Moroccan ambassadors, recently returned from postings abroad, would often lurk behind trees on both sides of the fairways. The King, or so I've always thought, begrudged them the independence and presumed high life they had enjoyed abroad and demonstrated his power by making them wait before a further assignment. So they would stand patiently behind designated trees for weeks or even months on end, whenever the King golfed, before getting the royal summons to step forward. Once, the Royal Golf Federation, of which the King was Honorary President, thought to surprise him by upgrading the old seaside course at Mohammedia, patterned on a Scottish links, to professional level. When he arrived to play, the

Monarch was outraged that such a decision had been taken without consultation, ordered the course put back exactly to its former slightly dilapidated state and dismissed the entire Federation board. Soon elaborate bunkers that Arnold Palmer himself might have designed were back to seaside rough.

As I've said, I worked on Morocco with four American ambassadors, three in the country and one while I was Director for Egypt and North Africa in the State Department. All were political appointees, both because Morocco is an appealing place to live much sought after by bundlers and other appointees and because the King strongly preferred it that way. The few career ambassadors in our bicentennial relationship with Morocco have had a much rougher time and one, the late Richard Parker, a fluent Arabic speaker, was actually declared persona non grata and asked to leave. This is not uncommon among kingdoms of the Arab world, and our best speaker of classical Arabic, Ambassador Hume Horan, was unceremoniously booted out of Saudi Arabia in the same manner. Their fault was quite simply to know too much and to pick up nuances of meaning never intended for foreign ears. The King also assumed, not always correctly, that political ambassadors were close friends of the President and thus a back door into the White House for gifts and special emissaries, circumventing the bureaucracy. With the right personal touch, he undoubtedly hoped to unlock a secret route to Camp David levels of billion dollar US assistance for Morocco.

A canard in the State Department is that no ambassador has ever been given command of an aircraft carrier, while retired admirals and campaign donors proliferate at one third or more of American embassies, usually the most important. In fact, political ambassadors come with a varied mix of skills and weaknesses, although few with the rare abilities of an Edwin Reischauer in Tokyo, Arthur Burns in Bonn or, perhaps more recently, Jon Huntsman in China. Overall, abuse of these appointments erodes morale in the career service, many of whom understandably view it as a corrupt political spoils system. Since so many American diplomats serve in hardship posts like Baghdad, Kabul or Khartoum and 248 listed on the State Department's memorial plaque have died for their country, it would be motivating for the best and brightest to aspire to some of the top posts as well. Furthermore, if ambassadorships are really to be used as fundraising rewards, like PBS mugs or tote bags, it's painful to see how little they often go for. Some in major countries are listed for as little as $50,000 on the appointee plum list, while others with unusual amenities and no particular security threats, Luxembourg or Bermuda for example, can cost fat cats serious money. Apart from the corruption aspect, I've always felt that it's insulting to our friends and allies to be priced and auctioned off on the cheap this way in the marketplace. Nor can the receiving country have any clue to what they are getting based on the often inane testimony of ambassadors-designate at their Senate confirmation hearings.

"With Ambassadors like you, Excellency, we'll make America great!"

How an embassy staff reacts to these newcomers parachuting in from the outside world varies greatly. I recall one new arrival in Rabat who announced at his first country team meeting of the senior staff, "Now I want to make one thing absolutely clear at the outset; if there is any fellowship going down in this embassy, I want to be part of it." In the pause that followed, the staff looked to me as "oriental secretary" for response, and I was on the verge of replying, "Well, Sir, there is a Friday night poker game and plenty of bourbon at the Marine House," when happily he continued. What he had meant was early morning Bible study, and by keeping silent I had avoided an unpromising start with someone who over time became a good friend and colleague.

I have, however, seen some senior staff work behind an ambassador's back to undercut him and sow doubts in his or her mind about the loyalty of career staff in order to maximize their own role as principal mentor and puppeteer. On the other hand, the only viable strategy for a foreign service officer is to make the new arrival as efficient as possible and to take fullest advantage for the embassy of their usually larger rolodex of contacts and business background. In fact, lacking prior embassy experience or sometimes even exposure abroad, a political appointee must depend on professional guidance and often gives staff greater responsibility than would a seasoned career ambassador, many of whom turn out to be micromanagers.

MR. ROCKEFELLER COMES FOR BREAKFAST

My first ambassador in Morocco, Joseph Verner Reed, was a bit unorthodox from a career perspective, but came with dazzling contacts, up to and including the President whom he called "Poppy," and boundless energy that few in the Embassy could match. He had been a longtime Vice President and Executive Assistant to David Rockefeller at the Chase Bank for whom he handled relations with

Iranian Shah Reza Pahlevi, an important Chase client, including his final hospitalization in New York. I have always thought without proof that it was Reed's whimsical humor that registered the Shah at the New York Hospital under the name of David D. Newsom, at that time Under Secretary of State.

In any case, it was not surprising that in my first week on the job as Political Counselor I was asked to meet Mr. Rockefeller at the Casablanca Airport, about an hour away, and escort him to the official guest house of King Hassan, another important Chase client. Apart from the official armored Cadillac, the Ambassador had a private customized van with tinted class and plush red seats that swiveled 360 degrees around a conference table. It was irreverently known within the Embassy as the "Reedmobile," and it was with this conveyance that I greeted Mr. Rockefeller, fatigued after a trans-Atlantic flight and short stopover in London. It was a heady feeling swiveling in such chairs with a planetary banker as the van traversed fields with Moroccan peasants toiling in the hot sun. Many would bid handsomely for such a privilege in a charity auction.

Rockefeller accepted with equanimity problems that immediately confronted us on arrival at the King's guest house. The previous guest, Colonel Muammar Qadhafi of Libya, as usual disheveled and hours behind schedule, had not yet departed and was still upstairs. To avoid an impromptu encounter or, worse, what the Navy would call hot-bedding, Moroccan Royal Protocol had arranged an elaborate breakfast for the Rockefeller party in a separate banquet hall. Down one side of the large buffet was an array of exotic dishes described as a "traditional Moroccan hunting breakfast" while on the other were every conceivable Western breakfast food from cereals to eggs in every form, bacon, sausages and even hominy grits. The hunting breakfast, by contrast, consisted of livers, kidneys, and other unidentifiable innards, steeped in heavy oil. The entire party except Mr. Rockefeller went straight for the bacon and

eggs, while he was careful to sample each of the Moroccan delica-
cies, which most travellers would eschew after a long flight and
time change. Breakfast was interminable, but by its conclusion
Qadhafi had decamped and an army of household staff tidied up
after him.

The King in those days was a night owl, sleeping late, golfing if
he felt like it in the afternoon and working and receiving visitors
late into the night. His first words to Rockefeller when they met at
midnight were that he was honored and pleased that Mr. Rockefeller had favored the hunting breakfast that morning. The King had
acted as his own intelligence chief and minister of defense ever
since the two coup attempts, and this exchange was proof of his
ubiquitous network and command of minutia throughout his Kingdom. Rockefeller, on the other hand, was no slouch either and had
clearly been well briefed before ingesting a breakfast he could only
have found unpalatable. It was a remarkable lesson for a junior
diplomat, translatable into almost any profession as simply "do
your homework." Along with the lesson, Mr. Rockefeller gave me
a Chase necktie, which I still perversely wear whenever visiting
CitiBank or the Bank of America.

GRAND STRATEGY

King Hassan was convinced that Morocco was strategic real estate,
guarding access to the Straits of Gibraltar and exercising moderate
leadership in a region threatened by Islamists and, during the Cold
War, by an Algeria aligned with Moscow. He further marketed the
Kingdom as the essential gateway for Americans and Europeans
into Africa. All of these assumptions appeared threadbare, however, as the Soviet Union collapsed and the First Gulf War demonstrated that the Straits of Gibralter were no longer vital to project
US power into the Middle East or Africa. In fact, few would still
risk a carrier in such tight quarters. Crises in the Balkans and else-

where also vied for declining US foreign assistance, and Morocco's share dropped precipitously from $140 million a year in my time there to $34 million the last time I checked.

This tectonic shift became clear when, not long after our wedding in Casablanca, my wife Eia and I escorted Senator Patrick Moynihan and his wife around Morocco for several days. The focus of the Senator's trip was to investigate the continuing need for the largest radio transmitter in the free world located at a sprawling Voice of America (VOA) site outside Tangier. This was an ongoing major investment, based on obsolete Cold War realities, with transmitters able to beam radio broadcasts across the Soviet Union, Africa and the Middle East. With the collapse of the Soviet Union, it had become a costly white elephant, now long since closed, and there were no good answers to Senator Moynihan's demands for justification from the VOA and Embassy staffs. As a parenthesis, I took a risk in giving Moynihan a copy of my book on the NAM, since it covered his period as US Ambassador at the United Nations and insistent calls for accountability by UN member states. To my surprise, he read the entire rather dull book overnight, commenting to his wife, as she recounted to me, "This man hates me." He never mentioned it to me, however, and we continued to get along passably well, so far as I could tell.

A similar unforgettable visit involving US facilities, in this case to Marrakesh, unfolded with Florida Congressman Claude Pepper, the oldest living member of Congress, then in his mid-eighties, who headed the Grey Panther movement for the elderly. He was accompanied by a phalanx of young Congressmen whom he basically confined to quarters at the plush Mamounia Hotel during periods when he was resting so that they would not get ahead of him or freelance on their own with independent business or contacts. The King had just completed a $72 million dollar interior renovation of the legendary Mamounia Hotel undertaken by the French interior designer Andre Paccard, de-Moroccanizing the hotel many felt, but also installing state-of-the-art gadgetry. On the first night there, Congressman Pepper turned over in his sleep, accidentally hitting the bedside control panel and activating the automatic blinds, TV, music, and lights, causing a minor panic among the staff.

The purpose of the Pepper trip was to discuss a new NASA agreement for extension and use of a military airfield outside Marrakesh as a back-up landing site for the space shuttle. I will never forget escorting Claude Pepper to call on a recently appointed young Governor or Wali of Marrakesh. Pepper, who as a child had accompanied his father to watch Orville and Wilbur Wright take to the air at Kitty Hawk, North Carolina in 1909, held forth at length on the history of manned flight. Neither the other delegation members nor the bewildered Wali got in a word edgewise. The agreement, however, was finalized and implemented. If the ill-fated Challenger Space Shuttle had survived a few more minutes on January 28, 1989, the Marrakesh field would have been its emergency back-up landing site. The field has otherwise never been activated to my knowledge.

OTHER GLITTERATI

Morocco has always attracted enormously wealthy expatriates, particularly to Marrakesh and Tangier, gaining a not always positive reputation as a Mecca for jet-setters and glitterati. People like Malcolm Forbes, Yves St. Laurent, Barbara Hutton, Mark Gilbey of Gilbey's Gin,[4] Doris Duke and Princess al-Sabah of Kuwait, to name a few, had spectacular places in Tangier regularly featured in Architectural Digest. Marrakesh attracted people like Guy and Marie-Helene de Rothchild, Countess Hettie von Augsberg, and Countess Boule de Breteuil, at whose Villa Taylor Churchill and Roosevelt relaxed following the 1943 Casablanca Summit and to which Churchill returned in later years, leaving behind on the walls watercolors painted while there. Society revolved around such luminaries who, in fact, were only rarely in residence, with circles radiating outward of would-be friends, admirers and outright voyeurs.

The late David Herbert, a victim of British winner-take-all primogeniture and author of "Second Son" about his elder brother becoming the Earl of Pembroke, described the Tangier social scene with great wit.[5] It was, he once told me, a city of incorrigible strivers and social climbers conniving for decades to reach the pinnacle of local society. And once they finally arrived after years of fawning obeisance, he said, it was a terrible anticlimax when they found that "at the pinnacle of society there was only me."

These circles were a world away from Embassy life in Rabat, like Washington a staid one-company government town. Usually the twain did not meet except in a crisis. Such an emergency occurred in 1989 when Malcolm Forbes was famously hosting Elizabeth Taylor for his 70th birthday in Tangier and had promised her an audience with King Hassan. As it turned out, the Royal Palace did not grant the audience and, in desperation, Forbes turned to the Ambassador who cashed in some chips to arrange it. In the end, Hassan eventually received Forbes and the diva at the seaside palace in Skhirat.

"Crises" of this kind invariably found their way to the Embassy, although the US still had a Consulate General in Tangier, now closed in one of many of budget cutbacks. It was, in fact, the oldest diplomatic or consular facility of the United States abroad, and the archives are full of correspondence dating from 1789 between Thomas Barclay, who was the accredited American envoy to the Sultan of Morocco, and both Thomas Jefferson and John Adams. It was Barclay who earlier had negotiated the first American treaty with Morocco at Marrakesh in 1786 to curb depredations of the Barbary pirates. President George Washington then famously wrote to Moroccan Sultan Sidi Mohammed on December 1, 1789, "Within our territories there are no mines, either of gold or silver, and this young nation, just recovering from the waste and desolation of a long war, has not, as yet, had time to acquire riches by agriculture and commerce. But our soil is bountiful, and our people industrious and we have reason to flatter ourselves that we shall gradually become useful to our friends."[6]

"The US Consul General with his Royal Lions."

In order not to contaminate the rest of the Kingdom with "infection by infidels," foreign envoys were quarantined in Tangier where President Washington established a permanent US Consulate in 1797. Later, a separate "international zone" administered by France, Britain and Spain was set up in 1923 and lasted until Moroccan independence in 1956.[7] The originial consulate or legation is today the only site outside the United States to receive official US Historic Landmark status from the Department of Interior. 19th Century Moroccan sultans were in the habit of presenting American Consuls General with lions which they insisted be properly maintained within the Consulate grounds. Meat for a lion came to a dollar per day, a huge sum in 1833 dollars, and Consul General James Leib wrote to Secretary of State John Forsyth in that year, claiming reimbursement of $439.50 for lion feed over the previous 15 months. Receiving no response and deeply in debt, Lieb was eventually declared insane and repatriated to America via Gibraltar and Cadiz, Spain.

A new US Consul General, Thomas Carr, presented himself to the Sultan in 1839 and was rewarded with a brace of two perfectly matched lions. His correspondence with Secretary of State Daniel Webster about the lions' care and feeding contains no record that Carr, like Leib before him, was ever reimbursed. The State Department was clearly then, as it remains today, pennywise and pound foolish. With the Consulate now closed, the American flag flies in Tangier today only at the Tangier American Legation Institute for Moroccan Studies (TALIM), now a museum in the original legation building, and at the American School of Tangiers. The latter achieved celebrity over 45 years under its late headmaster, Joe McPhillips, with commencement speakers like Oliver Stone, Jimmy Buffet and Tahar Ben Jelloun, as well as dramatic productions with costumes by Yves St. Laurent.

Tangier, of course, also had a separate expatriate culture revolving around the reclusive author Paul Bowles and, in earlier years, his wife Jane and writers like Jack Kerouac, Tennessee Williams, Allen Ginsberg and William Burroughs. Bowles first washed up in Tangiers in 1947, remaining there on and off until his death in 1999, and never fully unpacking a large steamer trunk that dominated his modest apartment. His vivid imagination was inspired by what he called "magic" flying in the Tangier night. I remember once he zeroed in on my stepdaughter Evi's T-shirt imprinted with "Downtown Gul Blad," apparently a popular Stockholm night spot. Bowles was convinced that there was some sort of occult message in it and was mesmerized by the words.

Over time, Bowles became a 20th century cult figure, inspiring many with his quirky works on Morocco and well cultivated expatriate image. I've often quoted Bowles on the mystery and exoticism of Morocco: "You say you are going to Fez, and when you say that you are going to Fez it means that you are not going to Fez, but I happen to know that you are going to Fez. Why have you lied to me, you who are my friend?"[8] It was McPhillips who returned Bowles' ashes to the family plot in Lakemont, New York, executing Bowles' final wishes despite the writer's longtime disenchantment with the United States and fierce fights with parents growing up in Brooklyn. Sri Lanka where he also lived for many years has preserved his old house at Taprobane Island, happily spared by Tyfoon Haiyan in November 2008, and now a very upscale guest house. Along with Morocco, Sri Lanka had hoped to stimulate tourism with a local Bowles shrine and was disappointed with Bowles' choice of final resting place.

Morocco's glitterati image did not necessarily sit well in Washington. Particularly in the State Department's Bureau of Near Eastern Affairs (NEA), Arabists in the mainstream regarded the Kingdom as in many ways left field. They did not view Morocco and the Maghreb in general as authentically Arab to the same degree as the Mashreq or eastern Arab world. Then too, the obvious fact that Morocco is an undeniably pleasant place to live, not requiring the kind of shared sacrifice common in other parts of the Arab world and enshrined in NEA culture, set the Kingdom apart. I always had the impression that the more ambitious Arabists tended to avoid service there and regarded an assignment to Morocco, particularly one as long as my own eight-year sojourn, as its own reward and not necessarily a stepping stone to onward assignment or promotion.

Geography, exotic backdrop and vigorous promotion by Ambassador Reed did, however, put Morocco on the itinerary for almost every official traveler to the region. For several years in the mid-eighties the Kingdom was visited by more members of the US cabinet and Congress than any post worldwide except for the largest like London, Paris, Bonn and Tokyo and at a rate of at least one cabinet visit per month in addition to innumerable other VIPs. I was involved, for example, in visits by Secretaries of State Haig, Shultz and Baker and once accompanied Attorney General Ed Meese for half a day with King Hassan at Skhirat. One comedy of errors occurred when the Ambassador hosted the young Shah of Iran, son of Reza Pahlevi, for a private lunch. It coincided with an inspection by a large security team advancing the visit of Vice President George H. W. Bush. The young shah, already skittish about security, was startled to see agents peering down from almost every tree in the residence garden.

A number of delegations, particularly from Congress, would fly directly to Marrakesh because of its Palm Springs-like climate, golf and legendary Mamounia Hotel. They would somehow just assume that the King would bestir himself, fly there and accord them an audience. Naturally, the role of the Embassy in brokering such expectations was not always an easy one. Some visitors like Senator Lugar, Chairman of the Foreign Relations Committee, or Congressman Steve Solarz, Chair of the House Africa Sub-Committee, were all work and a great boost to the Embassy. Others were not. I recall one huge delegation which embarrassed the Moroccans by insisting on visiting the most impoverished slums of Casablanca and then jettisoned $4,000 worth of taxpayer-paid jet fuel right on the tarmac in Marrakesh because of overweight purchases in the Moroccan souks. As a result, the plane had to stop for refueling enroute to their next destination. Such abuse, in my experience, is not uncommon, yet the State Department's subservience to annual budget appropriations from Congress in practice enforced a conspiracy of silence.

A POST OF ONE'S OWN

This is a very big deal in the Foreign Service and the dream of most career diplomats. So, I was delighted that, after 21 years service, mine turned out to be Casablanca. I was later nominated by my bureau at State as a candidate for Ambassador to Algeria, but as it turned out a new Secretary preferred someone with whom she had previously worked and the matter was dropped. I had also visited Algiers often and knew that it was a virtual prison sentence at that time with a Navy Seal posted outside the Ambassador's bedroom and ground transportation only by prearranged armored convoy. So, I always felt better him than me and moved on.

In hindsight, Casablanca was a career high water mark. Week after week, American tourists showed up after searching vainly for Rick's Bar, not realizing that Bogart and Ingrid Bergman's *Casablanca* was all Hollywood. The real Casablanca was and is the business center or New York City, if you will, of Morocco. The concentration of the country's industry and banking in Casablanca, almost 70 percent of GNP, exceeds that of New York, giving it great weight in the national economy. The challenge for us was to penetrate a sophisticated business and banking structure for which the existence of consulates was largely peripheral. If you just stayed in the office, the phone would not ring off the hook. On the other hand, once you got a foot in the door, top executives held strong opinions and would speak their minds to a degree unthinkable among government bureaucrats in Rabat. Casablanca had experienced serious rioting in 1981 and, with some 5 million of Morocco's then 25 million population, its struggle with urban and social problems was thought to be predictive; as Casablanca went, so, many believed, would go the Kingdom.

It was also an easy move, just an hour up the road from Rabat. Knowing the Embassy well by then, I was generally free to have as much or as little to do with it as I chose, returning for country team meetings and special events but skipping the housing board and other tedious committee work. The Consulate General in those days was one of the larger constituent posts on the African continent with 42 Americans and 27 Moroccan employees. These included a number of regional offices like a Marine Security Battalion led by a colonel with two captains and technical staff. The basement was like a small factory providing engineering services for Delta barriers, safes and security systems throughout southern Europe and the Middle East. Emergencies would arise, for example, whenever an ambassador's armored limo in Yemen or Bulgaria was accidentally impaled on a raised Delta barrier.

Idyllic as the setting was, the Consulate was locked in a life and death struggle with Alexandria in Egypt. The Congress had decreed yet another round of Foreign Service post closings, and every geographic bureau at the State Department was forced to pony up a hit list of posts for closure. It became obvious that we or the historic Consulate General in Alexandria, the second city and major port of Egypt, would soon be sacrificed to make the NEA quota. So, we were busting to prove our worth and lobbying in all directions for survival. We were not harmed that the NEA Assistant Secretary at that time, Ed Djerejian, had once made his name as the labor reporting officer in Casablanca, and the victory was eventually ours. Yet, there was no joy in it. Casablanca and Alexandria both offer unique windows on countries important to the US. The reality of Casablanca or Alexandria is not that of Rabat or Cairo, cannot be covered from the capitals and is important to take into account.

Such posts are also vital training grounds for leadership in a service where career DCMs and ambassadors have previously often managed little more than half a secretary. If one could go back and ask General Marshall or General Powell how they acquired leadership skills, I'm sure they would say it was through progressive expansion of responsibility as they rose through the ranks rather than from a quickie leadership course at Fort Leavenworth. Replacing consulates, long the only option for early leadership experience, with two-week leadership modules, in vogue at the State Department, is short-sighted policy, I've always felt.

THE JEWISH COMMUNITY

For centuries Morocco has had an important Jewish community, which is still the largest in the Arab world. When the Moors were thrown out of Spain in the 15th Century, much of the Jewish population there fell back to Morocco, although some went to places like Thessaloniki in Greece, where traces of their ancient Ladino language still survive. Many Moroccans, typically with names beginning with Ben, originally were of Jewish origin, and the two communities have coexisted under the protection of the Alaouite throne. Casablanca remains the center of Morocco's Jewish community, although, with the creation of Israel, the majority emigrated there, with some also settling in France, Canada, the US or Brazil. King Hassan, a master of the global chessboard, was convinced that several hundred thousand Israelis of Moroccan origin could one day play a decisive role in Israel's politics. It did not work out that way, however, and most Moroccan immigrants joined Likud rather than the Labor Party and were in no sense a Moroccan fifth column. Israel's former conservative Foreign Minister David Levy who grew up in Morocco is a good case in point. The situation evolved, however, with the 1986 visit of Prime Minister Shimon Peres to Morocco and the exchange of inconspicuous diplomatic missions disguised as interest sections.

Casablanca had a unique festival of the Mimouna during which Jewish houses were opened to all, and throngs of Jews, and Muslim friends as well, would go from house to house celebrating. Further in the countryside was the shrine of Ait ba Ahmed where each year thousands of Moroccan Jews would come from as far away as Brazil and Australia to eat and drink to heart's content for several days, dancing to loud music and basking in the glow of each other's company. Representing the Embassy or Consulate General, I and my family were greeted with extraordinary hospitality and plied with enormous quantities of food and strong drink at this remote shrine. My stepdaughters, Evi and Alexandra, disappeared at one point from the festivities, wandering into an area reserved for ritual slaughter of animals, and returned to us with bloodied pinafores.

Across Morocco, and particularly in Casablanca, the Joint Distribution Committee, commonly known as just the Joint, operated a wide network of schools, medical centers and homes for the elderly catering to the Jewish community. The latter ran the gamut from immensely successful figures like one of the King's three Royal Counselors, the Chief Royal Accountant and the Minister of Tourism to the impoverished elderly. The Joint was run by an ultra-orthodox Lubavitch Rabbi who would pay me a monthly visit at the Consulate. My secretary, who really ran the place, was a career veteran of the Foreign Service of Irish descent who has subsequently retired in Portugal. Mary had great warmth, rushing to greet visitors with her hand extended, but also came with an Irish temper. The Rabbi, for his part, was forbidden by his orthodox beliefs from taking the hand of a woman and would determinedly clutch his own behind his back. Mary took umbrage at this, viewing it as a rebuff. After several such episodes, I persuaded her that she had obviously impressed the Rabbi to such a degree that he would be overcome just by taking her hand. For the remainder of my tour, peace reigned, and we both looked forward to the Rabbi's visits and greeted him with smiles.

THE LEGACY OF WINSTON CHURCHILL

The magnificent Consul General's residence in Anfa, the most upscale suburb of Casablanca, which I was privileged to inhabit for three years, was acquired by the United States after the war and redolent with history. It was used by Prime Minister Churchill during the Casablanca Conference of January 14–24, 1943, which determined the future course and strategy of World War II, setting as the highest priority final victory in the Battle of the Atlantic and destruction of all remaining German U-boats and submarine pens in the Bay of Biscay and committing the Allies to unconditional surrender of Germany and Japan. Off the main entrance hall of Villa Mirador is a study and map room preserved in the manner of Churchill's time there. Photographs, some taken on the broad lawns of the Villa, show Churchill in private outdoor consultations with President Franklin Roosevelt. Group photos also depict him in meetings with Roosevelt, General de Gaulle, General Eisenhower, Moroccan King Mohammed V, along with his young son and future King Hassan II, Harry Hopkins, top American diplomatic troubleshooter Robert Murphy, General Patton, Averell Harriman, Free French General Giraud and many others.

"Diplomats at Work in Churchill Map Room."

It was both intimidating and exhilarating to live in such august surroundings, and many were the guests who spoke in whispered tones over coffee and cigars in the Churchill Library. One day, rooting about in Casablanca's sprawling souk or traditional market, I came across an old and quite good charcoal drawing of Winston Churchill which I was proud to add to the Library's collection. One felt, through proximity, close to the enormous decisions taken at Casablanca midway through World War II and to the larger than life participants who shouldered those responsibilities. Out of respect, we rarely used the Churchill room except for official events, leaving the Prime Minister's desk frozen in time and in a state of high polish.

President Roosevelt's inclusion of King Mohammad V and his young son and king to be in those proceedings struck a resonant chord with Moroccans, still under French colonial rule, and helped to pave the way toward a new postwar US-Moroccan relationship. President Eisenhower cemented this by returning to Casablanca toward the end of his presidency on December 22, 1959, to meet with Mohammed V after the latter's return from forced exile in Madagascar and independence of Morocco in 1956. While annoying Paris, Eisenhower's visit, as well as Roosevelt's wartime meeting, were US votes of confidence in the new King and the future of an independent Morocco.

The Casablanca Conference was often referred to as the Anfa Conference, since all participants were quartered in villas adjacent to Villa Mirador or at a Palace-owned hotel across the street. The Villa with its stately driveway flanked by royal palms, and comfortable facilities was still enticing to guests, official and not. I recall playing tennis on the Villa's clay court with Deputy Secretary of State John Whitehead and with Congressman John Conyers, losing, and not diplomatically, to both who were many years senior to me. A source of amusement to all was a marble mantelpiece above a fireplace opening onto both the living and dining rooms which was adorned with a large and voluptuous statue of a reclining woman, reputed by my predecessors to be the original Madame Mirador.

The visit I most cherished was from the great diplomat and statesman George Kennan and his wife Annelise. They had visited once years before when I was stationed in Athens and were now in March 1987 taking the measure of Morocco for the first time. While Mrs. Kennan shopped and toured Casablanca's vast souks with my stepmother, Mary Keating, the Ambassador took solitary walks through the winding lanes of Anfa, absorbing the atmosphere and describing in his final book the typically Moroccan sense of privacy and family life out of sight in inner courtyards sheltered from public view behind high walls. [9]

One morning at breakfast, Ambassador Kennan told me that he had never studied Islam and asked to borrow a copy of the Koran. I gave him a daunting 1862-page annotated copy of *The Glorious Kura'n* with side-by-side English and Arabic texts and went off to work. When I returned after a long day in the Consulate, he had outlined what he considered to be the ten major similarities and ten differences between the Bible and the Koran which he wished to discuss. It was an intimidating prospect for a non-theologian after a day's work to tackle such a topic with Kennan and in the shadow of Churchill.

Since the Casablanca consular district was vast, covering half the country and stretching to Marrakesh, the Atlas Mountains, and the Western Sahara, visiting those areas was part of the job, often with visiting VIPs. One I well remember was Jeane Kirkpatrick, whom I had worked with in New York on the NAM book. She was invited to lunch with old friends in Marrakesh, Guy de Rothschild and his elegant wife Marie-Helene, and brought me along as well. It was an unusual glimpse into another world sitting in their stunning villa in the Palmeraie of Marrakesh amidst major works of Picasso, Matisse and van Gogh.

Ambassador Kirkpatrick's meeting with King Hassan was also an experience. Normally formal and reserved, the King rose to the challenge of debating global strategy and they carried on for several hours. Jeane, as usual, gave as good as she got, and the King was clearly impressed. I did not see such animation during his audiences with a steady stream of other American visitors during my eight years there. Another vivid figure from the Casablanca era was the late, great jazz singer Nina Simone, down on her luck but still performing. Our dedicated consul, Sallybeth Bumbrey, kept a close watch over her and ran interference with Moroccan authorities when she was found with an illegal pistol.

THE CASABLANCA AMERICAN SCHOOL

Welfare of an American community abroad means a decent school for children, and when I arrived the one in Casablanca operated from separate, dilapidated houses with less than a hundred students and was on the brink of collapse. We had a new director, John Randolph, a former semi-pro baseball player, black beret in Vietnam and a really tough guy committed to the kids and getting the school back on its feet. By default, I became board chair, and we succeeded beyond our wildest dreams with a truly motivated board of Moroccan and American parents. Being part of that team is my fondest memory of the Casablanca years.

Some of the Moroccan board members had direct lines into the Palace and the upper reaches of Moroccan business. They were able to get ample free land for the school in the upscale "California" district from Mohamed Sajid, a developer who later became Mayor of Casablanca. Mohamed correctly calculated that a prestigious American school at the center of his vast land holdings would double and triple real estate values. The Board also secured attractive bank financing and, best of all, we were able to convince the legendary Dizzy Gillespie and his band to do a *pro bono* fundraising concert in Casablanca. Dizzy said that it was the best performance that he ever gave in Africa, and it really did raise the roof, filling the city's largest concert hall, with some tickets to build the new school reaching as much as $1,500 each.

John Randolph had a family recipe for South Carolina hominy grits, which happened also to be Dizzy's home state. We served them to Dizzy and his band, as well as John Conyers, on the sunny terrace at Villa Mirador the next morning. In the glow of one of Dizzy's greatest concerts and sitting on a terrace where Winston Churchill once sat, the mood was jubilant. We now had a total of $3 million from the concert, donors and the bank loan with which to construct a school. While Morocco was then sometimes described as a country of 25 million with 1 million consumers, the school demonstrated that, in Casablanca at least, philanthropy was alive and well. CAS came in under budget after a juried architectural competition as a state-of-the-art facility for 500 students, later winning prizes for innovative educational design. Moroccans have comprised between 60–70% of the CAS student body with strong enrolment also from Christian, Jewish, Hindu and other communities.

AZEMMOURI AND THE CONQUEST OF ARIZONA

One of the pleasures of living in Casablanca was Azemmour, an historic seaport at the mouth of the Oum Er-Rbia River, a short drive west along the coast. There, I became acquainted with Guy Martinet, the noted French historian and intellectual, and his wife, Susan Searight, a leading anthropologist. Guy had labored for many years in the Spanish National Archives, piecing together the obscure history of Azemmouri, a native son of the town. Sadly, Azemmouri and his extraordinary odyssey had until then remained shrouded in the mists of early US history and unknown on either side of the Atlantic.

Azemmouri grew up at the start of the 16th Century in his namesake town, ravaged for several decades by one of the worst droughts and famines in Moroccan history. Portugal invaded Azemmour in 1513, and the town was captured on September 1 by the Duke of Braganza during a battle in which Ferdinand Magellan was severely wounded. Between 1521 and 1522 thousands of starving Moroccan sailors went, more or less willingly, with the Portugese to be sold as slaves or indentured seamen in Portugal and Spain. Azemmouri ended up in Cadiz where he was sold to a Spanish captain, Andres Dorantes.

Sometimes described as a "Berber slave" and renamed Estebanico, Estevanico or simply Estevan, Azemmouri sailed together with his new owner for the New World in June 1527 as part of the six-ship fleet under Spanish Governor Panfilo de Narvaez, including 400 men and 80 horses. Narvaez had previously participated in Spanish voyages to Jamaica in 1509, Cuba in 1511 and Veracruz in 1520. After landing and reconnoitering in Cuba, the new expedition pushed on to Florida in April 1528 reaching the area of today's Tampa Bay. From there, Narvaez marched north with 300 men, including Azemmouri, in search of gold and silver. Finding none and suffering heavy losses in attacks by Timucua Indians, the survivors reached the area of today's Tallahassee. Further attacks by Apalachee Indians and fevers traversing swampy coastal lagoons decimated a third of his force, forcing Narvaez to construct four primitive rafts and continue along the Gulf Coast by sea.

Forty days later after misadventures at sea and further Indian attacks ashore, only two vessels reached Galveston Island with twenty-four survivors. The other two rafts, one with Narvaez on board, had foundered in a storm. In Texas the party dwindled to fifteen and finally only four survivors, including Azemmouri, of the disastrous Narvaez expedition. Over a period of five years, Azemmouri and his Spanish companions were held captive by Indian tribes, fleeing occasionally only to be recaptured by others. They gained grudging acceptance over time by practicing crude medicine among the Indian tribes and became known as "Sons of the Sun." In May 1535, they began an arduous journey westward preceded by their reputation as healers and assisted by Indians along the way.

Azemmouri's party eventually reached Cibola in what is now Arizona. There they were killed by Zuni Indians in 1539. Three Indians informed Father Marcos, an early Jesuit missionary in the region, of Azemmouri's death, and he, in turn, notified the Spanish authorities in Mexico of the circumstances, embroidering the account with tales of gold and precious jewels in the village of Cibola.[10] When Coronado led his expedition there the next year in 1540, he found no El Dorado but only a "small rocky village" of some 150–300 reddish clay dwellings.

Coronado, of course, received all the glory for first exploring the present day states of Arizona, New Mexico, Texas, Oklahoma, and Kansas including discovery of the Grand Canyon, while Azemmouri's epic and earlier 4350-mile journey across North America, ending in violent death at Cibola, 6,215 miles from home in Azemmour, has until recently been lost to history. Moroccans, who glory in George Washington's 1786 letter to the Sultan and in their bicentennial relations with the US, would normally seize upon this early Moroccan adventurer, but Azemmouri's forced conversion to Catholicism under the Spanish made him an unpalatable hero for many Muslims. For Europeans, the huge class distinction between Azemmouri and Coronado may also have played a role, and the story has thus long moldered in the archives. Few have ever heard, even in Arizona where he was killed, that vast regions of the southern United States were first explored on foot and by boat from 1528 to 1539 by a Moroccan from Azemmour.

As a footnote to the above, Guy Martinet passed away in 2003, leaving me with his rough manuscript and research on Azemmouri. In semi-retirement by early 2015 with time on my hands, I resurrected the idea of an historical novel based on this extraordinary Moroccan adventurer and even looked into possible foundation funding for such an undertaking. Imagine my total surprise and relief when my research revealed, full blown, *The Moor's Account* by Laila Lalani, published in late 2014.[11] Better she than me! It is a magnificent and creative book, which I recently reviewed for the Foreign Service Journal, replete with deep background on Azemmour and imaginatively written through the Moroccan and Muslim eyes of Azemmouri.

MANDATORY EVACUATION

When time was up in Casablanca, I made the short drive back to Rabat, becoming Deputy Chief of Mission (DCM) for the new Ambassador, Michael Ussery. He wanted someone with continuity and experience in Morocco, and I turned out to be that person. The defining moment in our two years together was unquestionably the First Gulf War which erupted on January 17, 1991 after six months of uneasy build-up following Saddam Hussein's invasion of Kuwait on August 2, 1990. While Morocco is on the furthest western periphery of the Arab world, 3,200 miles from the battlefront in Kuwait, the conflict and the State Department's overreaction to presumed threats in Morocco reverberated in many directions. The threat of war following the invasion of Kuwait did, of course, expose existing cleavages within the Kingdom. There were marches in which, for the first time, four or five hundred Islamic fundamentalists dared to show themselves outside the Parliament on the main avenue of Rabat. In December, 1990, fundamentalists burned to the ground the five-star Merinid Hotel in Fez.

An amusing episode occurred on the way to war. The Ambassador was briefly out of the country, and, alone after hours in the Embassy, I received a call from Moroccan Royal Protocol asking if it was true that Defense Secretary Cheney and General Schwarzkopf were coming to Morocco that evening. It was the first I had heard of it, and naturally I was dubious. To be sure, I called the

State Department's Operations Center and they told me in effect, "What are you smoking out there, go back to sleep." A few minutes later, about 6:30 pm, I got a call from Richard Haass on the NSC staff at the White House who told me that not only were Cheney and Schwarzkopf coming, but they would be landing at 7 pm at a military field near Kenitra, normally a 45-minute drive away. Scrambling to call in drivers from their homes, some in Sale across the Bou Regreg River, we raced there at 80 mph, reaching the field just as Cheney's plane was coming to a halt before the VIP pavilion. Normally, you orchestrate such visits for months in advance, and this was as easy as it gets.

Coordination between the Department and embassies is usually more seamless, and in this case nobody was to blame. Cheney and Schwarzkopf had been consulting with King Fahd in Saudi Arabia prior to war and had stopped on their return to meet with then-President Mubarak in Cairo. As they were airborne for Washington and approaching Moroccan airspace, President George H. W. Bush had called the plane to ask that they touch down in Rabat to bring "our old friend Hassan" into the picture as well. Undoubtedly, the Palace had been alerted to the visit by the pilot's urgent request for landing authority, and Cheney and Schwarzkopf were probably as surprised to be there as I was to meet them.

As Charge d'Affaires, I escorted Cheney to a hastily arranged audience with the King while Schwarzkopf rode in a follow car with Moroccan motorcycle police in front and back of our speeding convoy. Cheney was lost in his own thoughts, and I drew no response whatsoever when I observed that my son Richard and his daughter Liz were classmates at Colorado College. On arrival at the Rabat Palace, we were escorted into an ornate room where the King sat on a throne surrounded by advisors and cabinet members on small gilded chairs. Hassan asked whether Cheney would prefer his own French interpreter or the King's, and Cheney replied that "I would have much more confidence in yours," thus relieving me of that task. After some stilted conversation, Cheney interjected, "Majesty, I need to speak to you in private," and they moved to a side room for a relatively brief exchange.

Afterwards, I accompanied Cheney to the Embassy, where he made a report to the President by secure phone from the code room, and then deposited him and Schwarzkopf, whom I never heard utter a single word on Moroccan soil, back at the Kenitra field close to 1 am. I read later in the *New York Times* that the visit had been a huge success and that Hassan had agreed to provide a Moroccan battalion to guard a Saudi oil refinery outside Ra's al-Khafji near the border with Kuwait, thus along with Egypt and Saudi Arabia providing Arab cover for the allied coalition. The Moroccans, for their part, were able to make the distinction for domestic public opinion that they were not part of Desert Storm but were in the Gulf at the direct request of Saudi Arabia.

There was, of course, support on the street for Saddam Hussein, seen as a macho Arab standing up to the United States. On the other hand, even in Morocco, the Iraqis were blatant in their behavior, and educated Moroccans clearly knew who and what Saddam was. Only months before, my counterpart as DCM at the Iraqi Embassy had expressed private doubts about the direction that Iraq was heading during discussions with me and other diplomats as well. The Iraqis sent a hit team from Baghdad, tortured the DCM at the Plage des Nations, a popular beach outside town, and dumped his body, riddled with bullets from a signature caliber pistol used by the Iraqi *mukhabarat* or secret police, for all to see and fear their brutal methods. My colleague had a young family with children and, while the incident was kept from the press, news spread quickly and it did not endear Saddam to Moroccans who became aware of it.

As the threat of war approached, there were riots elsewhere in the region and a voluntary evacuation was ordered by the State Department, which Embassies in more threatened Tunis and Algiers took advantage of. In Morocco, however, except for the earlier hotel burning in Fez, things were peaceful. The Embassy was generally relaxed, officers were playing golf with their Moroccan counterparts, schools were functioning normally, and no one chose to depart on a voluntary basis. The Department, on the other hand, was under pressure from Congress to show that they were protecting staff and evacuating dependents from the Middle East. It was politically sensitive, however, to pull diplomats out of Israel or Saudi Arabia where they might actually get an Iraqi SCUD missile on their heads. So, in order to meet its quota for evacuees, the State Department ordered an immediate mandatory evacuation of 600 "non-essential employees" and dependants from Morocco, creating the false, public perception that it was the most dangerous place in North Africa.

There is a destabilizing, human impact when a large American embassy community like Rabat with consulates or branch offices at that time dispersed in Casablanca, Tangiers and Marrakesh is ordered to evacuate on a tight deadline and without knowing when actual warfare might commence. American Schools, in the middle of the academic year, for example, faced serious difficulty. The Casablanca School, which I remained close to, stayed open but lost a number of teachers. My own family found temporary safehaven in Finland. With families and "non-essential" colleagues gone, we simply waited. Personally, I've always felt that the State Department's designation of evacuees as "non-essential employees" is demeaning and offensive, raising, as it does, basic questions about why, being non-essential, they were posted abroad at taxpayer expense in the first place.

The United States had never before been involved in a major war against an Arab country in the Middle East and, of course, we were in new territory. As we had predicted, however, the situation remained calm, and Moroccan officials were most cooperative on security matters. I visited the Ministry of Interior, which obligingly agreed to issue Americans with temporary Moroccan license plates in place of the diplomatic ones that identified us with the Embassy. Finally, early in the morning of January 17, I received a phone call, not from the Department of State but from the better informed Canadian Ambassador, informing me that the aerial bombardment of Baghdad had begun. Even though Morocco remained dead calm and after the brief war ended in February many Moroccans privately regretted that Saddam was left in place, it took four months to secure Washington's permission to bring back evacuated personnel.

My family, for example, and for the second time in my career, were sent away to safehaven, in Helsinki where my stepdaughters were enrolled at mid-semester in a local school. The then undersecretary for management insisted that dependants could not return until there was a 10 percent reduction in the Embassy's personnel ceiling. We had already been through a series of such reductions and viewed this as blackmail by a Washington appointee who had never served abroad and had little grasp of the human dimensions and toll on families and schools from an extended and unnecessary evacuation.

LA GUERA OR BUST

"It's easy to offer to slaughter a camel when the guests are leaving."
—Somali Proverb

The Western Sahara is a vast, scarcely populated, rock-strewn desert of some 100,000 square miles. Once, travelling along Morocco's southern border with the disputed territory, my son stopped at the roadside to relieve himself and out of nowhere appeared hundreds of tick-like insects drawn to the only moisture in that desolate landscape. War has festered there on and off between Morocco and Sahraoui rebels of the Polisario, based in Algeria, ever since Spain relinquished control in 1975 and King Hassan II launched the "Green March" of 350,000 unarmed Moroccans into the territory. Morocco gradually built an earthen wall, known as a berm, topped with electronic warning systems to enclose most habitation, and warfare consisted of hit and run breakthroughs and attacks on the wall. Since a ceasefire in 1991 and former Secretary Baker's long tenure as Special UN Envoy for the Western Sahara, the area has been largely quiescent.

It was a paradox that State Department policy in those years generally prevented American diplomats from visiting the disputed region, although members of Congress could travel there at will with an Embassy or Consulate escort. The US Navy and Marines were also able with Moroccan permission to use the endless Saharan coastline to practice amphibious assaults. As Consul General, I received an exceptional authorization to observe one such live-fire US Marine over-the-beach assault in 1987, and it was a heady experience to helicopter out to the offshore Marine assault ship USS *Saipan* together with the provincial Moroccan Governor. There below decks, the toughest looking Marines I have ever seen, all in blackface, were polishing a formidable array of weaponry. From the deck, we could see landing craft struggling to reach shore through heavy surf and explosive fire.

Since our access to the Saharan region was otherwise limited, we counseled visiting Americans and US companies to avoid the area since we could not insure their protection in an emergency or provide normal consular services such as repatriation of remains or visiting them in prison to be sure that they received treatment at least equal to that afforded to citizens of the region, which itself was not 5-star. Given these strictures, the 1989 visit to Morocco of Occidental Petroleum's legendary CEO Armand Hammer and his single-minded pursuit of an Oxy concession for the Western Sahara put us on the spot. I was acting Charge d'Affaires again at the time and had no choice but to accompany the controversial oil baron to see the King. On the other hand, the prospect of American oilmen and engineers running around the Western Sahara, where lightning strikes by Polisario armed vehicles were still punching through the berm and the Moroccan Air Force retaliating with sorties of its own, was anathema to the USG. At 91 and in the year before his death, Hammer was spry and had just arrived in his own plane from Moscow after delicate negotiations with the Kremlin.

I had, of course, zero prospect of influencing their meeting and was a mere bystander. The King at that time appeared under the weather, and I could see that the sheer energy and larger-than-life, wheeler-dealer personality of Hammer, thirty years his senior, encouraged and buoyed him up. Hammer opened by noting that the King was reputed to appreciate good horse flesh and then brought out what looked like a deck of cards. Together, for most of the hour they pored over photographs of Hammer's prize stallions and brood mares. Finally, Hassan asked if there was anything that he could do for his guest. Hammer was obsessed that, after the Gangetic Plain in India, the Draa Valley in the Western Sahara was the last, major unexplored oil-bearing structure on earth, and asked for a seismic exploration concession for the entire region. The King replied without any questions something like, "you want it, you got it," and the meeting was over. For a diplomat, it was, like Mr. Rockefeller's earlier visit, a teaching moment in strategy and power. With Hammer's death the next year, however, Occidental did not pick up the concession and there were not to be American roustabouts or drillers in the disputed territory.

Ambassador Joseph Verner Reed travelled constantly throughout Morocco and, while being an ambassador is by no means just a popularity contest, he was better known to the average Moroccan than most of our ambassadors, before or since. Certainly, he saw far more of King Hassan and frequently took along with him some small gift like an exotic fountain pen for the royal collection or, perhaps, a golf item inscribed to Hassan from President Bush because of Reed's close ties to the White House of that time. The King appreciated these gestures

and when Reed, having already visited every province of the Kingdom, set his heart on visiting the forbidden no man's land of La Guera,
the King assented and intervened with the Mauritanians to obtain
special access literally to the ends of the earth.

La Guera is an abandoned fishing village with a ruined Spanish
fort at the tip of a peninsula on the southernmost extremity of
Western Sahara, across a bay from the Mauritanian fishing port of
Nouadhibou. It is inaccessible, surrounded by impenetrable barbed
wire and heavily guarded by Mauritanian troops. There is no over-
land access from the North, and the route from Rabat passed
through Dakar and on by road to Nouackchott and eventually
Nouadibou. The landscape had not changed since my visit nearly
twenty years before with the moonrock except that the dugout ca-
noes to cross the Senegal River had been replaced by a ferry. Along
the way, we were entertained by resident American ambassadors
and, observing Reed's high energy levels, one of them took me
aside to ask, "Is he always like this?" In general, career ambassadors in the neighboring countries envied the pomp and circumstance of the Kingdom and often joked about Reed's unorthodox
style behind his back. When their tours came to an end, however,
and a next ambassadorship was far from certain, they often sent
obsequious letters seeking preferment and Reed's intervention with
the White House. I saw several such entreaties which were no
credit to the career service.

La Guera, like most abandoned ruins, was forlorn and a bit of a
disappointment but, like Ithaca, it was the trip itself that made it
worthwhile. We were escorted by a Mauritanian Army team in all-
terrain vehicles along a circuitous route through the no-man's land.
The Ambassador was able to take photographs for King Hassan of
this former outpost of Moroccan glory from the Merinid, Almorav-
id and Almohades Empires, and we returned to Nouadhibou, there
to await an infrequent outbound flight to the Canary Islands. We
were invited to dinner with a Mauritanian entrepreneur from the

local fishing industry whom I had once worked with as Chargé d'Affaires of the Mauritanian Embassy in Washington.

Our host lived in a palatial, marble-floored villa outside the town, and a table was set for the three of us in an ornate, but stiflingly hot, Moorish sitting room. Before us were laid out three glasses and a bottle of Johnny Walker Black Label scotch, a rare luxury and great honor to be served in that corner of northern Mauritania, and only to be imbibed neat. As we talked, piteous cries came from the kitchen where, we were soon to learn, the not inconsiderable liver was being pulled from a young camel, another great honor to guests in that part of the world and also to be consumed neat.

Reed was fastidious about matters of food in any circumstances and, as a precaution, had lined the pockets of his traveling suit with rubber. He then commanded our host's full attention with gestures and fixed eye contact while covertly filling his pockets with the still pulsing liver. When they were filled, he surreptitiously transferred the remainder from his to my plate. Diplomatic courtesy and animal rights did silent battle in my mind, yet the animal was now dead and we could not tell beforehand what horrors were transpiring in the kitchen. Still, it is one thing to be accustomed to steak tartare or sushi and another to swallow something so recently alive with the animal's cries still echoing in the room. The Johnny Walker Black Label turned out to be a welcome, even therapeutic antidote. [12]

KING HASSAN II AND THE PEARL-HANDLED PISTOL

In 1996, I was privileged to return to the Kingdom in company with a senior American foreign policy official for an important meeting with King Hassan II. After the business was done and all the official talking points, as usual involving the Western Sahara dispute and relations with Algeria, had been made, the King took us aside to share an insight or rather a vision of the United States, Morocco and Algeria which I have never forgotten. Hassan was notably older and frailer than when I had last seen him and, in fact, passed away three years later.

"Let me tell you about the Algerians," the King began, "they are different from you Americans and we Moroccans. When Moroccans or Americans go to gamble, we wear our 'smokings,' we go to the best casinos and, when we lose, we take out our pearl-handled pistols and we do what we must. But when the Algerians go to gamble, they wear old clothes and they go to the worst bars on the waterfront of Marseilles and they drink the cheapest red wine. And when they lose, they take out their razors and they slit their throats."

Never had I heard Moroccan-Algerian differences described in these terms. This surprising image, apart from giving undue credit to the average American gambler, was evoked straight-faced and without humor that I could detect. I can only suppose that absolute power exists in a vacuum where strange notions can flourish and emerge full blown. If so, this bizarre stereotype must have been a throwback to earlier, more elegant times for Moroccans and Americans. Still, it was hard for American diplomats to make sense of such a pronouncement from a respected strategic thinker, and we did not include it in our reporting.

A BACKWARD GLANCE

It's hard to look back on eight years in Morocco without nostalgia and a sense of loss. Although I've returned many times and the country is still exotic, there is a certain knowledge that the jumble of experiences, heady times that we lived through and precious time there with family can never be truly recaptured. I remember, for example, early in my sojourn heading south with my daughter Eliza and son Richard to visit the dunes of Merzouga where Lawrence of Arabia is often erroneously said to have been filmed. Reaching the remote dunes with the indis-

The Fabled Kingdom 147

pensable Land Rover and guide in total darkness in order to see the legendary sunrise, we became aware of moving shapes around us in the desert landscape, undoubtedly sheep and goats, what the Moroccans call cheptel. With daylight, however, they proved to be about fifty intrepid Japanese tourists with tripod-mounted cameras who had stood their ground through the chilly night, waiting for the perfect photograph.

Of course, a close Moroccan friend is for life and, coming back, you can pick up where you left off. Some friends don't even appear to register that you've been gone for fifteen or twenty years. In some ways, it is as if time and friendship stand still. And yet the world around Morocco has shifted so dramatically since 9/11 with the rise of terrorism and encroachments of radical Islam. King Mohammed VI, whose portrait my talented wife Eia painted along with those of his father King Hassan II and sister Princess Lalla Meriam, has so far averted the ravages of the Arab Spring through deft power-sharing and streamlining of the government system. The implosion of Libya, the rise of al Qaida and ISIS in the Maghreb and the eventual return to Morocco of young men drawn to conflict in Syria and Iraq are all red flags, however.

The US and European allies would do well to strengthen our historic ties with this moderate and traditional kingdom. As someone who has watched with dismay and sadness the collapse of Somalia, Libya and Greece where I have lived so many years, Morocco remains one of the few successes, and it would be unspeakable to add it to the list as well. It must remain and be supported as a bulwark against the challenges that we all face.

NOTES

1. John Waterbury, *Commander of the Faithful*, Weidenfeld and Nicolson, London, 1970.
2. The pilot, the late Mohammed Kabbaj, was subsequently promoted to General and Chief of the Moroccan Air Force.
3. Waterbury, op. cit.

4. Note: Mark Gilbey was also the owner of Gorée Island in Senegal, one of the major transit points for the West African slave trade, which he sold in 1989 for $175,000 to a foundation organized by Secretary of State George Shultz as a permanent memorial, later visited twice by President Barrack Obama.

5. David Herbert, *Second Son, an Autobiography*, 1972.

6. President George Washington letter to Moroccan Sultan Sidi Mohammed of December 1, 1789, National Archives. Note: The text of this letter has traditionally been frontpaged in Moroccan newspapers every year on July 4.

7. I. Finlayson, *Tangier: City of the Dream*, University of Michigan Press, 1993.

8. Paul Bowles, *The Spider's House*, Random House, 1955.

9. George F Kennan, *Sketches from a Life*, Pantheon Books, 1989, pages 334–344.

10. Note: An alternative version from the historical archives has Azemmouri reaching Mexico directly by crossing the Rio Grande River and, on arrival there, being commissioned by the famous explorer, conquistador and nobleman Coronado to lead an exploratory mission back to Cibola where he was, in either scenario, killed by Zuni Indian arrows.

11. Laila Lalani, *The Moor's Account*, Pantheon Books, New York, 2014.

12. As a postscript to the above, I revisited Dakhla in the Western Sahara as an educational consultant in February 2011. Bidonvilles there had been eradicated and there was a high level of Moroccan investment, as well as flourishing fish canneries and hot-house vegetable and fruit cultivation (*sous-serre primeurs*). Per capita income was considerably above the level in Morocco proper, and the indigenous Sahraoui population, now under 10 percent of the total, was overwhelmed by Moroccan immigrants from the North. In fact, the Western Sahara had become the escape valve for unemployed masses in Casablanca and the big cities. Richard Jackson, "Observations from January 31-February 4, 2011 Consultations in Dakhla."

VII

Heritage as Handicap,
the Case of Greece

POINTS IN TIME

My first introduction to Greece was through Dr. Charalambropoulos, a dentist now long retired, to whom I was taken with an impacted wisdom tooth on the day of my arrival as Consul in Thessaloniki, August 15, 1972, the Feast of the Panaghia.[1] With profuse
apologies for the stifling heat and absence of his receptionist and
hygienist on the major summer holiday, the doctor got right down
to business. Circumstances had forced him into the practice of den-
tistry, he confided, but at heart he was a lyric poet and proceeded to
recite his work in a loud keening voice and literary *katharevousa*
Greek, for the most part unintelligible to me, throughout the protracted operation. Soon he removed his shirt, revealing a hirsute
back and chest. Next to the dental chair, a large hunting dog darted
in and out of a wooden doghouse on a short chain.

After two hours, Dr. Charalambropoulos fell over backwards
with a broken half tooth clasped in his tongs. He then warned me in
no uncertain terms that he would proceed to dig out the remainder

of the tooth but that the presence of a nerve controlling blinking close to his area of operations meant that I might never blink again. I told him that, when it comes to blinking, I would have to think about it and beat a hasty retreat. I can't help thinking, however, that my unblinking focus on Greece for the sixteen years that I lived and worked there may have affected my judgment, so that at this late date I no longer know whether to laugh or to cry. In any case, subsequent dentists never fail to comment on unique aspects of my remaining half-extracted tooth or, for that matter, to recoil in shock from root canals done earlier in Libya.

It may well be that, with children and grandchildren in Athens, I have overstepped the bounds of diplomatic objectivity and no longer see Greece as clearly as, for example, the Somalia that I once knew. It's also true that the same things can appear altogether differently depending on your age. Days of ouzo and retsina in the hot sun and the wild breaking of plates, or *spasimo*, on crowded dance floors to protest the Greek Junta, are no longer part of my daily routine. On the other hand, I took the milk train recently from Athens to Thessaloniki with ancient stops like Thebes, Domosala and Paleofarsala, and the once verdant fields of Thessaly looked to me more like dust bowl Oklahoma. Similarly, the overconfident politicians of the boom years have morphed into the dispirited, empty suits of today's Greek leadership. Thus if readers have indulged me up to now with amusement, it's time you turn to lamentation.

Many are the Greeks I've known who have moved so often between Greece and the United States that they are at once deeply at home and completely alienated in either country. The contrast between American order, education, efficiency and ways of doing business and Greece's chaos, human scale, personal warmth and general disrespect for law breeds a nostalgia and longing for whichever country where one is not, from which even non-Greeks like me are not exempt. It raises the question, however, just who are these Greeks and where do they belong in today's fractured world.

The Department of State used to periodically carve up the world map, reassigning countries arbitrarily to different regions and even continents. Greece, Turkey and Iran, for example, traditionally formed a single office within the Bureau of Near Eastern Affairs (NEA) which spanned the entire Middle East. While it is tempting to think of this taxonomy as genuflection to the expanded Ottoman Empire or the even greater conquests of Alexander the Great, the prosaic rationale was bureaucratic infighting among fiefdoms within the Department of State. In any case, during the Greek military junta years when the very idea of Greek membership in the European Union was unthinkable, Henry Kissinger moved the chess pieces around, shifting Greece, Turkey and Cyprus to the European Bureau (EUR).[2]

To be sure, NEA was well compensated by the addition of Algeria, Libya, Tunisia and Morocco, which had historically belonged to the African Bureau (AF). As usual, Africa was the loser, since the promise of an eventual posting to North Africa, like the mechanical rabbit at a dog track, had always been an incentive and hoped for reward for service in some of the Continent's less salubrious posts. I cite these bureaucratic maneuverings for the sheer hubris involved in arbitrarily reassigning millions of Greeks and Turks without consultation from one continent to another, but also, in the case of Greece, for the lingering ambiguity it reflects, just a few decades ago, about that country's proper geographic location and identity.

To be Greek, of course, is to speak Greek and to be Greek Orthodox, a clear-cut litmus test of identity, conveying pride in language, religion and heritage. Legendary, even compulsive, Greek hospitality is a projection of this pride. I have often envied the Greek who, hearing his or her language spoken in some remote outpost, rushes to embrace fellow citizens, since rarely have

American accents from an adjacent table led me to do so. On the other hand, such hard and fast criteria of Greekness have made Hellenes slow to accept minorities, whether Slavophones, Turks, Pomachs, Roma (gypsies), even Jews. Still, up to the present, a strong sense of Greek identity has provided resilience and coping mechanisms throughout the slow recovery from World War II, the Greek Civil War, the seven years of the military junta, EU entry and subsequent binge spending and, since 2008, economic collapse.

In my view, Constantine Karamanlis's decision in 1981 to join the European Union was an example of statesmanship, safeguarding Greece at one stroke from repetition of the six military coups, four attempted coups and one assassination which had marked the earlier part of the Twentieth Century in Greece. The fateful decision to join the Euro Zone in 2001, however, marred by falsified Greek accounts and total lack of EU due diligence, was poorly thought out and injurious from both Greek and European points of view. I can remember euphoric celebrations of the Millennium rejoicing over the impending disappearance of the 3,000 year old drachma. Confidence was high in the new Euro and waves of money sloshed into Greece at low interest rates previously reserved for Northern Europe. Such was confidence in backing for the Euro that Greeks borrowed beyond any ability to repay and with no restructuring of their underlying, small economy. EU banks, particularly German, rushed to foist near interest-free loans on the Greeks, and companies like Goldman Sachs and Bain Capital were by no means innocent. Needless to say, conspicuous consumption ground to a halt after 2008 in a chaos of haircuts, unemployment, pension cuts and austerity imposed by foreign creditors as a condition for further support. Greece today still remains poised on the "knife edge of default."[3]

Having lived through some of the critical junctures along this path of recovery, boom and bust, the reflections that follow are little more than subjective points in time drawn from the sixteen years that I lived and observed the Greek scene between 1972 and 2009 with annual visits thereafter. They can in no way do justice to the suffering and frustration of the Greek people, assign blame to the many parties who deserve it or list the multiple causes of the economic cataclysm.

THE JUNTA AND DEMOCRACY RESTORED

Thessaloniki, when I arrived in 1972, was five years into the April 21, 1967 Colonels' Coup. Vocal opponents were long since imprisoned or otherwise silenced. I had, of course, read Eleni Vlachos' *House Arrest* and attended the Washington premier of Costas Gavras's film *Z*[4] about the assassination of leftist parliamentarian Grigoris Lambrakis on May 22, 1963 on the streets of Thessaloniki. Such opposition sentiment as existed, however, was well beneath the surface and activists were wary of contact with representatives of the USG, which was widely believed to support the Junta.

Prior to arrival I had spent ten excruciating months confined, eight hours a day, to intensive Greek class in Arlington, Virginia. Along with the language, I absorbed from our instructors, probably the first Greeks that I ever met, the idealized vision of an earlier, more agrarian Greece, frozen in time, which they and many emigrants had left in the 1950s. We learned, for example, that the railroad station master or *stathmarchis* was an important power broker and even matchmaker in provincial towns and someone not to be trifled with. Today, by contrast, he is a forlorn figure in a bedraggled uniform still lurking on platforms where trains rarely stop. So I sallied forth with my tongue-twisting Greek sentences from World War II language manuals, not altogether prepared for the Greece I was to live in and come to love over sixteen years.

The city of Thessaloniki itself, the second largest in Greece with a long history dating back to 315 BC, was in many respects a sleepy Balkan town, still recovering from the 1923 influx of 1.5

million Greek refugees from Turkey and the loss of its vibrant Jewish community in World War II.[5] It was notable, however, as the headquarters of the Greek C Army Corps, the largest military concentration in the country, stationed there to counter a feared Turkish thrust into Thrace or presumed Bulgarian designs on a Mediterranean port like Kavala. Thus, the city had a palpable military air about it. During the Junta's uncertain last year following the ouster of Col. Papadopoulos, the interim President of Greece from 1973–74 became none other than C Army Corps Commander, Gen. Phaedon Gizikis, an austere and remote figure so far as I could tell.

In the grand scheme of things, the American Consulate General was a backwater, yet the polarized and dysfunctional Embassy in Athens offered scope for modest initiatives in Thessaloniki. Much has been written about American policy toward Greece during the Junta and specifically the role of the US Embassy which was then headed by Henry Tasca, a favorite of Richard Nixon. Tasca, like Ambassador Phillips Talbott before him, generally acted in a pro-consular manner and disdained direct contact with the colonels, delegating liaison to other agency personnel, many of whom were conservative Greek-Americans who supported the Junta.[6] The previous Consul General, David Fritzlan, was an experienced political reporter who sought to provide an independent voice from his consular district but was unceremoniously dumped by Tasca in a rare motion of no confidence. His successor, Edward T. Brennan, who by sheer coincidence was from my own small town of Beverly Farms, Massachusetts, was handpicked and had risen through the courier corps and specialized in administrative work. He generously encouraged me to do whatever reporting I could, and the Embassy, preoccupied with its own infighting, paid little enough attention to my scribblings.

The major events in the city's life at that time were annual full dress military parades. An endless array of tanks and armored vehicles would tear up the city's major thoroughfare for three hours or

more while jets screamed overhead and interminable military, para-
military, police and even high school formations passed in review
before the colonels' triumvirate of Papadopoulos, Pattakos and
Makarezos, legions of military brass and the Consular Corps
decked out in obligatory morning coats. Most affecting were the
last surviving veterans of the Balkan wars, fewer each year and
many in wheel chairs, who proudly struggled to complete the arduous route accompanied by mournful strains of the Greek national
anthem.

On such occasions and particularly on the feast day of Demetri-
os, the patron saint of Thessaloniki, a high mass or doxology would
be celebrated. Often the ruling triumvirate would occupy places of
honor with civilian Prime Minister Spyros Markezinis in morning
attire standing slightly behind like the tiny figure of a groom on a
wedding cake. A large military cohort and the motley consular
corps in full dress would occupy seats strictly designated according
to rank and arrival date, although often hotly disputed among the
rank-conscious consular corps. The military, by contrast, were always in the same order, unblinking as lizards behind dark glasses
and resplendent in campaign ribbons and dress swords. While the
liturgy progressed with chanting and incense, as often happens during Orthodox services there was a continual hubbub of friendly
conversation, business transacted and even intelligence collected
from around the periphery of the huge congregation. One could
sometimes glimpse figures like the legendary operative, Gust Avra-
katos, up from Athens to work the crowd and, at moments like that,
standing at attention in the reserved consular seating area seemed
somehow like a charade.[7]

The Consulate General in my time was in a stately building on
King Constantine Avenue with a broad walkway along the majestic
seafront of the Thermaic Gulf and view of the historic Venetian
White Tower, the emblem of the city. The small staff of four lived
with their families in apartments above the offices and flag which,

whenever volatile Greek emotions boiled over into demonstrations, gave the place a certain beleaguered feel. In normal times, however, it was a paradise with terraces on every floor overlooking the sea and, on clear days, snow-capped Mount Olympus across the bay. At sunset, families dressed in their finest would still stroll along the seafront in a classic Greek courting ritual to introduce eligible youngsters under strict parental chaperonage. Only in more recent years has Thessaloniki fallen to the lower ranks of European cities on indices of pollution and air quality.

The Consulate had its own auto repair facility, bomb shelter, miniature post office and a commissary in the basement, maintained by the AAFES USAF post exchange system and offering all manner of tax-exempt liquor, cigarettes and comestibles at obscenely low prices. Once the spouse of a senior American military officer attached to the NATO outpost was caught retailing cases of Budweiser to sleazy bars in an alley nearby, and the genial Consul General was forced to suspend her commissary privileges for several months. The Consulate was, in other words, perfectly self-contained, and we used to joke that, with the addition of a barbershop, there would be no need to deal with Greeks or their turbulent politics from one month to the next. One earlier Consul General famously had himself shaved in the office during staff meetings. One could have just picked up local nuances from the balconies sending them along to Washington without worrying so much about representation and contact work. There would be no tendency to over-report either, like so many of those posts that send in whatever they happen to hear, stamping it "secret" to bolster readership.

Socially, the town was dominated by a hierarchy of tobacco merchants, just a few leading families of whom were arbiters on all matters of custom and taste. Manufacturing was in its infancy and the larger plants like Hellenic Steel (a subsidiary of Republic), Goodyear, ESSO Pappas, Ethyl, Coca-Cola and several banks were controlled by American managers who, combined with dozens of resident American tobacco buyers, constituted a substantial presence. To be invited to staid late-night dinners with the tobacco crowd was considered the pinnacle of social achievement. Yet conversation over cigars and brandy always dragged on interminably about the then-falling value of the dollar, and I was invariably on the spot and poorly prepared to defend the dollar against full-throated attack.

Nor during the Junta period did big tobacco, at least in my hearing, ever speak out on politics. The subject was generally taboo, and even at weekly meetings of the Thessaloniki Central Rotary Club, which I had joined to improve my stilted Greek, attitudes were highly nuanced. Members were largely doctors, lawyers, businessmen and importers of medical and scientific equipment. After several years of political turmoil and uncertainty leading up to the 1967 coup, for them these were years of economic stability, and Rotarians, admittedly a privileged cross-section of society, appeared to be prospering and generally loath to bite the hand that fed them.

On the other hand, evidence of the security apparatus was everywhere, and all the Consulate phones were clumsily bugged. Not infrequently, you could even hear one of the secret listeners in the background asking "What is he saying, that one?" The work of the Consulate General was generally so banal, however, that our minders must have had quite a boring time of it. Less benignly, we once invited the editor of a conservative local paper for dinner and a phone call came through for him from Brig. Pattakos, threatening to "**** your mother" if a certain article was published the next day. He returned ashen-faced to the table, and the offending piece was withdrawn. The local press was for the most part a mouthpiece for the Junta but quick to vilify them when Col. Papadopoulos was overthrown. One flagrant Junta flak, Elias Kyrou of *Ellinikos Vorras*, ran a banner headline, "He (Papadopoulos) was the Trujillo of Greece" the day after his fall. His about-face was typical of many strident supporters of the Junta who became overnight its loudest critics.

For all of the Greek military based around Thessaloniki, with rare exceptions it was nearly impossible for American civilians to meet military personnel. Through friendship between our wives, I became friends with a completely non-political Lt. Colonel attached to an armored unit near Kozani. He had no political views that I could discern and was obsessed with the operational readiness of the unit under his command. One day, he discovered that the expensive cadmium batteries that powered the night vision sights on tanks in his unit had long expired and were inoperable. He protested to the regional commander and was advised not to pursue the matter further. Not to be deterred, he pushed it to progressively higher levels until, coming to the attention of Brig. Pattakos, he was imprisoned. Here was proof positive of the corruption and rot at the core of the Colonels' Junta. Because of sheer greed at the top, tank batteries across Greece were not being replaced, and the Greek army, whose raison d'etre was defense of country, would have been blindsided in the event of a Turkish tank attack by night across the plains of Thrace.

We were, of course, then in the midst of the Cold War which, despite the close-by borders of Yugoslavia, Bulgaria and Albania, intruded only rarely into the consciousness of the local gentry. I recall, during one foray across the border, that the Bulgarians rushed to indoctrinate our young son Richard and daughter Eliza with medals depicting the baby Lenin and that the former King's palace at Borovitz had been converted into a worker's paradise for winter sport. Closer to home, obligatory calls on consular homologues, both friendly and less so, were another way to take the pulse. I remember how my Yugoslav counterpart insisted on a rigid protocol of three glasses of high octane slivovitz plum brandy during morning courtesy calls. After extended inane conversation, and obviously following a Tito-era manual, he would abruptly demand when the third glass was served, "Tell me please on what wavelength is broadcasting the American military communications unit on Mount Hortiatis?"

In my time, the Consulate still maintained a thirty-five foot double-ended Greek caique or fishing vessel for the pleasure of the Consul General who sometimes entertained staff on sunset cruises around the Thermaic Gulf or even as far as Chalkidiki. It too was a Cold War relic, and its wooden hull concealed armor to withstand up to 50 caliber machine gun fire. In its day, the craft had been employed to infiltrate saboteurs along the Albanian coast. Less than four out of a hundred agents ever made it ashore and, years later, visiting the coast near Durres south of Tirana, I observed pill boxes at regular intervals and understood why. Enver Hoxha's break with Moscow in the early sixties and international pariah status made such operations superfluous, however, and the craft and its grizzled captain Christos now specialized in pleasure cruises only. Several former consuls general with a taste for the sea were outraged when a non-nautical successor eventually sold the worthy ship.

Another dimension of the Cold War, at least in the port of Thessaloniki, were almost monthly visits from the US Sixth Fleet. While these may have projected American power into the communist hinterland to the North, they also reinforced the prevailing Greek view of American support for the Colonels. Sailors will be sailors and, of course, a carrier in port means four or five thousand of them all at once. The fleet is a natural magnet for legitimate businesses, as well as promoters and hucksters of every stripe. We always worked closely with the local press to keep things positive, showing the sailors giving blood at the hospital, painting an orphanage or doing a choir sing at the old people's home. All the same, these civic efforts were sometimes overshadowed by what was going on downtown in the waterfront bars. There was always some idiot who would bite a girl in the ladies' room or worse, and it was sometimes ugly.

I remember one visit, from the USS Enterprise if memory serves, when everything seemed to go wrong. It was so foggy that we had to send an "immediate" cable to establish that the huge carrier was even in port. Everything was backed up, and the General, the Bishop, the Governor and the Mayor were all waiting to receive the Sixth Fleet Commander's courtesy visits and then be ferried out in the Admiral's launch and piped aboard the carrier for lunch. Painting started late at the orphanage kitchen too and the place was torn apart before they realized that brushes would not do the job and spray guns and compressors were needed, causing several hundred orphans to miss dinner. At the University, the ship's rock band blew out the fuses, cancelling the concert. In the sports palace, however, the Greeks had their revenge. Tired of losing to nearly professional athletic teams with virtually unlimited practice time onboard carriers, they quietly sneaked in the Greek Olympic wrestling team and cleaned up the mats with our boys.

Meanwhile on the waterfront, an inebriated sailor overturned a tureen of hot spaghetti on a table of minor Greek actors. Sensing a publicity windfall, the latter pressed charges against the spaghetti thrower or *spagetoriktis* as he was labeled in the Greek press. The case was just one of the unsettled claims, shore patrol phone bills, apologies, thank-you's and, of course, AWOL personnel which make up the detritus of such visits. In the latter category, four sailors woke up after the carrier's departure in Kozani, several hours across the mountains, with no money and no recollection how they got there. Still, as is traditional after fleet visits, the Consul General was presented with the ship's insignia mounted on a handsome plaque, which was duly added to the Consulate's collection, spanning many years, of a hundred or more such mementos.

In such a small post, you had to be able to back-stop the others in order for anyone to take leave or travel and, so, I often found myself stamping visas, issuing passports and helping Americans in distress abroad. Like the monthly ship visits, it was operational work and a relief from sending unread economic and political dispatches into the maw of an opaque Washington bureaucracy. People abroad seem to think that Consuls have tremendous influence and, of course, the consuls themselves have a certain stake in furthering this illusion. I remember a stream of drop-in visitors seeking preference on every conceivable matter, to get a boy into school, to angle for a government job or to hint at using the diplomatic bag. A cafe across the street was crowded with would-be interpreters and influence peddlers cajoling rubes from the countryside that they could never receive US visas without paying their exorbitant fees as intermediaries. Then there were the mad inventors, one of whom used to sit at a designated cafe table every night at 10 pm waiting for a signal which never came that the USG would buy his specially designed submarine patent.

There were serious cases too, of teenagers smuggled out of Bulgaria in car trunks to defect or hippies sentenced to hard labor in a Greek prison for a bit of marijuana in their backpacks. It was all in a day's work. You recorded births, witnessed marriages if invited and advised on preparing remains for shipment home. I remember one sailor, I think his name was Hanraghan, who asked me to witness his marriage and came in the day before to confirm again that I would be there. He was off a USN oiler, one of the series with Indian names, and in a state of agitation. Clearly, the bride's conservative Greek family did not approve the match and the long orthodox ceremony would be trying. The priest, a bearded figure out of a fresco, intoned the liturgy, periodically summarizing the proceedings in broken English for Hanraghan. The groom, however, was past comprehension by then, and the service concluded with him slumped in a chair with the bride standing protectively over him. Afterwards, still unsteady on his feet, Hanraghan asked if he could pay something for my services, which I, of course, declined. I never heard how the marriage held up, if they made good, or if they are happy in Utah where he planned to start a mink farm.

In our third and final year in Thessaloniki, the political pot began to stir with the ouster of Papadopoulos on November 25, 1973, the Turkish invasion and occupation of Northern Cyprus on July 20, 1974 and the growing realization that a return to the normal chaos of Greek politics was in the offing. Reporting up to then had involved little more than occasional trips to Xanthi and Komotini to observe whether the Muslim minorities there were being treated fairly under the 1922 Treaty of Lausanne or skimming out by low-flying helicopter to inspect promising oil wells sunk off the Island of Thassos with US investment.

Now, the atmosphere had changed overnight, and I was mesmerized to see Andreas Papandreau, a gifted economics professor at Berkeley, harangue a delirious crowd of several hundred thousand Greeks in Aristotle Square at the heart of Thessaloniki during the run-up to November 17, 1974 parliamentary elections.[8] Speaking extemporaneously for three hours from a hotel balcony above the square, Papandreou's rhythmic cadences and swaying motion, fortified some said by strong drink, electrified the crowd and helped insure his PASOK Party's stronger than expected showing which, in turn, altered the future of Greece.[9]

Some readers may remember Sir Craig Smellie, the British MI-6 chief whom we had known in Libya, a huge florid-faced Scotsman of at least 6 feet, six inches.[10] Improbably, I saw him, dressed in a kilt and sticking out like a sore thumb amidst some half million wildly cheering Greeks in the square. Making my way over to him with difficulty, he cut me dead because he was supposed to be incognito in MI-6 Greek language training for a final assignment to Athens and was under strict orders not to acknowledge his presence to anyone in public. He later made contact through channels and we had an agreeable dinner. Poor man, he died shortly afterwards in his retirement post.

The United States was widely blamed by Greeks for fomenting or at the very least doing nothing to prevent the brutal Turkish invasion of Cyprus which has partitioned that island right up to the present time. Popular outrage in the summer and fall of 1974 took the form of near daily demonstrations in front of the Consulate General with crowds of many thousands tightly packed along the seafront and narrow back streets. Rumors of impending violence and Molotov cocktails were rampant. While remaining behind himself, the Consul General preemptorily ordered that my family with two small children in elementary school relocate for the duration of our tour to the bucolic grounds of the American Farm School outside the city. It was a request that I would not have made but deeply appreciated, since the deafening chants of the crowd at all hours were not easy to explain to young children, and to this day my daughter Eliza, a lifelong philhellene, is troubled why people seemed to hate us so.

Founded in 1904 with support from Princeton University, the Farm School now sends graduates to Princeton and was at that time a window into an older, more agrarian Greece, also a paradise for young children with its dairy, piggery, rabbit hutches and other infinite surprises. It's legendary director, Bruce Lansdale, and his wife Tad were outspoken critics of America's passive policy toward the Junta and did much to redeem our image among their wide circle of Greek acquaintances. I recall a dinner with regime opponents after Vice President Spiro Agnew's ill-fated visit to Greece when conversation centered on an underground theatrical production, called "Easter with the Gargalianians" which mocked the pomp and circumstance of Agnew's return to the Peloponnesian village of his ancestors.[11] There is always resentment of the emigrant who comes back in the big car and brags of his success which Agnew was prone to do before his own fall from grace and felony conviction for bribery. Present at the Lansdales' was Alexandros Papadongonas, a Greek Navy officer, released after prolonged torture on the prison Island of Leros, whom I later encountered as Minister of Merchant Marine when the Junta fell.

The different Greece we stepped into at the Farm School was also good preparation for assignment to Athens. The School, like Anatolia College where I later became President, had played a major role in integrating many of the 1.5 million refugees from the Smyrna catastrophe of 1921, and the impoverished villages on the slopes of Mt. Hortiatis still remembered this as well as American aid after World War II and took immense pride in sharing their modest feta cheese, olives and wine with the occasional American visitor. The rutted dirt track running through the foothills to our children's primary school required a jeep and passed through verdant pastures, but is today a paved road through an underused industrial zone.

The Farm School was also an easy jumping off point for the pristine Chalkidiki Peninsula, now, with the exception of Mount Athos, marred by unplanned tourist development, but nevertheless still a paradise. Mt. Athos, the Holy Mountain, was a leap even further back in time. I had cultivated the acquaintance of Father Mathaios, a monk of Chaucerian appetite and girth, who served as Ambassador of Vatopedi, one of the largest and richest monasteries, to the Athos capital city of Karyes. He would occasionally appear at the Consulate with huge flagons of raw red wine and poorly bound leather books which I always made a point to purchase for the novelty of his company and world views. One day, he invited us to lunch at his Embassy in Karyes, an invitation not to be turned down.

In those days anyone, with or without nautical experience and safety gear, could put to sea in Greece. Since females of any species have been prohibited on the Holy Mountain for thousands of years, I embarked on the long trip by outboard motor around Chalkidiki to Athos with my son, aged ten, my younger brother Bruce, and a friendly Greek tobacco man. We encountered a violent summer storm or *burini* with hail stones the size of golf balls and were lucky to take shelter on the Island of Amouyani. Pressing onward, we reached the modest jetty of the Russian orthodox Monastery of Pandeleimonas, built for 4,000 monks and at that time housing only four, where the suspicious Russians denied us lodging and offered only stale and moldy bread on the rocky and windswept jetty.

"The Shearing."

We reached Daphne, the port for the capital city of Karyes, the next morning and proceeded by rickety bus up a long and perilous road to present our duly stamped letters of introduction, or *thiamoniteria*, to the central government of the Holy Mountain. There, the authorities took umbrage at my son's Beatle-like long hair as provocative and an offense against decency. He was led protesting to a primitive barber where monks on the floor busily stuffed pillows with his hair as it fell. The Embassy of Vatopedi, close to the equal of the US Embassy in Athens in sheer size, turned out to be a near derelict vestige of earlier times with Father Mathaios presiding in solitary splendor over a huge banqueting hall. Course after course were served as he discoursed on the history and treasures of Vatopedi.[12] Worried about the risky anchorage for our small boat, I reminded him of the fixed departure time for the bus back down the mountain, but he assured us that he had already made provision for our return.

When we emerged after three hours into one of the hottest afternoons of summer, the bus was still in place filled to standing capacity only with angry, red-faced priests and workmen. The wily Mathaios had simply sent word ahead that it was to be held in place until the arrival of the American Consul. All were yelling "which one's the consul?," and I replied in my best Greek "it's that one," motioning to my good Greek friend with whom I've laughed over the story for many years since. All the way down the mountain, the mob's wrath was directed at him, and it was a teachable moment for Costa to experience firsthand what it was like to be an American consul at that time and place.

Economic crises in the outside world and a revival of religiosity have brought new life to Mount Athos since our visit. And yet, reflecting on the Holy Mountain as we saw it still functioning nearly as it had in medieval times, I am struck by the gap between then and the world today. There is always a disconnect between "quaintness" and authenticity, on one hand, and development and consumption on the other. Greece was and is one of the most beautiful countries on earth, yet its preservation requires careful long term planning and limiting development to the scale and contours of its age-old landscape and culture. Not that the Athos monasteries were necessarily ever a better, more peaceful world. Later, when I revisited the Holy Mountain, one monastery, Esfigmenou, had broken with the Orthodox Patriarch for His unpardonable offense of shaking hands with the Pope and was in a state of outright war with its neighbors. Over its entry a large banner proclaimed "Orthodoxy or Death!," and at least one monk died in the subsequent fighting between monasteries when his tractor overturned during a breakout run for supplies.

At that time, Greece's mountains and seas were so pristine that one could experience over and over the exhilaration of seeming to see them for the first time. It was, of course, a simpler, unostentatious time with pleasure in tradition, close friends and shared experience. Even the Colonels—malevolent as they were with their network of torture chambers and prison islands—were country rubes by comparison with the corruption and patronage politics which were later to beset Greece. Insecure in their own educational backgrounds, they were almost comic in their efforts to express themselves in Katharevousa, a stilted hybrid Greek unintelligible to the common man.

Returning to Chalkidiki years later, I picked up a farmer hitchhiking to Polygiros, the regional capital, to visit his son in the hospital, the victim of a serious car accident. He told me that he had never met a Greek-speaking American and wanted to tell me about the "real Greece." His son would die, he said, because corrupt bureaucrats in Athens had skimmed off money earmarked for hospital equipment. Only one man had ever worked for the people and introduced roads and electricity to Chalkidiki, and only one man had ever upheld the dignity of Greece as an equal with foreigners. His name was George Papadopoulos and "all of us in Chalkidiki feel the same way," he assured me.

THE BIRTHPLACE OF DEMOCRACY

The offer in summer 1975 to extend for two more years in Greece at the Embassy in Athens while democracy was being restored under Prime Minister Constantinos Karamanlis was a no brainer that I jumped at. While the Commerce Department did not welcome it, preferring someone from their own department, the Deputy Chief of Mission, later Ambassador Monteagle Stearns and as close as I came to a mentor in the Foreign Service, insisted on my assignment as Commercial Attache. With the fall of the Colonels, the mission and attitude of the American Embassy had changed overnight. With sudden freedom to speak out after seven years of enforced silence, there was a palpable atmosphere of anti-Americanism, and most Greeks remained convinced that the United States had both supported the April 1967 military coup and incited or at least failed to restrain the July 1974 invasion of Cyprus by Turkey.

The latter conviction was fueled by the fact that President Lyndon Johnson had successfully deterred Turkish Prime Minister Ismet Inönü from an earlier threatened Turkish invasion of the Island in 1964. Greek wrath was particularly concentrated on the person of Secretary of State Henry Kissinger who, all Greeks were certain, tilted toward Turkey because of its greater weight in the Cold War and because of alleged friendship with his former Harvard student, Turkish Prime Minister Bülent Ecevit. Few Greeks whom I met were willing to acknowledge that, at the time Turkey invaded Cyprus, the US Government was close to dysfunctional during the July/August 1974 Watergate crisis and resignation of President Nixon.

The huge American Embassy, located on Athens's main Queen Sophia Avenue, was a glass "wedding cake" structure, designed by Walter Gropius, and very much in vogue in the Sixties along with comparable embassy creations elsewhere by Edward D. Stone. Built in the JFK era of embassies as showcases for American openness and values, it was in no way designed as a fortress and was basically at the mercy of tens of thousands of angry Greeks who regularly demonstrated against it over Cyprus and alleged backing for the Junta. During my time, it frequently sustained damages to its glass facade until heavy perimeter fencing was eventually installed. The explosion of anger and pent-up rage that followed the Colonels' ouster undoubtedly reflected both Greece's prior four-century occupation by the Turks and the tight controls on freedom of speech and expression during seven years of stifling military rule. Still, I could not help noticing during several visits to Turkey that, while ten million Greeks were obsessed with Turkey's alleged misdeeds and nefarious conspiracies, few of Turkey's seventy-five million citizens or its media seemed to give Greece a second thought.

In this perfervid atmosphere, the new and virtually only mission of the US Embassy was to restore some measure of trust and normalcy to relations with the Greek Government and people with whom we have had close ties going back several centuries. Putting the past aside was easier said than done, however, since the elite and political class still harbored deep feelings of resentment against the United States and were slow to rebuild contacts frozen during the Junta or to respond to overtures from political or economic reporting officers. I remember an old *New Yorker* cartoon in which fifty centaurs prance on stage while the director yells, "You idiot, I said fifty senators, not centaurs." In this case, however, central casting in Personnel did get it right in selecting an experienced and charismatic ambassador, Jack Kubisch, backed up by an old Greek hand and superb manager, Monty Stearns, to preside over the difficult restoration.

I was fortunate to be assigned as Commercial Attache, with a one-year overlap with my predecessor to learn the ropes, since access to Greeks was simply easier on the commercial side and people were more than happy to do business and expand trade with the United States. As an early example of this, I was surprised to be called in by Greek Merchant Marine Minister Alexandros Papadongonas, to discuss American participation in a project for a 600-bed seamen's hospital to be funded from the Seamen's Retirement Fund.[13] While I had previously met him at the Farm School, this was notable since the Greek Navy was more royalist and opposed to the Junta than the other services, and one destroyer, the *Velos*, had mutinied during NATO exercises off Italy.[14] A number of young navy officers, including Papadongonas, had paid the price with brutal beatings and long imprisonment.

The major event that impacted my work in Athens was the collapse of Lebanon during the worst fighting of the Civil War there in 1975–76. This resulted in a complete exodus of large American regional companies which had covered the Middle East from Beirut. Three hundred of these behemoths, some with as many as 3,000 personnel, settled in Athens, at least temporarily, and required considerable Embassy hand-holding in relocating and working with the Greek Government on regulations, which had not previously existed, for operation of offshore corporations. Agreement was eventually reached between the Ambassador and Minister of Coordination Papaligouras, a brilliant, driven man with great humor who was working and smoking himself to death before our eyes. The final regulations did not, however, offer the same tax incentives as Beirut, nor were the Greek infrastructure and bureaucracy in the least accommodating. As a result, Greece missed a fleeting opportunity to become a business hub for the Eastern Mediterranean, and the companies gradually drifted away to Cyprus, London or back to the Middle East. For a number of years, however, returnees to Cairo would still revisit Athens to phone headquarters before Egypt had a modern phone system.

Once I was asked to deliver a credible death threat to the recently relocated regional head of one of the major American banks. There was good reason to believe that a hit man from Lebanon would assassinate him in a matter of days at a specific point on his route to work. I recall that his executive assistant refused to interrupt an ongoing business meeting or acknowledge that someone from the Embassy could have anything of sufficient urgency to do so. When I eventually barged in, however, the manager was quite shaken and grateful for the information which I had been instructed to share with him alone.

The influx of US companies provided a wonderful hunting ground to recruit for and expand the American Pavilion at the annual Greek trade fair held in Thessaloniki. We doubled the pavilion size with 65 exhibitors and even a few airplanes one year. This line of work was quite operational and satisfying since you could see results, and I had also worked on the Pavilion while in Thessaloniki. The fair was always in early September and traditionally included a large photo of the President at the entry to the US Pavilion. Only, in 1974, photos of President Ford were not yet available following Nixon's August resignation. The theme for the exhibit that year was waste materials and waste treatment, and when I went to inspect the pavilion just before the opening reception with the Ambassador and many dignitaries expected, there at the entry, larger than life, was Richard Nixon's portrait over the caption in bold letters, "Recycling Waste Materials." While I was able to make a last minute switch before guests arrived, I've always thought that it would have made a great New Yorker cartoon.

Business in Greece, boosted at least temporarily by disintegration of Lebanon, was marked by intense rivalry among a handful of entrepreneurs, particularly in the shipping sector, for control of Greece's most valuable assets. Wealth was highly concentrated, and the massive consumption, overwhelming debt and blatant corruption of the political parties was still years ahead. I recall touring the Hellenic Shipyards with its Director, the nephew of Stavros Niarchos, and marveling over the hulls of giant vessels moving simultaneously down the automated factory floor with computerized laser cutouts. It was a world class operation, and Greek shipping had a special glamour then before the bubble burst in the shipping industry and a socialist government nationalized the yards. I recall, as if it were yesterday, lunch at a coastal villa high above the Aegean at which the Director arrived late by helicopter to greet his guests, bringing to mind Tony Perkins in the classic movie *Phaedra*.

Years later, as President of Anatolia College in Thessaloniki, I called on Constantinos Drakopoulos, by then senior statesman of the Stavros Niarchos Foundation, and reminisced with him about visiting his shipyard. He described with great emotion seeing his life's work nationalized and run into the ground by an inefficient, bloated government bureaucracy. I, in turn, talked about the frustrations of operating a private, non-profit American educational institution under a huge government bureaucracy, constantly changing regulations and outright hostility from many of the public universities. Finally, bringing out my tin cup as college president, I gulped and told him that our Board Chair had put up a million dollars for a new library and could the Foundation possibly help. With no hesitation, he asked whether the Chair, George Bissell of Boston, would be willing to match a gift of $2 million from the Foundation. It was then the Chairman's turn to gulp when I called him, but he came through with flying colors. It was also my first experience with fundraising and by no means typical, since average cultivation time for a million dollar gift is usually seven years or more.

Historically and by geography, Greece has always been an outward looking crossroads country. This, of course, attracted every manner of Greek, American and third country middlemen, as well as con artists. American congressional delegations, or CODELs as they were known, were also regular visitors because of Greece's reputation for natural beauty, hospitality and as a jumping off point to Europe, Africa or the Middle East. Staff would share the escort duties, and early on I was tagged with a large group from the House Post Office and Civil Service Committee. Their improbable objective was to study best practices that the United States might emulate from the millennial postal systems of Greece and Egypt. They advised me at the outset to keep official calls to the minimum required by decorum and indicated a preference for spending the balance of their time at the Old Faliron racetrack. Furthermore, I was instructed to provide them with a Greek embassy employee who played the horses and could advise on their bets. The hard part was finding an employee on the local staff who would own up to such a vice, but eventually someone sheepishly stepped forward, and the Congressmen apparently enjoyed their outing, some even winning a few bets.

Seeing the fortified Green Line in Nicosia and separate Greek and Turkish sectors not long after the 1974 partition of the island helped me to better understand the tragedy of Cyprus. An eerie silence prevailed in the abandoned and ghostly resort of Varosha at Famagusta in the Turkish sector. By contrast, the Greek sector was bustling, and consultations with my counterpart in the US Embassy and with Cypriot businessmen revealed optimistic prospects for growth. It appeared to me that partition of the Turkish and Greek populations into north and south had released new business energies, previously tied up in marginal agriculture in the north, for more productive use in the Greek sector. By comparison, business along the northern coast appeared stagnant. When a senior US official and head of our delegation, in a spectacular lapse of judgment, attempted to purchase carved wooden seats from an abandoned Orthodox church in the Turkish sector, planning to sneak them back to Athens on the Embassy plane, I was relieved that the US Ambassador to Cyprus, the late Bill Crawford, barred his way, threatening to blow the whistle in Washington.

After three years daily immersion in the Greek language, while in Thessaloniki, I was re-tested by my former instructors and received unconscionably high marks which, as with Somali years before, got me into almost immediate trouble. There were undoubtedly Greek-American staff in the Embassy with native fluency in the language who had no need for the FSI training with its somewhat archaic grammar and vocabulary and received lesser test scores. Be that as it may, I was designated in a telegram from Washington to be the American certifying officer for the equivalency of Greek and English texts of the

1976 Defense and Economic Cooperation Agreement (DECA) and its subsequent implementing agreement the following year. As with the earlier episode of Somali threats against Vice President Humphrey, I was in a nearly untenable situation and very uncomfortable with the terminology and legal niceties which meant little to me in English, let alone Greek.

The most harrowing incident of my time in Greece occurred following the Ambassador's holiday party on December 23, 1975 for Embassy staff, a few diplomatic colleagues and selected Greek friends. With us was Dick Welch, the recently arrived and declared CIA Station Chief in Greece, along with his wife, Kiki. Mutual friends had introduced me to Welch in Washington as he was preparing for a preceding assignment. He was an immensely well-educated and cerebral person, fun to be with and a passionate Phil-hellene and student of ancient Greek. It was a splendid evening of good cheer and fellowship, and all left reluctantly and in high spirits at its conclusion. The Welches lived just around the corner from us in the close-by suburb of Palio Psychico, and soon after getting home we learned that he had died moments before in a hail of gunfire outside his front gate, ambushed by unknown assassins.

The Welch assassination was the first of 30 killings, including four other Americans, carried out by a small group of Greek thugs and petty criminals whose identities only became known twenty-seven years later when the first culprit was finally rounded up on June 29, 2002 through a series of mishaps and pure coincidences.[15] Among the victims were prominent Greek business leaders, two senior Turkish diplomats and British Brigadier Stephen Saunders whom my wife Eia and I had known in Morocco. While they took the name November 17, marking an attack by the Colonels' regime on the Athens Polytechnic School on November 17, 1973 in which a number of students died, there was no serious political or ideological group behind these random lowlifes who financed their activities through a series of eleven bank robberies.

The Greek authorities were slow to investigate November 17 or even to acknowledge the possibility that there might be Greeks behind it, preferring instead to consider it as a foreign plot, perhaps originating in the Middle East or Balkans. Once, I was provided information obtained from the relative of someone who had been in prison and who claimed to have heard other inmates discussing Welch's murder. I passed the details and names involved along to the Embassy security officer who, I believe, turned them over to the Greek authorities. Certainly, my source soon totally disappeared from the face of the earth, and I still regret how the matter was handled.

The killing of Dick Welch was a lasting shock to the Embassy community in Athens, particularly those who had been celebrating with him just moments before. Yet, terrorism and near constant danger has become a fact of life for American diplomats in recent years, the flip side of the thrill and glamour of serving one's country abroad. During my three decades in the Foreign Service (1965–1999), dozens of American ambassadors and diplomats were assassinated or died heroically in the line of duty at US embassies and consulates around the world. Though few Americans realize it, the list of these victims running from 1780 to 2016 now reaches 248 American diplomats who have died for their country.

In my own small orbit, those whom I had met or knew personally included Amb. Cleo Noel (Khartoum, 1973), Curt Moore (Khartoum,1973), Amb. Rodger Davies (Nicosia, 1974), Richard Welch (Athens, 1975), Amb. Francis Meloy (Beirut, 1976), Amb. Spike Dubs (Kabul, 1979), Dennis Keogh (Windhoek 1984), Amb. Arnie Raphel (Pakistan, 1988), Bob Frasure, (Bosnia 1995), and Steve Kaminski (Croatia 1996). This is fairly typical, and colleagues with greater exposure in dangerous areas lost many more friends than I. More recently, we have all mourned the loss of Ambassador Chris Stevens and three colleagues in Benghazi on Sept. 11, 2012. I had been privileged to work with Chris in the State Department's Bureau of Near Eastern Affairs and to share with him a fascination with Morocco and

North Africa. With his self-deprecating humor, I have no doubt that he would have been appalled by the partisan bickering that has cast a pall over his sacrifice and service to the nation.

Departing Athens in 1977, I looked back on my years there as a watershed for Greece and for the Embassy as well. Gone was the pro-consular American attitude which had lingered after the War as US economic and military assistance shaped the "miracle" of Greek recovery, as well as America's hands-off stance during the Junta which was read by Greeks as quiet encouragement. It was fascinating to observe both the Greek Government and Embassy management work their way through this process. The knee-jerk tendency of Greeks to blame foreign powers and conspiracies for whatever went wrong was slow to dissipate. I remember, for example, once at a reception being snubbed by Merlina Mercouri and her American husband Jules Dassin, who refused to shake hands with an American diplomat. They, or for that matter Andreas Papandreau as well, having made their reputations and careers in the United States, might have thought twice, it seemed to me, before casting the first stone. Overall, however, US-Greek relations appeared to be on an upward trend, eased by a succession of experienced and relatively low-key American ambassadors. Prime Minister Karamanlis had firmly anchored Greece within Europe, confirmed by its admission to the European Union in 1981.

MORE FOREIGN SERVICE THAN
TODAY'S FOREIGN SERVICE

I retired from the Foreign Service in 1999 after thirty-four years in government. Believing that an ambassadorship is the capstone of such a career, I had accepted with alacrity when my bureau at the State Department put my name forward for Algeria, a challenging and not inconsequential assignment. Yet when the Secretary, as was her perfect right, preferred someone from her immediate entourage, I decided that three decades of government service was enough for one lifetime. As it turned out, there is life outside of government, and I came to regret that I had not made that discovery sooner.

As you belatedly reach the senior ranks of the Foreign Service, you are no longer an oriental secretary ferreting out secrets from bedouins over sheep's eyes in the desert, but a bureaucrat and manager like any other. Thus, the skills of motivating people, establishing priorities, thinking ahead etc. differ little from those needed to run a college, NGO or company branch abroad. At the same time, since 9/11 but starting well before, embassies and consulates have been forced into a bunker mentality with an almost single-minded focus on terrorism.[16] Free circulation and the ability to carry out the traditional role of a diplomat representing the values and ideals of the United States abroad have been circumscribed in critical parts of the world.

Thus, once back in Thessaloniki, I came to feel that serving as president of an American college was in many ways more foreign service than today's Foreign Service. I could travel about at will without concern for security or diplomatic hierarchy. Once, attending a conference in Beirut for American college presidents in the Mediterranean region, I met for drinks at a local watering hole with a former colleague then serving in the beleaguered Beirut Embassy and surrounded by six bodyguards with automatic weapons, and not only did I not envy him, but came to pity his life inside such a cocoon. I also felt, as a practical matter, that all the guards and weaponry made us more rather than less conspicuous targets.

In academia I came to feel greater satisfaction in measurable results than I had ever experienced in government. If you are running a college, you know precisely where you stand at any point in time and cannot easily fake it. Annual enrollment figures, the budget, fundraising, graduate placement and other precise indicators provide a clear bottom line in a way that the

status of US-Mauritanian relations or trends in Islamic funda-
mentalism simply do not. Finally, the formula of government
pension plus salary was a pleasant surprise, since Foreign Service pay, free housing and educational allowances go a long way
abroad, but are a very tough stretch for most families at home.

By way of background, Anatolia College, which I was privileged to head from 1999–2009, is one of the oldest American educational institutions abroad with deep roots in modern Greek history.[17] It sprang from the "haystack" prayer meeting at Williams
College in 1806 whose 200th Anniversary celebrations I returned
from Greece to address at Williams in 2006. The original meeting
took place literally under a haystack where a group of Williams
students sought refuge from a thunderstorm and, during a sleepless
night, laid the groundwork for America's Congregationalist missionary outreach around the world.

Their impromptu meeting, in turn, led to establishment in Boston in 1810 of the American Board of Commissioners for Foreign
Missions and, after prolonged and unsuccessful negotiations with
the founder of the Modern Greek state, Ioannis Kapodistrias, to
build a school in Greece, to establishment of the Bebek Seminary
outside Constantinople in 1840.[18] The Seminary split in two in
1862 with half secularizing and remaining at Bebek until this day
as Robert College and the other half moving to Marsovan near the
Black Sea where it too eventually became secular, taking the name
Anatolia College in 1886.[19]

Turkey closed Anatolia College, however, in 1921 in the build-
up to the Smyrna catastrophe of the following year, and Anatolia
accepted the invitation of Greek Prime Minister Eleftherios Veni-
zelos to relocate to Thessaloniki in 1924. It was thus a refugee
institution amidst a tide of one and a half million Greeks uprooted
from Turkey and still takes pride in these origins and service. With
the exception of World War II, when the campus was occupied as a
regional headquarters by the Nazis, Anatolia has continued to edu-

cate Greek and international leaders in all fields at the elementary, secondary, undergraduate and MBA levels.

Many of its archives were destroyed during the German occupation and eventual liberation of the campus by British Gurkha troops. The campus may well have sheltered the infamous Austrian Chancellor and UN Secretary General Kurt Waldheim and others involved in the deportation of Thessaloniki Jews to Auschwitz. The campus remains honeycombed with underground Nazi tunnels, bomb shelters and command and control centers, now closed for safety reasons. Still, as President I had a key and could be persuaded to give the occasional VIP or student tour.

The Board of Trustees, long headquartered in Boston across from the State House and around the corner from the old Board of Commissioners for Foreign Missions which has now merged into the Congregationalist Library, was conservative in both selection of presidents and avoidance of debt at all costs. During my time, the majority believed that a president of Hellenic origin could be vulnerable to outside pressures for preference in hiring or other favors and that a visibly American president without roots in Greece would be regarded as more impartial.[20] The Board did recognize at that time, however, that command of modern Greek was a requirement for the job, since it is the language of instruction at the elementary and secondary levels and used in staff meetings. While a decreasing minority of Americans still study classical Greek, which differs widely from the modern version, these dual requirements tended to limit candidates to broken-down former diplomats like myself and my predecessor for a quarter of a century, Dr. William McGrew. I am pleased to report, however, that the Board's policies have since been relaxed, and the first Greek president in nearly two centuries, Dr. Panos Vlachos, was sworn in during August 2013.

The 50-acre Anatolia campus, nestled in the foothills of Mount Hortiatis and overlooking the Thermaikos Gulf and on a clear day snow-capped Mount Olympus, was an oasis of tranquility and greenery in a city now ranked as one of the most polluted in Europe. In the early Twentieth Century, a student and Armenian refugee, Haigaram Baronian, wrote of the original Marsovan campus that "It was like heaven on earth," and his words still ring true today for the campus in Greece. Outside the school gates, however, in both Turkey then and Thessaloniki today, the reality was and is quite different.

In the nearly quarter century since I had left Thessaloniki, gone were the many American businessmen and their families who had formed an important pillar of the international community. While this was initially seen as a triumph of Hellenization, in the end most of these enterprises closed or, following the collapse of 2008, relocated outside of Greece. Gone too was the vital tobacco industry and its leading families who had been the social center of the town, as the few remaining producers relocated their operations to take advantage of lower labor costs next door in Albania. Gone were the majority of foreign consulates, once a bustling presence in the city's public life.

Finally, gone as well, with one notable exception, were the regular US Navy ship visits to Thessaloniki. Shortly before I left for the second time in 2009, the amphibious assault ship USS *Saipan* came limping into port for a final visit just before it was decommissioned and sold for scrap in 2009 after 35 years of service. From its decks, I had once observed a live-fire, over-the-beach amphibious assault off the coast of Western Sahara, and it was a treat to go onboard with my stepdaughter Alexandra and to reconnect with its battalion of 2,000 Marines.

Thessaloniki had long ago lost its battle with Athens to be considered the co-capital or *simprotevousa* of Greece. In fact, Athens and its massive central bureaucracy had become a colossus astride the Greek economy. Yet the business and city leaders in their Macedonian pride and stubbornness persisted in this unequal combat. I would often fly to Athens to seek various permits from the Ministry of Education or grants from the many foundations based there. The morning plane was inevitably filled to capacity with cheerful businessmen optimistic that they would finally secure vital financing, authority to open a new business or the myriad permits necessary to operate in Greece. The evening plane back was invariably filled with the same crestfallen and despondent travelers, rebuffed by the bureaucracy and forced to return yet again another day to face the bureaucrats, regulation and widespread corruption.

The vision for Thessaloniki, I have always felt, should never have been head to head competition with Athens but, in US terms, the model of Boston as a preeminent academic and intellectual center. With two major public universities, including the largest in Greece, Aristotelian University, as well as two preeminent American educational centers, Thessaloniki had the fleeting opportunity to be an educational beacon for the Balkan hinterland as neighboring countries emerged from the educational and cultural shambles of communism. Instead, Greece was held back by lack of consensus or vision among government, business and academic leaders, to say nothing of the Church, each locked in their own petty squabbles and self-interest.

An intractable and long-running dispute over the official name of Macedonia further soured the atmosphere, and at my college I saw a robust contingent of bright Macedonian students dwindle to just a trickle. Nor was Greece able to seize the potentially much larger opportunities for regional leadership after the collapse of the Soviet Union. Instead, it was inundated by a wave of impoverished Greeks uprooted from Armenia, Georgia, Azerbaijan and beyond. I happened to visit a former nearly empty tuberculosis sanatorium at Asvestohori, now filled again with patients bringing back the disease from these lands.

I once asked the Rector of Aristotle University whether Princeton, which I attended, could be called a university since it lacks a medical or law school, and he insisted that it could not, since a real university must offer all branches of human knowledge.[21] Not since medieval times, in my view, has one institution spanned all fields of human knowledge. Even Harvard degrees are scrutinized by a Greek review board (DIKATSA) and returning graduates are often required to take additional courses in Greece for degree recognition and the right to work. It was thus a particular victory for our institution to receive a major grant directly from the EU as the leader of a research consortium in the area of artificial intelligence and robotics. Limited EU research funding is typically spread across all twenty-eight member states and awarded to public universities only through education ministries, thus ceding most cutting-edge research to the corporate sector and losing competitive ground to North America and Asia.

Lack of Greek Government recognition for private colleges and often outright hostility from public universities, fearful of competition from the private sector, meant that we had to scramble to find public-spirited donors and foundations. Macedonia Hall and the other historic campus buildings, many dating to the 1920s, required constant maintenance. At the same time, the computer age and modern educational technology required a network of fiber optic cables across the 50-acre campus. Before I'd even heard of Facebook, I remember receiving a message from a recent Albanian graduate asking me to be her friend and to follow her career progress. She had just become a director in the Albanian Foreign Ministry and I could hardly say no. The exchange became public, showing me to have only one friend in the world, and our computer savvy alumni were embarrassed that their President was some kind of friendless-homeless loner, and I received hundreds of friend requests, drawing me unwillingly into the vortex.

One of our Trustees was deeply involved in a two billion euro project for electrification of gas which, he promised, would include a hundred million Euro educational foundation centered at his *alma mater*, Anatolia College. Gas from Kazakhstan would be converted to electricity inside the Ukrainian Free Zone and exported tax-free to meet Western Europe's energy demands at highly competitive costs. All, including financing through Credit Suisse, was in readiness, and I attended several dinners at his seaside villa at Lagonissi outside Athens with major players like President Nursultan Nazarbayev of Kazakhstan, then-Ukrainian President Viktor Yanukovych and Greek President Stephanopoulos. Yanukovych, an intimidating giant of a man, spoke little English and no Greek, so conversation with Greek Archbishop Christodoulos, whom our host Costas insisted be part of the Anatolia-based foundation, went only so far.

After at least three years of these negotiations, Ukrainian relations soured with Russia, and Transneft, the Russian state pipeline company, on orders from Putin, blocked transit of Kazakh gas across Russia to the Ukraine. Putin, in other words, cost our struggling college a cool 100 million euros. If he hadn't been such a jerk about it, my astute vice president had already projected that I might have gotten away with just showing up mornings at the college for Greek coffee for the rest of my natural life. Our trustee and alumnus, Costas Keletzekis, who lived for this one last score, had travelled regularly to Russia, Kazakhstan and Ukraine well into his late eighties to secure agreement, and died broken-hearted in March 2009 along with Anatolia's dreams for a foundation on such an unimaginable scale.

Costas was in all respects larger than life, inhabiting a world that no longer exists and not the type of Greek you are likely to meet today. In fact, he could have stepped out of any number of museum portraits of the great Greek brigands and pirates like Kolokotronis or Karaiskakis, known as "klephts and armatoloi" during Greece's independence struggle against the Turks. He grew up in Iran, where he later became President of the large Greek expatriate community, and was packed off for seven years at Anatolia College in remote

Thessaloniki, graduating in 1937. He made his fortune dredging harbors like Bandar Abbas in Iran, earning just a quarter of what his competitor, John Latsis, was pulling in for the same work in Saudi Arabia. Still, he was able to buy Pacific Dredge, parleying it into one of the world's largest shrimp fleets and on from there into oil and gas. I remember breakfast at his villa on its own peninsula overlooking the Aegean at Lagonisi. Driving into Athens afterwards in one of several Rolls Royces, he spoke simultaneously on cell phones to Moscow in Russian and Tehran in Farsi. When we reached a designated corner in downtown Athens, a valet from his city residence stood waiting with a hanger of neckties from which Keletzekis made his selection for the day. Nor was he all about money and deal making, but also an accomplished poet in both English and Russian, favoring the romantics.

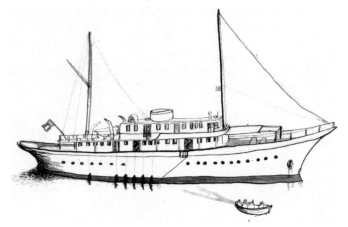

"Cruising the Saronic Islands on the **Madiz.***"*

Preliminary discussions for the scholarship foundation were held on an historic 148-foot yacht, Costas' pride and joy, built for Lord North in Scotland in 1902 and the only surviving vessel from that time with the coveted Lloyds Registry rating of "+100A1" more than one hundred years after its launch in the Firth of Clyde. The ship had conducted auxiliary patrols during the First World War and, during the Second, played a role in both the evacuation from Dunkirk and the

Battle of the Atlantic. It was often used by King George VI, as well as Queen Elizabeth and her mother, the Queen Consort. It was later the setting for Agatha Christie's Poirot episode, "Problem at Sea." My wife Eia, stepdaughter Alexandra and I embarked on it for an unforgettable week's cruise in the Saronic Islands along with a group of trustees and their wives. Costas, our host, ran a very tight ship, and it was fascinating to watch the interaction of Greek-American Trustees, several of them successful venture capitalists with egos of their own, with their Zorba-like host and captain. Obedient to his every wish, they ate whenever he commanded, napped when he gave the order and were clearly in awe of their octogenarian host. Yet in those rarified surroundings the seed was planted for an undertaking which could have transformed the college, but sadly succumbed to politics in the Caucasus.

Lest I mislead you, daily life was by no means just a cruise among Aegean islands. The constant need for students, funding and academic partnerships led me to forage about regularly in the "near abroad." Istanbul[22] was my favorite city in the region, and I had reason to go there often because of a partnership with Koc University under a $3 million USAID grant for transportation and trade facilitation in the Balkans. Koc was one of the finest private universities in Turkey, perched high above the Bosphorus and with every conceivable academic bell and whistle. Its dynamic President, Attila Askar, was married to Elsie Vance, the daughter of Secretary of State Cyrus Vance, for whom I had once worked and greatly respected. Money was no object in construction of Koc University which resulted from an intense rivalry between Turkey's two major industrialists, Rahmi Koc and Sakip Sabanci, to see who could build the best and grandest university.

Koc Holding is, in fact, a state within a state, said at that time to control up to 7% of the products and services that an average Turk consumes each day. My courtesy call on the family patriarch, arranged by one of our trustees, was memorable. Setting off from

Istanbul's European side with a driver with whom I shared no common language, we reached a small village in Asia, worried to keep Mr. Koc waiting and totally lost. No one in the village, it appeared, had heard of or were willing to speak to strangers about either Rahmi Koc or Koc Holding. Finally, one local pointed to a rutted and unmarked dirt road which led inauspiciously up a mountainside. Reaching the summit at long last, we came on a complex resembling nothing so much as CIA Headquarters in Langley, Virginia with much the same perimeter security, but considerably more refinement and taste within. At the center were the exquisite offices, reception and dining rooms of Rahmi Koc.

Mr. Koc, an internationally known yachtsman and ocean racer, was immensely hospitable and talked warmly of his long association with Greece and the basic similarities of Greeks and Turks. Partnership between Anatolia and Koc University was sealed, and he volunteered to help in a quixotic endeavor to restore the decrepit clock tower from the shuttered old campus in Marsovan to the campus in Greece. The wooden tower, in danger of collapse, had been the hallmark of the earlier campus, which had gone through many permutations as a military base and hospital and was now largely derelict and abandoned. The clock itself, the first of its kind in Turkey when Anatolia purchased it from Switzerland in 1902, was now long gone, but according to missionary accounts, its hourly chimes had once prompted the people of Marsovan to be the first to abandon Asian timekeeping and adopt the western system.

The concept was to truck the otherwise worthless tower to Thessaloniki to mark the one hundred and twentieth anniversary in 2006 of the school's operation as Anatolia College. Even the Greek Foreign Ministry lent support to our effort, but the Turkish Government remained adamantly opposed. It officially designated the tower from an American Christian school serving mostly Armenian students as part of Turkey's cultural patrimony, never to be removed from the homeland. Although Mr. Koc obligingly offered to

buy the worthless relic, which by this writing may well have collapsed, and lend it indefinitely to Anatolia, mistrust between the
two countries proved too great to overcome.

This and other trips to Istanbul brought me face-to-face with the
vastly different economic realities of Greece and Turkey. My wife
Eia and I would stay at a magical hotel with Ottoman decor and a
multi-star rooftop restaurant overlooking the Sea of Marmara on
one side and the Sultan Ahmet Mosque and former Hagia Sophia
Orthodox Cathedral on the other and pay exactly half of what it
cost me each month at a run-of-the-mill Athens hotel. At the time, I
attributed this imbalance to greater Turkish competitiveness and
relative inefficiency in Greece's highly regulated tourism sector. In
hindsight, I now understand that Greece was inescapably locked
into unrealistic German levels of efficiency and competition while
Turkey, outside the Eurozone, could freely control its own currency, the Lira. It was not, in other words, a level playing field, and the
imbalance had little to do with the efficiency of Greek hotel workers and everything to do with the rigidity and flawed structure of
the Eurozone itself.

My escapade in Bulgaria was of an altogether different and sinister nature. I had recently arrived at Anatolia and needed to consult
at regional United Nations headquarters in Sofia regarding several
million dollars in funding we had received for Transportation and
Trade Facilitation in Southeastern Europe (TTFSE). I had been
warned by senior Greek Trustees about car theft in Bulgaria and
took pains to secure the company car at a well-known hotel on the
central Queen Sofia Avenue. The receptionist indicated a space
close to the front entrance and assured me there was twenty-four
hour surveillance. She also inquired whether the car had an electric
alarm system. The next morning it was gone, and new faces at the
front desk denied any hotel responsibility and asked me for the
prior receptionist's name. After verifying that there was no alarm
system, she had obviously informed accomplices that she had a

pigeon. Then, like clockwork, a band of nimble-fingered boys jim-
mied the lock and hard-wired the ignition before an old man casual-
ly sauntered up, like any owner, and drove off. Typically, within
minutes, I later learned, a team of mechanics would have disassem-
bled the vehicle for shipment and reassembly in Russia.

Although the US Ambassador assured me that stolen cars were
routinely located and returned intact, I also later learned that even
Embassy vehicles equipped with sophisticated GPS tracking de-
vices were regularly turning up in Siberia. Adding insult to injury,
cars are noted on a driver's passport on entry into Bulgaria, and I
had to spend a Kafkaesque day testifying under oath in a Bulgarian
criminal court that I had not illegally sold the vehicle before I could
even leave the country, never to return. Naturally, the fine print of
the Greek insurance policy specifically waived all coverage for
theft in Bulgaria, and it was without doubt a poor start with Trustees for a new college president.

Going back to its earliest origins, Anatolia has been the college
of choice for the Armenian and Jewish communities, first in Asia
Minor and then Thessaloniki. I worked hard to maintain these ties,
twice visiting Yerevan, the exotic capital of Armenia, and seeking
out scholarships designated for promising Jewish and Armenian
students. The history of the Jewish community was particularly
haunting because at the dawn of the Twentieth Century it had been
the largest single community in Thessaloniki, then a vibrant cultural center known by some as "Jerusalem of the West." Ninety-six
percent of Jews living in Thessaloniki were deported, quite possibly under orders of Nazis occupying the campus, and killed during the Holocaust, the largest percentage of the Jewish population
lost in any major European city.

The year 2005 was the sixtieth anniversary of the liberation of
Auschwitz-Birkenau by allied soldiers and a solemn event in Thessaloniki attended by Israeli Minister of Transportation Meir Shee-
trit and German Foreign Minister Joschka Fischer among dignitar-

ies from around the world. The commemoration caused me to delve into the fate of Anatolia's many prewar Jewish students, and I was surprised to be told that the question had not previously been posed and that most of the school archives had been burned for warmth and cooking by Gurkha troops liberating the campus. We enlisted a faculty member with deep roots in the Jewish community and a Muslim intern from my office to delve more deeply and, working with Yad Vashem in Israel, they came up with a list of 94 former Anatolia students who died or remain unaccounted for in the Holocaust.

The question then became how, sixty years after this unspeakable tragedy, to honor these students without exploiting their loss as just another pretext for fundraising. Governor Mike Dukakis and his wife Kitty, a longtime member of the US Holocaust Memorial Council and founding member of the US Holocaust Museum in Washington, showed us the way. Mike is an Honorary Trustee of Anatolia and a regular presence at its Michael Dukakis Center for Public Policy and Service, which he lent his name to and helped to make possible.

Together, Mike and Kitty organized a moving service of remembrance and celebration at Los Angeles's Temple Tifereth Israel, one of the most important Sephardic congregations in the United States. It brought together hundreds from the city's Greek and Jewish communities including at least one Holocaust survivor as well as former President of both the Academy of Motion Picture Arts and Sciences and Paramount Pictures, Sid Ganis and his wife Nancy, Greek-born Cantor and operatic talent Alberto Mizrahi who flew in from Chicago to perform, the Consuls General of Greece and Israel, and Orthodox "Priest to the Stars," Father John Bakas, among other notables. The climax of the evening was a rendition by star Greek singer Anna Vissi of "Mala: Music of the Wind" (*I Moussiki tou Anemou*), a haunting song from a theatrical opera about the Holocaust in which Anna had starred as the heroine, Mala

Zimetbaum, executed at Auschwitz-Birkenau on September 15, 1944.

It was, in short, an unforgettable evening of Jewish and Greek music and reminiscence. The names of the ninety-four lost Anatolia students were listed in the program, and in an emotional moment afterwards, the nephew of one victim came forward, learning for the first time with certainty the fate of his aunt. The list had been meticulously assembled from scattered and incomplete archives with confusing name variations and overlap. I was at once hoping against all hope, but also fearful, that someone in that large audience would cry out, "There's been a terrible mistake, it's me, I'm right here," but it was not to be and the hall was silent. The event resulted in generous funding, including from Hellenophiles Tom Hanks and his wife Rita, to dedicate a special classroom to the Holocaust, insuring that its terrible reality remains alive for generations to come of Anatolia students.

I think of the eleven years at Anatolia as a series of widening concentric circles, and during the final two I served as President of the Association of American Colleges and Universities Abroad (AAICU), the network of American private, non-profit and accredited colleges and universities around the world. These institutions are an important and under-appreciated soft power resource for the United States. The Association is comprised of some twenty institutions stretching from Kyrgyzstan and Pakistan in the East through the Persian Gulf, Lebanon, Egypt, Greece and on to Britain. Many of these institutions like the American Universities of Cairo and Beirut and the American Colleges in Greece are deeply embedded in local societies and for decades have shaped the elites of government, business, academia, and the arts. It is no secret that the largest single block of delegates assembled in San Francisco in 1945 to create the United Nations came not from Harvard, Oxford or the Sorbonne, but from the American University of Beirut.

Such American institutions have earned the high esteem in which they are held the hard way by throwing in their lot with the countries and people they serve for the long haul and often in the most trying circumstances. Nowhere is this more true than in Lebanon where the American University of Beirut, one of whose presidents was assassinated on the job and another long held hostage, has kept hope alive for many Lebanese by standing firm in crisis after crisis. Over time, such American institutions have created a fabric of human ties between their countries and the United States that are of inestimable value, in times of crisis and misunderstanding. Graduates in academia, government, business and the professions travel often to the United States and are at home in both cultures. Thus, while presidents, administrations and ambassadors come and go every few years, it is the American colleges and universities which are there for the long haul and are thus viewed in a different perspective. During the George W. Bush administration, for example, the universities were seen in many regions as "the America we want to believe in" as opposed to a perceived hostile force.

The decline of Thessaloniki relative to Athens only accelerated as Greece joined the Eurozone in 2001 and the lion's share of massive new money flows flooded the capital. Yet, evidence of consumerism gone wild was nevertheless everywhere. I attended the opening of the first Carrefour megastore, part of a French global chain and on a scale close to Walmart. Greek shoppers by the hundreds were lined up beforehand and, in a frenzy of shopping, filled carts to overflowing with an astonishing array of goods. Their enthusiasm was boundless, but when I happened to return months later, the mood was sour as the same shoppers, now harried and out of sorts, queued to weigh fruit and vegetables and then endlessly again to pay at the register. In the meantime, many of the small family butchers, grocers, bakers and fruit stores, longtime landmarks at the neighborhood corner, had started to vanish in a seemingly irreversible process.

In a caricature of Greek history, the stage was now set for a period of unbridled consumption and excess. In my simplified version, Greeks had retreated to their mountain fastnesses during four centuries of Turkish occupation or *turkokratia*, there to preserve Hellenic values and ideals in their purest form. Descending from these redoubts when the Turks were finally driven from the Greek mainland only in 1913, survivors then endured the privations of two world wars, a bitter civil war, prolonged recovery and a military junta. It was only to be expected that they would now hasten to compensate for past under-consumption. Not surprisingly they abandoned traditional Greek virtues of austerity and saving in favor of excessive spending and debt, yielding to the blandishments of low-interest funding from banks, hedge funds and other malefactors.

Even to the untrained eye, rampant consumption and expansion was ubiquitous. Panorama, a sleepy one-road village when I left in 1975, was transformed into a Bethesda-like suburb of upscale homes and gated communities when I returned a quarter century later. Tax evasion and fraud by doctors, lawyers, bureaucrats, corporations and millionaires squirreling funds out of Greece was everywhere to be seen. The longtime mayor of Thessaloniki, a former track star, was finally convicted and jailed in 2013 for embezzlement of some 51 million Euros. At the micro level, a village doctor, whom I asked in 2015 for a receipt, told me that any written record would oblige him to triple my bill.

I left Greece in summer of 2009, yet the full impact of the 2008 economic collapse did not appear until 2010. I have observed it with growing alarm during annual visits to my daughter and grandsons in Athens. I have strong views about the multiple causes of the crisis, but these are beyond the scope of this informal memoir, and I have attached as Annex I my best analysis of how and why the crisis developed, published in the September 2015 issue of the Mediterranean Quarterly.[23] My time at the college was, by contrast, one of expansion and growth. The waves of cheap money that sloshed over the country following Greece's mistaken 2001 entry into the Eurozone also boosted philanthropy, and the trustees' insistence on NO DEBT kept us on the straight and narrow. The result was a spectacular new library, theater, classroom wing, soccer and track field, primary school and MBA program, all of which would be unthinkable start-ups today.

Nor does this small country seem likely to emerge anytime soon from the "intravenous drip" of debt repayment or the frontlines of a refugee crisis engulfing all of Europe. Flying back to Greece via Istanbul in mid-2015, the landscape looked the same from 30,000 feet. The same Mediterranean and white coastal villages sparkle on both sides of the border. Today, however, one imagines the refugees and migrants below swimming the Evros River and struggling through minefields. Seven hundred fifty thousand had reached Greece in the first ten months of 2015, making it the entry point of choice to Europe and casting a shadow over one of the most evocative landscapes on the planet. Bright are still the memories of lifelong friends and resonating times past, but were they really as I remember them and are those times truly now gone? Probably not, although realities of today confound memories, raising doubts whether remembered times of laughter and spontaneity were somehow glamorized in the eyes of a youthful beholder.

The present period is, beyond doubt, the worst national trauma for Greece since the Second World War and Civil War. Yet the Phoenix, debased as it was during the Junta, is still a Greek bird, and survival in a new form is certain in the long run. The flexibility and coping skills of Greeks, honed in adversity over three thousand years, are legendary. Nor is it a bad thing that many Athenians, representing half the Greek population, are relearning country skills and seeking a simpler life in ancestral villages, vacant for decades in readiness for their return. The reappearance of bicycles and even pedestrians in congested city streets is also reassuring. Athens has no need to emulate Beijing with its choking smog, limited visibility, required indoor days and respiratory disease. The Akropolis glistening white against a clear blue sky and the ramparts of Thessaloniki where Saint Paul preached to the Thessalonians must and will once again serve as inspiration to the world and powerful symbols of Hellenic history, culture and ideals.

NOTES

1. Also known as the Assumption, Dormition, Assension, and Dekapentavgoustos.

2. The tectonic shift of Greece, Turkey and Iran was not necessarily part of, but occurred simultaneously with Dr. Kissinger's personnel policy of globalization, colloquially known within the Department as "glop," under which hundreds of language and area specialists were assigned to opposite ends of the earth so that the Secretary could have the advantage of advisors who thought globally and "saw the big picture." The policy was the death knell of the oriental secretary, already long on the endangered species list.

3. Dr. Jeffrey D. Sachs, Director of the Earth Institute at Columbia University, September 17, 2013 Lecture Sponsored by the Harvard Business School Club of Greece, at the Bank of Greece, in Athens.

4. Based on a 1966 novel by Anatolia alumnus Vassilis Vassilikos, the film *Z* was directed by Costa-Gavras and starred Jean-Louis Trintignant, Yves Montand and Irene Pappas.

5. I particularly recommend Mark Mazower's *Salonica, City of Ghosts*, Alfred A. Knopf, New York, 2005.

6. See Robert V. Keeley, *The Colonels' Coup and the American Embassy*, Pennsylvania State University Press, 2010 and Seymour M. Hersh, *The Price of Power: Kissinger in the Nixon White House*, Summit Books, 1983.

7. George Crile, *Charlie Wilson's War*, Atlantic Monthly Press, New York, 2003.

8. For a particularly insightful analysis of the man and his personality, see Ambassador Monteagle Stearns, *The Gifted Greek: Andreas Papandreau in Greece and America*, pending publication, 2016. Stan Draenos, *Andreas Papandreou: The Making of a Greek Democrat and Political Maverick*, IB Taurus and Co., London, 2012 also deals with Papandreou's career prior to the April 21, 1967 military coup.

9. See Norbert L. Anshuetz, Oral History, July 13, 1992, Association for Diplomatic Studies and Training and Seymour M. Hersh, Op.Cit. Note: Hersh cites several sources including Tasca's own congressional testimony that the Greek intelligence service (KYP) and Greek-American entrepreneur Tom Pappas

were used as conduits for Greek funding to the committees for the election of Richard Nixon in 1968 and 1972.

10. See Chapter "Within a Proper Embassy" from Libyan section above regarding earlier reference to Sir Craig Smellie.

11. Vice President Agnew served under President Richard Nixon and resigned in 1973 amid charges of fraud.

12. The Holy and Great Monastery of Vatopedi dates from the Tenth Century and is a favorite contemplative retreat for Prince Charles of Great Britain, as well as at the center of a 2008 scandal with the New Democracy Party involving millions of Euros in fraudulent land transactions.

13. See Wikileaks Cable 1975Thessa00383.b, written and signed by the author, at: http://www.wikileaks.org/plusd/cables/1975thessa00383.html.

14. In retrospect, it is somewhat surprising that Greece was allowed to remain a NATO member and participate in NATO military exercises throughout the seven-year Junta, although there was a partial NATO embargo in place on military sales.

15. For details, see *Greek Urban Warriors: Resistance and Terrorism, 1967–2014*, by John Brady Kiesling, Lycabettus Press, 2014

16. See Jane Loeffler, *The Architecture of Diplomacy.*

17. William McGrew, *Educating Across Cultures: Anatolia College in Turkey and Greece*, Rowman and Littlefield Publishers, Lanham, Md., 2015

18. Kapodistrias (1776–1831) served as Greek Head of State from 1827 until he was assassinated on October 9, 1931 on the steps of a church in the then Greek capital of Nafplion.

19. Also known as Mersifon and located near modern Samsun.

20. The Department of State historically followed a similar policy of not assigning hyphenated Americans to their country of family origin because of assumed security vulnerabilities or divided loyalties. By the 1980s, it was generally recognized, however, that Hispanic Americans or Greek Americans, for example, could often bring special expertise and be highly effective in their country of family origin.

21. The Greek word for university (*panepistimio*) literally means "all sciences."

22. See Tassos Boulmetis' film, *A Touch of Spice* (Politiki Kouzina), Village Roadshow Productions, 2003 for a sense of the nostalgia and deep loss many Greeks still feel about this unique city.

23. Richard Jackson, "The Unraveling of a Greek Tragedy," *Mediterranean Quarterly*, Vol. 26, No. 3, Duke University Press, summer 2015.

VIII

Epilogue

We are poor passing facts,
warned by that to give
each figure in the photograph
his living name.
— Robert Lowell, "Epilogue"

Like characters in Thorton Wilder's *Our Town*, I have always thought that it is hard to know at any particular point in time if one is truly happy or where the experience you are living through will find its place in the arc of career and personal life. This is particularly true of a lifetime spent moving every few years between different countries, cultures and languages. As the race begins to run its course, however, those happy stretches you'd give your right arm to relive jump out with greater clarity, both in the road taken as well as the opportunity costs of paths not taken.

Beyond bilateral relations and career, there is an aesthetic and spiritual dimension to experiencing a foreign culture over a period of years. It lies in the people and culture, the quality of light and nature itself. For me, the sense of place was most dazzling in

Greece where, unusually, I lived for sixteen years and Morocco where I spent eight, both still indelible in the mind's eye.

In my case, retirement from government in 1999 after three decades of Foreign Service was a watershed between the ordered and introverted world of government and the independence and uncertainty of life on the outside. I soon realized, however, that there is indeed intelligent life outside government. In marketing Foreign Service skills to academic and NGO employers, I very soon learned that diplomats are generally seen beyond their own charmed circle as less cutting edge than they, for the most part, consider themselves to be. Peripheral assignments like executive secretary or school board chair invariably have greater resonance with employers than bread-and-butter jobs like country director, desk officer, consul general, DCM or charge d'affaires which are so ferociously fought over within the Service.

In short, the concept of a lifelong diplomatic career, like that of the proverbial salary man in Japan, is a bit outdated, and transition away from it requires retraining and creative packaging, particularly in technology where most of government lags behind. That said, fluency in esoteric languages, as well as comfort living and negotiating in foreign cultures are not common in the US and can indeed be marketable.

As a traditional career, law or diplomacy for example, winds down with increasing work demands and decreased energy levels, years begin to pass as if they were months, and when the music stops, as it eventually does for all, many are caught out, off their stools as it were. And yet the desire persists to return to the action, for one last posting, somewhere in the mind's eye with the trappings and authority of age but the excitement and passion of youth. Beyond the eleven-year adventure that I have described at Anatolia College in Greece, this quixotic quest has taken me through a series of consultancies in exotic venues like Mongolia, Romania, Albania, New York, Latvia and Western Sahara. [1]

The common denominator for most of these excursions was the ambition of many countries to emulate American universities, eight of which are ranked most years among the world's top ten. Yet these countries were also, for the most part, impatient and in their haste discounted the decades and even centuries that have gone into developing our greatest universities, clinging instead to the vision of a Harvard or an MIT descending full blown from on high, reputation already established, and immediately attracting students from around the world to glistening new campuses in Ulanbaatar or Dakhla in the Western Sahara.

Nor was there usually much grasp of the concept of non-profit education among would-be sponsors and trustees eager for return on their investment and incredulous that a board would not only be unpaid but also asked to make annual contributions from their own pockets. My modest role was to inject reality on issues of accreditation, curriculum and start-up as part of a team lead by an ambassador with whom I had worked closely and including experts on finance and real estate. It was a collegial effort and appears likely to bear fruit in an American-style campus in Mongolia and possibly one still to come in Albania.

I've always felt that stress, that much maligned word, is positive and invigorating. That is, the days when you complete more than you thought humanly possible in twelve hours are energizing while those when you space out a few make-work projects, completing them indifferently and without passion, are deeply frustrating. And so, to re-emerge periodically from retirement in Florida to a world of deadlines and cross cultural research usually brings a welcome rush of adrenaline.

Each project has its own idiosyncracies. In Romania, for example, the task was to evaluate a vast former Soviet military base, stretching to the horizon in all directions with dozens of barracks and warehouses, as the improbable venue for an American university. The sheer scale and need for thorough de-mining, let alone the dearth of tuition-paying students, made it a long shot. Albania, by contrast, had low labor costs and a burning desire for quality education, but was suffocated by a proliferation of unscrupulous for-profit colleges, all claiming to be American and undermining the brand. In both cases, deeply entrenched corruption among government officials and parliamentarians owning and passing special legislation for their own for-profit schools made for an unusual operating environment.

The Western Sahara, by contrast, was a welcome return to North Africa, after eight years spent in Morocco. The issue there was the desire of Dakhla, a bustling port city, and its dynamic governor to have an American university or vocational institute to rival the state university in the regional capital, Laayoune. In fact, this vast desert region with 700 miles of pristine beach could not possibly support another higher education campus, let alone the hoped-for influx of foreign students to one of the world's most remote areas. Yet it is a place of stark beauty, flourishing today with a vast fishing industry and bulk, year-round fruit and vegetable exports to Europe.

"*Gaze on my Works, ye Mighty and Take Heart.*"

Most exotic for me was Mongolia, the largest landlocked country on earth with unlimited steppes and a millennial nomadic tradition. There, discovery of some of the world's richest mineral deposits and construction of one of the largest open pit and underground mines at Oyu Tolgoi had created expectations for visible public benefit projects like an American university to reassure the restive urban and rural poor that all new wealth would not be siphoned off into just a few pockets. The blueprint that our team left may yet take its place in the urban landscape of Ulaanbaatar. There, it will be dwarfed, as everything is in Mongolia, by the 131-foot silver statue of Genghis Khan, rising out of nowhere on the steppes, and, unlike Ozymandias, continuing to dominate his country nearly one thousand years later. On these same steppes, I saw with my own eyes Przewalski's wild horse, first reported in the 15th Century and later studied in 1881 by a Russian colonel whose name it bears, hunted to extinction in 1969, and reintroduced into the Mongolian wilds by a Dutch Foundation in 1992.[2]

Departing Mongolia via China allowed me to visit my son Richard in Hangzhou, renowned by Marco Polo for its beauty, where he lives and is helping to create the world's first fully bilingual English-Chinese artificial intelligence platform. Richard's once-a-week cook and cleaning lady, with whom I had no common language, spoke of me to her husband, who it turned out was the grandson of the legendary Ma Yinchu and curator of the Ma Yinchu Museum and Institute in Hangzhou. It was an only-in-China moment when he subsequently picked me up by limousine and at the Museum conferred on me the distinction of being the Institute's first Honorary Ma Yinchu Fellow. There, dominated by a huge statue of Ma himself, I was able to delve into how this centenarian father of Chinese population policy happened, in the last spasm of the Qing Dynasty, to study at Yale and Columbia, was punished under Mao, and at age 97 rehabilitated as Honorary President of Beijing University.[3]

Recalling my visits to China brings me inevitably to the subject of family and work-life balance, mostly absent from this account. Nomadic and expatriate life, of course, weakens one's ties to home, and immediate family becomes the vital touchstone, source of continuity and only shared witness to the journey and its improbable events. At the same time, it is easy to underestimate the stresses and strains of perpetual transition and uprooting, particularly for spouses and children. The latter quite understandably must eventually choose their own identities and make their way at places along the route as my children and stepchildren have done in Hangzhou, Athens, Brussels and Helsinki. A strong support network of extended family and friends from a life spent largely in place is not a resource or platform on which they or other diplomatic children can necessarily count. Nor, as in previous generations, is there any longer a family place where all are welcome, offering security and continuity whether or not they can often get there. Such losses are part of modern life, accentuated by a peripatetic career, and for which Skype and its Chinese rival, WeChat, remarkable as they are, can never compensate.

There is a cottage industry of books today on work-life balance, many but not all gender based. Secretaries of State regularly genuflect to the role of family and getting the balance right, but, at least in my experience, relentless hard work combined with plain luck, are still what lead to promotion. Certainly, I have had the balance wrong most of the time, habitually escaping argument or unresolved issues at home for long hours and even weekends in the office. Diplomatic life abroad and bureaucratic life at home also impose strains, albeit different, on families which require constant tending. Abroad, however, there is more chance for shared purpose and partnership between couples than in the anonymous suburban environment of Washington. In any case, I have been twice married and twice made more or less the same obtuse mistakes, even in the same country, Greece. Both my first wife, Stuart, and my present wife, Eia, have been central to whatever I've accomplished and whoever I am today. Paradoxically, however, now that I have time on my hands, the dream which burns so brightly for all of us, of children and grandchildren around a weekly dinner table is a real stretch, only partly offset by observing distant birthday parties on Skype.

Being out of the system for over a decade, I've come to view the ship of state as inward-looking and reactive, its absolute power, once insured by secrecy and a monopoly on intelligence, now eroded in a world of Snowdens, Mannings, and Assanges. Meanwhile, NGOs of every imaginable stripe have flowed into the vacuum, and global corporations often give American embassies a wide berth. Not that I would take back the experiences that I and my family had in Somalia, Greece or Morocco, the broadened intellectual horizons they offered and the bird's eye view of other countries. On the contrary, I like to think that some of the bizarre and lighthearted experiences recounted here might even lead adventurous readers to consider the world's second oldest profession.

I've written above that the cultural shock of return to a rapidly changing United States is usually greater than that of landing for the first time in a new post abroad. Diplomats, often in the compressed timeframe of two or three years, develop the skills of analyzing the economy, stability and culture of a foreign country. Their work is carried on, however, in the perfervid environment of capital cities and in the company of other diplomats, journalists and think tanks. On the theory that the outsider's perspective, like that of Alexis de Toqueville, is often more incisive than that of residents immersed in the reality of everyday life, retired diplomats tend to persist in their analysis once at home.

Yet it is a daunting and disorderly task, scattered randomly in retirement across America, for them to make sense of its economy, demographics and bewildering politics of today. The 2016 election is a case in point with its harsh rhetoric, plain rudeness and embarrassing ignorance of the world beyond our borders or the degradation of Planet Earth. Not infrequently, widows of former colleagues, both American and foreign, express to me relief that their husbands did not live to see the undoing of what they worked for in public service careers, inspired by idealism. The cynical mantra of politicians on the make that government is the enemy, trumpeted for decades, has finally seeped into the culture. The result is distrust and disfunctionality, backfiring on even the most obtuse politician, their calling and the country. [4]

I remember taking a taxi to Reagan Airport on my last day of work in the US Government. The driver, like many in Washington was a young Somali, and I asked him in vestigial Somali whether "riding is holding with hands" and whether "spring and the fool can both bring gifts," traditional proverbs meaning basically whatever one wants them to. The floodgates opened, and we spoke about Ali Shermarke and Abderrazak Hagi Hussein and Aden Abdullah Osman, leaders from Somalia's brief heyday before he was born, and of the hopes that ruined nation once had. In his family of teachers most are dead, and he and two siblings only escaped to Kenya to make their way.

Riding into retirement, it seemed to me that I had come full circle. Somalia has gone from the impoverished but proud and starkly beautiful new country that I once knew to the grim landscape of a failed state; my own first-post idealism has turned with time to skepticism, and it is surely no longer possible to believe, as we once did, that the course of history or US influence on it is anything like an arc of unbroken progress. There is, in short, a world out there that unfolds according to its own rhythms and beyond reach of the morning meeting or the bureaucrat's in-box. In fact, there is a yawning gap between the two. It has become a truism to say that American embassies are besieged without and in the grip of a siege mentality within and that Uncle Sam is distrusted in much of the planet. Now that I've experienced both, the bottom line relative to the private sector is that in government there is no real bottom line, and one can all too easily coast by without the risk taking and commitment that are otherwise essential. This is by no means a complaint, however, since I believe that only in America could one transition seamlessly from diplomacy to academia to consulting and freelance writing with the challenges and rewards of each.

NOTES

1. I include New York in this unlikely grouping as it is *sui generis* and in some respects a country unto itself.

2. Przewalski's Wild Horse, also known as Khalka, Dunzgarian Horse, and Equus Przewalskii, is the only truly wild horse in the world today with a genetic code differentiated from either domesticated or feral wild horses.

3. See Annex II for the author's "Ma Yinchu: From Yale to Architect of Chinese Population Policy," reprinted with permission by the American Association for Chinese Studies from the *American Journal of Chinese Studies*, Volume 19, April, 2012.

4. See at Annex III, Richard Jackson, "The Founders' Intent," reprinted from The Sunday Dialogue, *New York Times*, Jan. 17, 2016.

Appendix I

Richard L. Jackson, [1]
"The Unraveling of a Greek Crisis." [2]

The mood was somber and the security tight on 1 October 2013 when Columbia University professor Jeffrey Sachs addressed a by-invitation-only audience of Greek cabinet ministers, bankers, and industrialists in the Karatzas Auditorium deep inside the fortress-like National Bank of Greece in Athens. [3] The high-net-worth audience was composed mostly of septuagenarians from the very establishment whose failed policies and decisions had led the country to the brink of collapse. Elegantly dressed, most, if not themselves actually on the infamous Lagarde list, [4] at least had substantial fortunes outside Greece. There was obvious tension as Professor Sachs began to speak about the scale of investment and export-led growth that would be required if Greece was to avoid default.

Sachs is, of course, a frequent presence in countries at or nearing default, with a long track record of restructuring failing economies, successful in the cases of Bolivia, Estonia, Poland and Slovenia but less so in Russia. He is a spellbinding speaker, erring if he does on the side of over optimism as in the Millennial Campaign goal to eradicate global poverty by 2020. He minced no words describing the Greek depression, with its 28% loss of national income since 2010, massive debt and record unemployment, worse than in the Great Depression. Distinct from 1929, Greece was a one-country depression, and creditors and friends could help at the margins by allowing lower interest rates on Greek debt and longer repayment. There would not, however, be more "heroic efforts" from the European Union, he predicted. Sachs' words have been born out as Greece's Prime Minister elected in early 2015, Alexis Tsipras, confronted the reality that, without a further EU bailout, Greece would be on the brink of default and that additional funds would not be forthcoming without clear agreement on repayment, reform and reduced spending.

In 2013, Sachs counseled that Greece should cease to look only to Berlin and Brussels and aggressively pursue export-led growth with China and the Middle East. Further elements of the prescription were lower corporate taxes, a revamp of Greece's dysfunctional tax code, German-style training and apprenticeships to address 65% youth unemployment, and long-term planning in tourism, construction, agribusiness, wind and solar power.

As of 2015, there was a lack of consensus, political will or ability to take any of these steps. Greece remained on what Sachs termed the "knife edge of default" ranking ninetieth on the Global Competitiveness Index.[5] The noted Greek economist Ghikas Hardouvelis (who later served as minister of finance from June 2014 to January 2015) asked for help in unlocking further bailout funds to end the recession before launching an export campaign; Sachs replied that immediate efforts to increase exports were the only hope to save the economy.

The gulf between the beleaguered Greek establishment, hunkered down within the bastion of the National Bank of Greece, and the reality outside of steady decline, unemployment, drug use and homelessness was stark. It was unmistakable as the cavalcade of departing limousines snaked through the deserted streets of Athens past the blackened and gutted 140-year old neo-classical Attikon Theater, destroyed along with two other theaters by demonstrators on 12 February 2012 and just down the street from the former Marfin Bank, which arsonists ransacked, burning to death three bank workers, one pregnant, on 5 May 2010.

This was not then, in other words, a "normal" country, and it was even less so in 2015. On any given day, events in Greece seemed to confirm this:

- A Golden Dawn deputy attacks a Muslim colleague in Parliament as "anti-Greek" and declares that Golden Dawn believes "Constantinople was and will always be the Greek capital."[6]
- A two-day strike of civil servants begins across Greece, including at public hospitals and in the transportation system.
- Neo-Nazi Golden Dawn thugs in black and camouflage uniforms knife to death a Greek artist.
- Rolling five-day strikes by school teachers begin, with opposition party leader, now elected Prime Minister of Greece, urging students to occupy their schools in sympathy.
- Public university rectors threaten indefinite closure of all higher education if they are not exempted from government-wide personnel reductions.
- Further property taxes are announced with the then opposition party, Syriza, threatening to sue foreign property investors.
- Twenty percent of residents are removed from old age facilities so that they can help support children and grandchildren from their dwindling pensions.

All of these events occurred in the course of only one day in September 2013.

Going further back, the Greek Government and the EU conspired together in acquiescing in phony accounting to speed Greece's 2001 entry into the eurozone. In this, they were aided and abetted by Goldman Sachs in obscuring billions in Greek debt from budget overseers in Brussels.[7] Goldman Sachs president Gary Cohn visited Athens in 2001 to foist complicated financial instruments on Greece, circumventing EU deficit rules by hiding transactions as currency trades rather than loans. Equally, the two major political parties at the time, Panhellenic Socialist Movement (PASOK) and New Democracy, shared responsibility with German and other banks and financial institutions for pushing Greeks into a paroxysm of spending and debt beyond all hope of repayment. Greedy individuals and institutions in Greece and well beyond needed little prompting to seize the opportunity for corruption and self-enrichment.

Finally, a culture of entrenched interests, cronyism and contempt for successful upstarts has smothered entrepreneurs who for generations have fled Greece to become leading business figures all over the world. In the long term, Greece's renowned classical heritage has also been a double-edged sword, a source of pride and survival in crisis, but also of complacency and entitlement in better times. It was surely the latter, for example, that cost Greece the coveted Centennial Olympic Games in 1996 although it clawed its way back to host the 2004 summer games.[8] In a country of myth, for a time including huge billboards urging tourists to "live their myth," there is always the risk of becoming captive to one's own rhetoric. Exceptionalism, in other words, whether the Greek or American variety, has its downsides.

A Moment of Truth

The painful social costs in Greece have been apparent since 2010 in Europe's highest unemployment, slashed pensions and lost educational and job opportunities for an entire generation, the most privileged of whom have largely fled abroad. Shuttered stores, omnipresent for sale or rent signs, beggars and rampant drug use round out the scene. In harm's way, along Athens' grand avenues and squares, once desirable commercial properties stand empty and unrentable. Suicides have moved from one of the lowest rates in Europe to one of the highest. Flagship Greek companies like Viohalco, S and B Minerals and Fage have moved their headquarters to Brussels or elsewhere out of Greece. Wages in Greece have fallen abruptly by 28 percent since 2010, and there was a precipitous 40 percent drop since 2008 in the disposable income of Greeks.

Massive European assistance has come at a high cost in both interest payments and detailed foreign supervision of a once proud nation. Prior to the January 2015 elections, the troika, consisting of the International Monetary Fund, the European Commission and the European Central Bank, maintained a tight rein on the bailout, with payments doled out gradually to enforce targets for budgets, salaries, pensions, personnel reduction, tax revenues and the sale or liquidation of money-losing state enterprises. Austerity measures reduced the budget deficit from $49 billion, or 15% of gross domestic product (GDP), in 2008 to near zero by 2013. Yet this may not be such an accomplishment with the economy continuing to spiral downward and with crushing annual debt service payments of $16 billion.

Popular reaction to foreign control by the troika was vociferous, and German chancellor Angela Merkel has long replaced Henry Kissinger as the most reviled foreigner. One taxi driver joked with mordant humor that Greece would be better off returning to the Ottoman Empire in the hands of Turkish President Recep Tayyip Erdogan. Deep down, the presence of foreigners imposing conditions on Greece's hiring, budget and tax systems has been resented as an affront to national sovereignty. As often happens under extreme stress, Greek politics became increasingly polarized between Right and Left.

Former prime minister Antonis Samaras projected that by 2019 Greece would return to economic levels of 2008, a lifetime away for the unemployed and elderly, and thus faced mounting popular opposition and anger leading up to his crushing defeat at the polls in January 2015. In this highly charged environment, the unspoken fear was some form of social collapse or gradual loss of central control, increased criminality, and possible devolution of power to independent-minded regions like Crete. To date, popular protests have come in waves ranging from generally peaceful mass strikes uniting most Greeks across the political spectrum to outrageous violence from extreme minorities of both the Left and Right. Mass rallies were frequent before parliament in Constitution (Syntagma) Square, and a carefully choreographed ballet often unfolded between heavily armored police and masked youths with protection against tear gas. With surges back and forth, the two groups would exchange tear gas canisters without apparent harm to either side.

A Violent Streak

After the largely middle-class and middle-age protesters dispersed after demonstrations, a small nucleus of "mask wearers," or *koukoulofori*, took to smaller back streets where over several years they systematically burned down stores, banks, theaters and symbols of authority. The *koukoulofori*, said to number less than three hundred people, were middle-class youth from upscale neighborhoods whose names and addresses were known to the police, but like those on the Lagarde list they enjoyed immunity. The harmless ballet of tossing tear gas canisters back and forth in any case showed police off to advantage on Greek television. Such occurrences were so commonplace that, during December 2011 protests against President Vladimir Putin in Moscow, Fox News used generic riot footage from Athens with Greek lettering visible on the National Bank of Greece as backdrop for its Moscow coverage.[9]

There may also have been a more sinister protection racket involving the stores and buildings not destroyed. It is reported that the owner of one of the burnt-out theaters pleaded with *koukoulofori* not to burn it down, but did not have the three hundred thousand euros they demanded and watched helplessly as it went up in flames. An activist involved in many protests reported that she had observed several instances of *koukoulofori* complicity with the police. [10] In one instance, a masked man was overcome with tear gas and police escorted him to their own first aid area behind the parliament. She also claimed to have seen another *koukouloforos* bomb and destroy a store on a side street and then take shelter in police ranks while demonstrators fled in the opposite direction. In this manner, a small group was able to terrorize Athens with impunity until being gradually eclipsed by the neo-Nazi group Golden Dawn.

Golden Dawn has existed in Greece in one form or another since 1980 as a marginal, xenophobic, neo-Nazi gang, but it gained traction following the 2008 economic collapse, winning eighteen seats in the Greek parliament in the 2012 elections and placing a strong third behind Syriza and New Democracy in the January 2015 elections. Few protested when they murdered two immigrants and carried out countless assaults and beatings of immigrants, gays and foreigners including tourists, all the while boosting popular support through food banks solely for Greeks in impoverished districts. It was not until a group of some thirty uniformed thugs from Golden Dawn assassinated a Greek artist and singer, Pavlos Fyssas, in 2013 on the streets of Athens that Greek authorities reacted by arresting and charging six members of parliament, including Golden Dawn leader Nikolaos Mihaliolakos, with murder and twenty-nine other instances of criminal violence. As of May 2016, the case was still ongoing.

As with the *koukoulofori*, however, the Police stood idly by during several years of assaults and criminal violence, and there is reason to believe that many on the force are actually supporters of Golden Dawn. Police connections with both Golden Dawn and their apparent ideological opposites, the *koukoulofori*, highlight the underlying issue of corruption and the grey area between organized crime and ideology. It is no coincidence that the November 17 terrorists, claiming to man the leftist ramparts, turned out to be little more than petty thugs and bank robbers.

The emergence of a fascist, neo-Nazi party is a shocking wake-up call in a country that suffered atrocities and mass starvation during the Nazi occupation. In the longer run, however, the ebb and flow of violence appears rooted in modern Greek history, and it is not surprising that it would emerge with such virulence during a time of social strain. Against the violence and repression of the Second World War, the Civil War and the Junta, the 1948 murder of CBS journalist George Polk, the 1963 murder of Grigorios Lambrakis, the thirty assassinations carried out over twenty-five years by November 17, the 2008 killing of fifteen-year-old Alexis Grigoropoulos, the 2010 burning to death of three Marfin Bank employees, and the 2013 killing of Pavlos Fyssas by Golden Dawn are signposts along the way. That such violence became commonplace in the birthplace of democracy, philosophy, critical thinking, and idealized beauty sullies these high ideals.

OUTCOMES

A stark clash of opposites was evident on July 29, 2011, the day that *koukoulofori* destroyed large sections of central Athens and the Stavros Niarchos Foundation broke ground at Paleo Faleron for the visionary new Greek National Library and National Opera complex, designed by renowned architect Renzo Piano. Never have two more different visions of the future been juxtaposed with the sea to one side of the Faleron site and flames and black smoke covering the center of Athens. Faced with such polarization, the governing coalition of New Democracy and PASOK were immobilized and unable to sustain a consistent policy or long term planning. Lack of consensus prevented action on critical issues, from an enforceable tax code to export promotion.

Absent measures to slow and reverse the slide from recession into outright depression, it was inevitable that anger over prolonged unemployment, hardship and falling living standards would reach a breaking point. The vacuum, not surprisingly, was filled by Tsipras and Syriza, committed to ending austerity, at least partial debt relief and re-negotiation of bailout agreements with the EU. Such a bold and popular plan, on the basis of which Syriza won a landslide election, nevertheless, required a well thought-out Plan B in the event that the gap between campaign pledges and EU conditionality could not be bridged.

As the crisis has deepened since 2010, a number of outcomes to the present dysfunctional system can be considered :

* Adoption of a European Central Bank, treasury or federal reserve system responsible for fiscal and monetary policy and responsive to the needs of all members, not just the northern tier. The need for this has been evident for decades but vigorously resisted on grounds of sovereignty, individual states' economic interests and disparity of treatment between seventeen eurozone members and eleven EU members outside the eurozone. Opposition to the concept is even stronger today following the emergence of conservative parties across much of Europe and acute problems facing the continent.
* Successful renegotiation of the existing bailout with reduced interest rates and a relaxed repayment timetable, perhaps linked to GDP growth. This would require the Greek government to live with an extension of the current bailout program with existing obligations, but it would continue to safeguard Greece's eurozone membership, albeit with a continuing debt burden estimated as high as $353 billion. In the words of a *Wall Street Journal* editorial, it would be a "fifty-year IV bailout drip."[11] As of May 2016, the impasse was further complicated by division between the IMF and the EU, principally Germany, over the sustainability of Greek debt and the need for serious debt reduction.

- A facilitated exit from the eurozone and soft landing with continued membership in the EU. With Ireland, Portugal, Spain, and even Italy showing signs of recovery, the domino theory is less ascendant, and a quiet, well-managed exit by Greece might actually resolve rather than create problems for the eurozone. Lawyers in Brussels have argued about the legal rationale for this, with some asserting that there is no provision for a eurozone exit, which would then require departure from the EU as well, but others maintain that the EU predated the Euro and Greek membership would be unaffected. If so, Greece could be 30-40 percent more competitive returning to the drachma. While the word "Grexit" has become a shibboleth in Greece for fear of inspiring panic, many Greeks have been quietly thinking along these lines.
- Default and chaotic exit. This remains in the background as the consequence of overconfidence or a misreading by Greece and/ or the EU of each other's positions. It raises the specter of social unrest, capital flight and controls, closure of banks, and even military intervention. The example of Argentina's 2002 default after severing the dollar-peso parity is not reassuring. After a year of famine and hardship, Argentina emerged stronger because of external increases in world food prices and the country's vast agricultural production capacity. In the case of Greece, its industries are badly eroded by neglect and Chinese competition. Proud mill towns in the North, for example, are ghostly relics as merchants have turned to low-cost Chinese imports. Shipping is largely offshore, and tourism cannot thrive in uncertainty or panic.
- Worldwide economic crisis whether caused by China, the eurozone itself, an act of Congress, or otherwise. In such a calamity, Greece's debts would likely be erased, and being already in depression the country might paradoxically be better prepared as world trade fell to lower levels.

Each of these scenarios has implications for China, fast becoming a major player in Greece. Its continuing interest in the purchase of the Piraeus Port for sums estimated up to $5.8 billion is well known. In the meantime, China enjoys a long term lease for port facilities, has invested $400 million in modern equipment, agreed in November 2013 to an additional $308 million in new pier construction, and also covets ports in Thessaloniki and Crete. Major Chinese companies are also investing in Greek solar energy and telecommunications sectors. All represent a Chinese bet on Greece as a platform from which to penetrate European Union markets, although a return to the drachma would reduce the value of these investments. China appears to value its new presence in the Mediterranean as its ability to quickly evacuate Chinese citizens from Libya during fighting there demonstrated. Greece is thus a cog in the wheel of China's worldwide push for access to new markets and raw materials. Russia, by contrast, is a less reliable partner, seeking regional influence and willing to offer economic blandishments in return for presumed political influence. Both are cards that the Syriza Government has not hesitated to play in its dialogue with the EU, with mixed success to date.

Following the acrimonious four-month bridging period negotiated by former finance minister Varoufakis in early 2015, which Greece entered in order to reach a sustainable agreement for additional EU funding and growth, there remains ample blame to go around for a catastrophe many years in the making:

- Successive Greek governments that cooked the books.
- The eurozone that welcomed Greece without due diligence.
- German, US and other financial institutions that pressured the Greeks to borrow.
- The massive greed, corruption, and self-interest among Greek politicians, business leaders, and political parties.

All have brought this on themselves and on their innocent countrymen.

Negotiating an interim agreement exposed divisions among eurozone members over emphasis on austerity and the impact on the EU of a possible Greek departure. For Prime Minister Tsipras, it exposed a yawning gap between the populist platform on which he was elected and the vital need for fresh credit, with unwanted conditionality, to avoid default. While even the interim extension of the bailout was contentious and went down to the wire, the Tsipras government will have an ongoing challenge of retaining the confidence of both its base and its eurozone partners. As a spectator rather than participant in the drama, the United States will continue to counsel restraint among the parties, while quietly gauging financial implications if a rupture occurs, as well as possible implications for the North Atlantic Treaty Organization and beyond.

Projections that the Greek GDP should return to pre-crisis levels by 2019 and achieve a positive debt-to-GDP ratio by 2040 remain meaningless to most Greeks, concerned as they are with immediate survival and unable to think in long-range terms. The present period is, beyond doubt, the worst national trauma since the Second World War and Civil War. Yet the Phoenix, much debased by the Junta, is still a Greek bird, and survival in a new form is certain in the long run. The flexibility and coping skills of Greeks, honed in adversity over the past three thousand years, are legendary. Nor is it a bad thing that many Athenians, representing half the Greek population, are relearning country skills and seeking a simpler life in ancestral villages, vacant for decades in readiness for their return. The reappearance of bicycles and even pedestrians in congested city streets is also reassuring. Athens has no need to emulate Beijing with its choking smog, limited visibility, required indoor days and respiratory disease. The Akropolis glistening white against a clear blue sky and the ramparts of Thessaloniki where Saint Paul preached to the Thessalonians must and will once again serve as inspiration to the world and powerful symbols of Hellenic history, culture and ideals.

Addendum: As of 2016, the conditions and uncertainties described above continue to prevail in Greece. I am encouraged, however, by the January 20 election of Kyriakos Mitsotakis as leader of the New Democracy party, despite the crushing 210 million euro party debts which he inherited. Mitsotakis spoke several times at Anatolia College events during my time there, and I formed a high opinion of his integrity, incisive mind and knowledge of the financial world. While this paper was submitted in March 2015, it has in my view generally stood the test of time. I have, therefore, made only a few minor factual updates to it as of mid-May 2016.

NOTES

1. Richard L. Jackson served in Greece for sixteen years in 1972–2009 at the US Embassy and as president of Anatolia College.

2. Reprinted with permission from *The Mediterranean Quarterly*, Duke University Press, Volume 23, Number 3, September 2015

3. Jeffrey Sachs, presentation at the Karatzas Auditorium, National Bank of Greece, 1 October 2013, sponsored by the Harvard Alumni Association of Greece, attended by the author.

4. The Lagarde list contains the names of about two thousand potential Greek tax evaders with undeclared accounts at the HSBC bank in Geneva. It was provided by the French minister of Finance (Christine Lagarde) to her Greek counterpart in October 2010.

5. The Global Competitiveness Index is an annual report published by the World Economic Forum (WEF) and based on Sach's Growth Development Index. It is designed to assess institutions, policies, and other factors in terms of their ability to provide sustainable levels of economic prosperity. See WEF, "Greece, Global Competitiveness Report," 2014-2015 (Geneva: WEF,2015), www.3.weforum.org/docs/GCR2011-12/CountryProfiles/Greece.pdf.

6. As reported in *Ekathimerini* (Athens), 18 September 2013.

7. Louise Story, Landon Thomas Jr., and Nelson D. Schwartz, "Wall Street Helped Mask Debt, Fueling Europe's Crisis," *New York Times*, 14 February 2010, www.nytimes.com/2010/02/14/business/global/14debt.html?pagewanted =all.

8. For more, see Yanna Angelopoulos-Daskalaki, *My Greek Drama* (Austin, Tx: Greenleaf Book Group, 2013).

9. Andrew Osborne, "Fox News Uses Athens Riots Footage for Russian Protests," *Telegraph*, 9 December 2011, www.telegraph.co.uk/news/worldnews/europe/russia/8947476/Fox-news-uses-Athens-riots-footage-for-Russian-protests.html.

10. Based on conversations by the author with a local enterprise owner and regular participant at demonstrations in the center of Athens, 2014.

11. "The Next Fifty Years in Greece," *Wall Street Journal*, 10 October 2013.

Appendix II

Richard Jackson, "Ma Yinchu:
From Yale to Architect of Chinese Population Policy." [1]

ABSTRACT

This paper traces the evolution of Ma Yinchu (1882-1982), the architect of China's family planning policy, although himself a strong foe of forced abortion, from his formative studies at Yale and Columbia Universities through his internment under Chiang Kai-shek, rise to power under Mao Tse-tung, subsequent internal exile for two decades, and rehabilitation, following Mao's death, as Honorary President of Beijing University. It examines the impact on his life of every major event in Chinese Twentieth Century history, including the Sino-Japanese War, the Maoist Revolution and disastrous "Great Leap Forward," the Cultural Revolution and, finally, the emerging mixed economic system of today. In conclusion, the paper poses several unanswerable questions such as how a graduate of America's finest universities, deeply influenced by Kant, Hegel and Keynes, could survive and even flourish over a seventy-year career in Twentieth Century China. How could his steadfast opposition to abortion co-exist with implementation of the one-child policy there? What could have been his private thoughts on the 1959 famine and horrors of the Cultural Revolution? Was the strident anti-Americanism in Ma's writings and speeches to some extent necessary camouflage for his ongoing career? Finally, did Ma and his generation of Chinese students in the United States represent in some sense a missed opportunity to serve as a bridge between the two countries?

The Ma Yinchu Museum, located at the center of Hangzhou, capital of China's richest province, is the former residence of a giant of 20th Century China, Dr. Ma Yinchu, who remains almost completely unknown in the United States. As an honorary Ma Yinchu Fellow for Population Studies in Summer 2011, I was able to better understand both Ma's unique contribution to the emergence of a new China and the impact on his life of every major event in modern Chinese history from the Sino-Japanese War, to the Maoist Revolution and disastrous "Great Leap Forward," the Cultural Revolution and, finally, the mixed economic system of today.

Ma's hundred-year life story (1882-1982) begins under the failing Qing Dynasty in 1906 with an undergraduate scholarship to Yale University, followed by a doctorate in economics from Columbia. His promising academic career in China is interrupted by war with Japan and imprisonment under Chiang Kai-shek. Resuscitated under the patronage of Zhou En-lai, he convinces Mao Tsetung of the negative impact of population growth on economic development and promulgates his "New Population Theory" in 1957. A year later, Mao reverts to the traditional belief that national power is based on the largest possible population, and Ma is ostracized as a Malthusian in internal exile for 20 years only to be completely exonerated following Mao's death and, in his late nineties, made Honorary President of Beijing University, China's most prestigious. He dies in 1982, venerated as the father of China's policy of limiting population growth but also as a strong foe of abortion and supporter of women's rights. Today, the Zhejiang Ma Yinchu Population Welfare Foundation serves as a model for the development of NGOs and civil society in China, with impressive outreach toward disadvantaged young women, the elderly and the rural economy.

The vicissitudes of Ma Yinchu's life and career raise a number of intriguing questions which I would like to explore here, although the full answers may never be known. Among them: How could a graduate of America's finest universities, deeply influenced by thinkers such as Kant, Hegel and John Maynard Keynes survive and even flourish over a seventy-year career in 20th Century China? How did his vigorous campaigns for delayed marriage and contraception and his abhorrence of abortion coexist with implementation of the one-child policy in China? What could have been his private thoughts and reactions to the 1959 famine brought on by Chairman Mao's failed industrial policy and to the horrors of the Cultural Revolution? How did the strident anti-Americanism evident in his writings and speeches evolve from his US education and was it, to some extent, necessary camouflage for his ongoing career? Finally, had the United States not been obsessed with the "Red Menace" and excesses of the McCarthy era, could Ma's career have developed differently and he and other US-educated Chinese graduates have served as a bridge between the two countries, offering a different social and economic model for China and lessening at least some of its revolutionary excesses?

THE EARLY YEARS

The dispatch in 1906 of 120 of China's brightest young scholars, including Ma Yinchu, to study in the United States and elsewhere abroad must have represented a last spasm of the Qing Dynasty, tottering on the verge of the 1912 Sun Yat-sen Revolution. It can be seen as a final desperate effort to master the mentality and ways of the West, by then occupying so much of China. Ma, in any case,

arrived in 1906 as a freshman at Yale, with relatively strong Eng-
lish-language skills acquired at a missionary school in China.
While he made friends among faculty and classmates, Ma concentrated almost entirely on his studies in order to win acceptance into
Columbia University's doctoral program in economics from which
he received his degree in 1914. Dwindling scholarship funds required him to seek out a series of menial jobs. His Ph.D. thesis was
a thorough study of how new financial methods had helped to
eliminate graft and inefficiency in the finances of New York City
and was subsequently published as a college economics text in use
at Columbia and elsewhere. [2] After Columbia, Ma completed a year
of post-doctoral studies in accounting and statistics at New York
University.

In these years, Ma read widely, working his way through a wide
spectrum of Western thinkers, who influenced him greatly and
whose works he frequently cited in later writings such as Hegel,
Kant, Sigmund Freud and John Maynard Keynes. For example, in
his pivotal 1958, "My Economic Theory, Philosophical Thinking
and Political Stand," Ma writes, "Here I classify unemployment
into voluntary and involuntary unemployment, which seems to me
the same as the Keynesian theory in his analysis of unemployment." It is also possible that his lifelong opposition to abortion, so
common in China in later years, may have been influenced by
ethical precepts absorbed during ten years in the United States and
earlier study at a missionary school.

Ma returned in 1916 to a collapsing and disorderly China moving toward civil war and invasion by Japan. He, nevertheless,
launched a successful career as Professor of Economics at Peking
(later Beijing) University and was promoted to Dean of Teaching.
In 1923, he was the Founding President of the Chinese Economics
Society. His outspoken speeches, while serving as an economic
advisor to Chiang Kai-shek, and opposition to perceived corruption
in the nationalist forces landed him in prison camps in 1940, first at

Xifeng and then at Shangrao. Of particular interest, his release from prison to house-arrest in Chongqing in 1942 was accomplished through the personal intervention of Patrick J. Hurley, then President Franklin Roosevelt's personal representative in the Far East and later Ambassador to China, who used the ruse of visiting Ma in prison to force the Chiang Kai-shek authorities to relent.[3] After the defeat of Japan in 1945, Ma resumed his academic career, teaching at the University of Shanghai. He was notably on the rostrum for the 1949 Beijing Conference on Foundation of the Peoples' Republic of China, consolidating the power of Mao Tse-tung and the Communist Party. Shortly thereafter Ma Yinchu was appointed President of Zhejiang University from 1949-1951 and of Beijing University from 1951-1960. In both posts, he gained a reputation as a diligent administrator committed to the welfare of both students and faculty.

Ma's View of the US: Ma was, first and foremost, a highly educated economist who was among the first in China to identify and speak publicly about the contradiction between unlimited population growth and China's development and emergence as an economic power. This put him directly at odds with China's strong rural tradition of large families and eventually with Chairman Mao himself. When China later enforced a rigorous one-child policy, Ma was further at odds with the government over the brutal means employed which he could not condone. He was thus regularly on the defensive and the object of vicious attacks, first as a decadent "Malthusian" and later as a Western-influenced liberal. Under the circumstances, it is not surprising that he chose to distance himself from the United States and that, during a period of unbridled Chinese nationalism following the Communist Revolution, his works contain frequent criticism of US policy. He, nevertheless, retained American friends particularly among the economics faculty at Columbia, and through membership since 1914 in the American Economic Association (AEA).

Ma Yinchu vehemently denounced the postwar Sino-US Treaty on Commerce and Trade. Writing in Wenhui Bao, an influential Chinese daily, on March 4, 1947, he rails that, "The whole of China has been stained by American tint [*sic*] and there is not a single piece of clean land to be found. The Sino-American Trading Treaty is supposed to be mutually beneficial to both countries, but only Americans are benefitted." And again, "The arrogance and prejudice of the American soldiers are intolerable. Their contempt of Chinese is shown in their killings of Chinese people and rapings (sic) of Chinese women. If we do not wish to see the only hope of China be destroyed by US Imperialism through their puppets, we must continue to carry out our traditional sacred task to fight against imperialism and feudalism, i.e. to start a revolution...." If our assumption is correct that Ma's decade in the United States was probably a time of loneliness but also of extraordinary intellectual growth which shaped his subsequent career, these writings can perhaps be partly attributed to Chinese nationalism of that time and anti-Americanism actively encouraged by the Soviet Union. Later, the blatantly anti-Chinese rhetoric of the McCarthy era and direct conflict between American and Chinese troops in Korea can only have reinforced Ma's hostility. One can thus only speculate about any residual ambiguity in his mind regarding the United States or the degree of genuine conviction and political expediency in his writings about it.

Survival Against the Odds: Occasional criticism of the United States, however virulent, simply cannot explain Ma's longevity and long-term survival throughout all phases of the Chinese Revolution despite differences with the central Government on major policy issues. Clearly, he was both an astute politician in compromising or recanting when necessary to preserve his primary goal of a rational approach to population control and at the same time enjoyed a measure of high-level protection. The latter, by all accounts, came from Zhou En-lai, China's first Premier, second in command under

Chairman Mao, and the architect of Chinese foreign policy. Zhou, like Ma himself, had deep family roots in Zhejiang Province and frequently visited. It is noteworthy that, when Ma was imprisoned during 1941 under Chiang Kai-shek, Zhou and his wife presented a poem honoring his heroism. There is also reason to believe that Ma Yinchu's presence on the rostrum of the 1949 First Session of the Chinese Peoples' Consultative Conference in Beijing, which established the Peoples' Republic of China, was due to the influence of Zhou. Finally, it is known that Zhou gave specific orders that Ma, then in internal exile in Zhejiang Province, not be harassed by rampaging Red Guard youth during the Cultural Revolution. A portrait of Zhou En-lai always hung in Ma Yinchu's residence, whether in Pukou, his birthplace, Hangzhou or Beijing and is today on display in his office at the Ma Yinchu Museum in Hangzhou.

Ma Yinchu's career and role as the first credible spokesman for family planning in China played out in a period of confusion and policy reversals as the Communist Party consolidated control. In fact, the Chinese Government had already begun a marginally effective promotional campaign for family planning in 1953 before either Ma launched his "New Population Theory" or Mao pronounced on the issue pro or con. Ma tested the waters for his new theory, preparing a presentation for the 1955 National People's Congress (NPC) but encountered strong opposition to it from deputies from his own Zhejiang Province and withdrew it. When, however, the National Agricultural Development Plan for 1956-1967, endorsed by Chairman Mao, contained language on the "campaign and promotion of birth control," Ma judged that "the conditions were ripe" and submitted his "New Population Theory" to the Fourth National People's Congress in 1957, prefacing his remarks there with fulsome praise of Chairman Mao. The full text of his theory was published in The People's Daily on July 5, 1957.[4]

Ma was immediately subjected to a storm of criticism and when Chairman Mao himself reverted to the traditional Chinese position that the country's strength lay in the largest possible population, his standing was completely undercut. He was particularly attacked as a bourgeois and Western "Malthusian" and forced to recant publicly a sentence from a speech at Beijing University, "If Chinese population increases rapidly, the Chinese people may be compelled to invade other countries due to being badly off in life," acknowledging that "After a second thought, I knew that what I had said was absolutely wrong" and that "Now I pledge I will not hereafter make such a mistake." Others took offense on grounds that family planning and population control had never been a topic of discussion by the Communist Party in Moscow and therefore had no place in Beijing's deliberations.

The result, in any case, was that Ma was dismissed from all official functions including the Presidency of Beijing University. So precipitous was his fall that Ma Yinchu was often cited as a cautionary tale by the next generation of Chinese population specialists for whom family planning remained a highly sensitive subject.[5] While he was in internal exile for two decades, the central Government began in 1971 to seriously encourage late marriage and contraception, followed by introduction of the one-child policy in 1978 and its widespread application beginning in 1979. Although Ma's recommended policy measures were adopted in 1971, his personal vindication would have entailed a loss of face for Mao Tse-tung and was, therefore, postponed until a decent interval after the Chairman's death.

In fact, Ma's collected writings are remarkably consistent throughout on both his differences with Malthus and strong opposition to abortion. Regarding the former, Ma always rejected Malthus' pessimistic conclusion that population would grow geometrically, outstripping food production and resulting in war, plagues and starvation to maintain balance. He saw instead the potential for breakthroughs in food production and was remarkably idealistic about achieving "truth, goodness, perfection and sacredness" through rational family planning and more efficient use of resources. In his world view, developments in the sciences and mechanistic theories such as those of Sigmund Freud had overlooked the mental quality of human beings and tended to "degrade mankind to the low level of animal." He was drawn, by contrast, to the prospect of improvement and change that he drew from writings of Kant and Hegel.

Equally with regard to both implementation of family planning and firm opposition to abortion, Ma's writings are consistent and clear. He never wavered from postponement of the age of marriage and vigorous promotion of contraception as the cornerstones of effective family planning. His prescription for achieving this was to offer monetary rewards to couples limiting themselves to two children and to levy taxes on those with three and progressively heavier taxes on those with four or more. Revenues from the latter would fund rewards for the former, so that there would be no costs to the state in his scheme.

Ma Yinchu's lifelong opposition to abortion was based on four pragmatic grounds: First, it is killing; second, it is harmful to women's health; third, it downplays the importance of contraception and often substitutes for it; and fourth, it increases the burden on already stretched Chinese medical resources. Of these, the first appears to have been Ma's primary concern, and Ma writes in his "New Population Theory," "Abortion kills the fetus in the mother's womb which has the right to life. Abortion should not be permitted unless the pregnancy endangers the mother's life." When asked separately about his views on uterine curettage and induced abortion, Ma responded, "Though Mr. Shao Lizi[6] stands for it, I myself oppose it. Abortion does considerable harm to the health of mothers."

Summing Up: While Ma's earlier career and survival may have been assisted by the patronage of Zhou En-lai, his complete exoneration, after the deaths of both Mao Tse-tung and Zhou En-lai, and

the honors bestowed on him in 1979 under Chairman Deng Xiao-
ping resulted from widespread recognition of the correctness of his
views and a sea change in Chinese thinking about family planning.
Although his appointment as Honorary President of Beijing University at the age of 97 is, of course, symbolic, it nevertheless
shows that positions within senior ranks of the Communist Party
were by no means monolithic on population policy. It is also noteworthy that Ma's steadfast opposition to abortion, so contrary to
Chinese implementation of the one-child policy, was tolerated to
the extent that Ma Yinchu continues to be venerated as a major
figure in 20th Century China, and a flourishing philanthropic foundation and museum today bear his name. While every Chinese
province has a family planning foundation, that of Ma Yinchu is the
only such semi-independent institution, with considerable corporate and individual donor support and the ability to select its own
projects, albeit with government approval. Belated recognition of
Ma and his contribution to Chinese development and population
policy, nevertheless, came at the high cost of two decades of enforced idleness during his still productive later years as well as,
according to some analysts, the "disappearance" of up to 43 million
Chinese girls. Emerging from these lost decades, Ma would have
found a nearly unrecognizable landscape. While the one child policy with its excesses of forced sterilization, late-term abortions and
sex-selective abortions was rigidly applied to an estimated 35 percent of the population, growing prosperity, while uneven, also
helped, as Ma had predicted, to lower birth rates, stabilizing China's population at an estimated 1.3 billion, still the world's largest
and close to 20 percent of the human race.

Paradoxically, family planning appears to have benefitted some
urban women whose enrollment at colleges and universities rose
from 24.2 percent in 1978 to 50 percent of undergraduate and 47
percent of graduate students in 2009. This is clearly because, at
least in urban areas, girls now received resources previously allo-

cated to boys only.[7] Since growth tends to reduce family size, such progress would have also resulted from Ma's program of delayed marriages and contraception, albeit more gradually. As Harvard's Dr. Vanessa Fong puts it, "Concentrated parental investment by low-fertility parents produces highly educated children."[8] An unintended consequence of the one child policy in China's cities is also an obsession with change in all forms as today's generation of only children, sometimes known as "little emperors," are outward-looking, focused on individual wants and receptive to innovation and change in all forms.[9]

From today's vantage point, Ma Yinchu is at once timeless and clearly the product of an earlier age. He grew up in and helped to reverse the thinking of a generation for which happiness was considered as having a son early and five generations living under one roof and "unfilial conduct" was defined as having no heir. He himself came from a large rural family and had many siblings. For that matter, prior to development of his "New Population Theory," Ma fathered seven children, five daughters and two sons, one of whom pursued a lifelong career at the UN in New York with three grandsons living in the United States today. While a committed disciple of family planning, Ma also showed compassion and humanity in later life by counseling and financially supporting a wayward nephew who fathered nine children.[10]

Reflecting the world around him and the need for balanced economic growth, Ma wrote in 1932, "We do not wish to compete with Western countries for world markets. Our expectations are very limited. We are satisfied to live on our own food, wear our own clothes, and use our own products."[11] Today China supplies the world with goods of every description and in 2009 surpassed the United States in consumption of all forms of energy by 4 percent. What Ma Yinchu would have thought of modern cities such as Shanghai, Guangzhou or Shenzhen can only be conjectured, and certainly they would have been unrecognizable to him. Planned observances in Hangzhou in 2013 to mark the 130th anniversary of Ma's birth, as well as the 2014 Centennial of his doctoral thesis publication at Columbia University, presented opportunities to reflect on Ma's impact on China's explosive development through rational family planning.

Just as we can never know the reaction of this classically-educated centenarian to the new China of today, we can only guess at his innermost thoughts as he observed firsthand the most turbulent century of China's millennial history. Certainly, the devastating Chinese famine of 1959, a direct consequence of Chairman Mao's disastrous "Great Leap Forward" industrial policy, was a terrible vindication for Ma's New Population Theory. Equally, the widespread destruction of China's cultural heritage during the 1960s must have been anathema to Ma's refined sensibilities.

Finally, at least from the perspective of a foreigner in China, the presence of a man of such obvious intellectual integrity at a critical juncture of modern Chinese history, along with a large cadre of other highly educated graduates of top Western universities, is also a story of unfulfilled potential and missed opportunity. Washington, swayed by lobbyists of Chiang Kai-shek, was convulsed with red-baiting and McCarthyism as Mao Tse-tung consolidated his power and proclaimed the People's Republic. Vilified and shunned by the United States, Mao, who had not previously travelled outside China, visited the Soviet Union for two months in October 1949 in search of guidance for the enormous problems that he faced and support. Josef Stalin, who up to then had seen China as a rival, craftily converted Mao to a rigid Stalinist orthodoxy, completely unsuited to the circumstances and needs of China. America's myopic vision and provincialism in demonizing Mao, opposed by China experts such as John Paton Davies and John S. Service at a cost of their careers, forfeited to the Soviet Union any meaningful role in China. Not until the 1972 Nixon trip to China and return visit to the US by Deng Xiao-ping in 1979 did such an opportunity come again. Like Deng, enthusiastically trying out a NASA space simulator in Houston, Mao too might have been inspired by dynamism and innovation in the United States and adapted some elements into his trial-and-error planning for China. While these are mere "what-ifs" of history, the unmistakable cost to China was millions of lives lost and untold hardship for several generations, affecting all from peasants to visionaries such as Ma Yinchu.

NOTES

1. Reprinted with Permission by the American Association for Chinese Studies from the *American Journal of Chinese Studies*, Volume 19, April 2012.

2. *The Finances of the City of New York*, Dr. Ma Yinchu, Longmans, Green & Co., 1914.

3. From September 12, 2011 interview in Hangzhou with Ma Da Cheng, Grandson of Ma Yinchu and Curator of the Ma Yinchu Museum in Hangzhou.

4. *Ma Yinchu's Collected Papers on Population*, Zhejiang People's Publishing House, 1997. Note: Subsequent unattributed quotations in this article come from this work.

5. "Silencing Anti-Rightists: The Shameful Matter of Ma," p 56-57. In Susan Greenhalgh's *Just One Child: Science and Policy in Deng's China*, University of California Press, 2008.

6. Ma is referring here to Shao Lizi, a hardliner from Zhejiang Province who served as China's wartime Ambassador in Moscow and later as a member of many of the top Communist Party Committees in Beijing. *Wenhui Bao*, April 27, 1957.

7. Dr. Vanessa Fong, Harvard University Professor and expert on Chinese family planning policy, as quoted by Alexa Olsen, Associated press, August 31, 2011

8. Dr. Vanessa L. Fong, *Only Hope: Coming of Age under China's One-Child Policy*, Stanford University Press, 2004

9. Richard L. Jackson, "A Tale of Two Parks," *Foreign Service Journal*, January 2011

10. Reminiscences of Ma Benna, *Shan Xi*, No. 3, 1981

11. "Are There Plans for a Fundamental Solution to the Negative Influence of the Chinese Family System on the Rural Economy?" *Spectator*, No.6, December 1932

Appendix III

Richard Jackson, "The Founders' Intent" [1]

SUNDAY REVIEW: SUNDAY DIALOGUE
THE FOUNDERS' INTENT
JAN. 16, 2016

Editor:

Arguably, the world is changing faster than at any point in history—in global warming, migration, technology, terrorism, national borders and genetics. The overriding challenge for the next president will be to coolly assess, prioritize and act on these daunting threats and opportunities.

Our first instinct is to recoil from change, taking refuge in a simpler, more prosperous time, 1950s Middle America, for example. The Constitution also looms large as a touchstone, to which literalists brook no challenge. If we can just turn back the clock following the letter of its 1787 precepts, change can be held at bay.

Yet the founding fathers were not at all terrified by change, but instead embraced it in the Constitution. They would, no doubt, be appalled by the political discourse of today and by those who claim to be disciples asserting a monopoly over their thinking and masterpiece. Their genius lay precisely in knowing that future crises could not be imagined in their time, leaving us the flexibility to respond to change and avoiding the pitfalls of rigid prescriptions.

Overreaction to change can also sap our strength. American exceptionalism, once shorthand for our can-do spirit and self-confidence, has been stood on its head as a bulwark against change on immigration, taxes and health. Seen from abroad, where I served for three decades, it conveys arrogance and a belief that entities like the World Court, and treaties on the Law of the Sea, the environment and human rights, simply don't apply to us.

Our next president must not shrink from long overdue reforms, but must lead with them. Both the president and Congress must keep in mind Chief Justice John Marshall's 1821 dictum that "a constitution is framed for ages to come, and is designed to approach immortality as nearly as human institutions can approach it." Put differently, effective governance lies somewhere between revisionism and textualism.

RICHARD L. JACKSON
Wellington, Fla.
The writer is a retired diplomat, college president and freelance writer.

Readers React:

The single most urgent function of our Constitution is to ensure that the rights of those who lack the votes to enact policy are not wrongfully diminished or debased because of their minority status. That imperative is timeless and should not be subject to changing mores, concepts or language.

But to the extent that the Constitution also serves as a blueprint for governance, it is foolish to worship words or concepts crafted in another time to deal with a very different world. Many of the founders had perspectives about slavery, race, punishment, women's rights and social relationships that are out of step with modern thought and philosophy. Because they knew that change was inevitable, and necessary, they bequeathed to their posterity a document that can live, breathe and adapt.

To insist that today's legal and moral issues be resolved only by reference to the Constitution's 18th-century language is not justified. That approach straitjackets our society and inhibits its continued growth and world leadership.

GERALD HARRIS
New York
The writer is a retired criminal court judge.

I would go even further than Mr. Jackson: Constitutional originalism, which opposes constitutional flexibility, is a bankrupt philosophy. To the extent that we know their views, the founders disagreed about most important matters, and generally understood the need to adapt to changing circumstances. Given that we are today a postindustrial society governed by a preindustrial document, thank heavens that the Constitution itself is often naggingly vague; it could not have otherwise survived.

Of course the document's text and "original meaning," to the extent it can be discerned, still matter. But those who swear fealty to originalism play a legal fool's game by pretending that the most profound societal changes somehow cannot or should not factor into present decisions.

ROBERT J. SPITZER
Cortland, N.Y.
The writer, a professor of political science at SUNY Cortland, is the author of "Saving the Constitution From Lawyers."

What is the point of writing a constitution unless you intend it to be applied as faithfully as possible? The founding fathers don't need Mr. Jackson to come to their defense. No one has accused them of being terrified of change. They deliberately provided a constitutional process for amending the Constitution.

In fact, the founding fathers provided a second mechanism for amending the Constitution: It requires Congress to call a constitutional convention to propose amendments when two-thirds of the states apply for such a convention. But if you mention that option, you will find all the liberals running as fast as they can in the other direction. Who exactly is terrified of change?

Liberals don't want "we the people" to amend the Constitution in the ways prescribed by the founding fathers. They want liberal justices to stealthily amend the Constitution. That has worked for them in the past. Mr. Jackson's prescription—"effective governance lies somewhere between revisionism and textualism"—is completely vacuous. Who would get to choose when the text controls and when revision is called for?

IAN MAITLAND
Minneapolis

The "original intent" lobby runs into a logical dilemma it has yet to resolve: Do you defer to the founders' original intent, or do you defer to their words literally? Do you look at what they were trying to achieve, the general principles they were trying to apply, or do you assume that those are self-evident from words they chose?

That question becomes more complicated when the very definitions of the words change over time. What is intended, for example, by the words "the right to keep and bear arms shall not be infringed"? Does that mean all arms of every description, for all people regardless of age or past criminal record? Or the words "a well-regulated militia." Are those words meant to apply to a group of armed government protesters who deem themselves a militia? Or in order to be "well regulated," does a "militia" need to have a state or federal charter?

WILLIAM MANTIS
St. Paul

A major obstacle to constitutional reform and greater flexibility in the interpretation and application of the Constitution is the belief by many Americans, and the doctrine of some American religions, that its creation was inspired by God, and consequently a perfect document of perpetual applicability.

Those founding fathers who composed and ratified it considered it the best they could produce to meet the needs of the time and of the future insofar as they could see it. The most gifted of them could not have imagined our world of today. Other nations with written constitutions often revamp them as changing times demand. Arguably, we should do the same, though always with careful, thoughtful deliberation and never in haste.

JOHN C. FRANDSEN
Auburn, Ala.

Some so-called conservatives claim that the Constitution should be read only in the most constricted manner possible and that amendments are the only legitimate means to resolve vital new questions. Should those brittle prescriptions ever be broadly adopted, their folly would soon be evident, but not before risking our entire legal system, if not the Republic. Even if the arduous amendment process could be made to address every unforeseen issue, our Constitution would become ever longer and more complicated, its great principles diluted until one day it would be a broken-down pile of words on its way to the scrap heap of history. Yet these ideas are "conservative"?

BRAD WHEELER
Lewisville, Tex.

The Writer Responds:

As usual, I am struck by the incisive comments of New York Times readers. I did not mean to imply, as Mr. Maitland suggests, that the founding fathers were in any way afraid of change or in need of defense. It is their self-proclaimed literalist disciples of today that concern me. As Judge Harris writes, the founders purposely designed a document that can "live, breathe and adapt" to changes that they could have never foreseen. The specific questions aptly posed by Mr. Mantis are ones that thankfully the Constitution gives us the flexibility to confront "with careful, thoughtful deliberation and never in haste," just as Mr. Frandsen proposes.

I do not, however, share Mr. Wheeler's fear that the amendment process could one day leave the Constitution a "broken-down pile of words" for "the scrap heap of history." Instead, at least for the time being, I take heart in President Obama's full embrace in his State of the Union speech of "change that's reshaping the way we live, the way we work, our planet and our place in the world."

RICHARD JACKSON
Wellington, Fla.

NOTE

1. Reprinted with Permission from the Sunday Dialogue, *New York Times*, Jan. 17, 2016.